GW00750947

I AM A..
FLiGHT ATTENDANT
& THAT iS MY
SUPERPOWER

Always with Love... ♥

jessica dsb

I am a Flight Attendant & that is my Superpower

ISBN 978-1-7777-279-0-1
Printed in Canada

Inflore
DESIGN

Design by Karina V Gonzalez
www.infloredesign.com

Contact@infloredesign.com

GRATITUDE

by Jessica De Serre Boissonneault

I would like to first thank my Lord and savior. Without him, I wouldn't be here. Thank you to my grandma and grandpa who are watching me from heaven. I miss you both dearly and cannot thank you enough for loving me like you did!

A very special thank you to my mom. My hero, the reason I am the strong, determined woman I am today is because of you. I was an unexpected, beautiful surprise in your life, and you loved me from day one. I am eternally grateful for all the sacrifices you have made for me.

Thank you, Dad, for always loving me and showing me what family stands for; eternal love and commitment. Thank you to my step-mom, Lidia, who has been an angel in my life since day one. You have shown me how family stick together no matter what, and the importance of supporting each other. Thank you, stepdad, for loving my mom and being there for all of us as your own kids.

Thank you to my love, Kossi. The way you love me, the way you care for me as your Queen, the way you have been my #1 supporter from day one has undoubtedly been one of the reasons I am writing this book right now. I am eternally grateful for you, my love. Your constant coaching throughout this project was priceless. Thank you.

Thank you to my lovely daughter. You have given me the greatest gift of being a mom. I wake up every morning in gratitude for watching you grow and getting to complete projects (like these) to empower you to do what your heart desires. Thank you to Alixia and Dylan. My life wouldn't be the same without you two bundles of joy. Believe in your dreams, my loves.

Thank you for my book mentors; Mr. Gordon So, Ms. Randi Goodman, and Mrs. Merav Richter. Without all of your valuable time and mentorship this book would have not been created in this particular timing. Thank you.

GRATITUDE

A special thank you to my friend and super coach Mrs. Hailey Patry for all your support, your time, your wisdom, and your mentorship. And most of all, for your unconditional love. Your continued support and coaching gave me the confidence to go ahead with my dreams!

A special thank you to Mr. Byron Nelson for being such an impactful, special human being in my life. Your mentorship, coaching and love made me believe that my dreams were possible! Possible to achieve!

Thank you to my friends and family. I could list many many names of individuals that have had, and still do have, an immense impact in my life. Please know I am very grateful, and that you have had an impact on the women I am today.

Very importantly; thank you to ALL the authors, all 20 of you. This book wouldn't have happened like it did without each one of you adding your colors! A special thank you to Karina V Gonzalez. You have been my rock throughout this project. Thank you for your incredible talents and most of all, thank you for your patience, love, and positive energy. Thank you, Jaime for your contribution to the foreword of this book. Your love and energy were definitely an added bonus into this project. Thank you, H.K, Amber and Christina for your contributions to the creation of this book. You ladies made sure this book would be ready and perfect for our readers! Amber and Christina, you added your colors. Your devotion, patience and professionalism are priceless. I am honored to have amazing, vibrant human beings like you in my life. Thank you all for your hard work. You have all exceeded my expectations 10 times over!

A HUGE thank you to our sponsors who have contributed to this project. Thank you for making a difference. Your generosity will always be remembered. For the readers reading this, I highly recommend flipping to the back of this book and getting to know each one of our unique, loving sponsors!

With much gratitude.
Always with love, 🖤 jessica dsb

FLIGHT PLAN

PRE-FLIGHT CHECKS

Jamie Mcniven Smith

DEPARTURES

Jessica De Serre Boissonneault

IN-FLIGHT CHECKS

Christina Degano (Narayani)

FLiGHT PLAN

ARRiVALS

Jessica De Serre Boissonneault

&

Christina Degano (Narayani)

SUPERHERO FLiGHT REVIEWS

SUPERPOWER BUSINESS HUB

SUPERHERO SPONSORS

PRE-FLIGHT CHECKS
by Jamie Mcniven Smith

*"The biggest adventure you can take is to live
the life of your dreams." Oprah Winfrey*

Being a flight attendant was always my dream ever since I was a little boy. I was fortunate enough to have been on my first flight at the age of 4, when my family emigrated from Scotland to Canada in 1979.

My parents loved to move and travel often, so, by the time I was 16, I had been on more airplanes than many people have in a lifetime.

When I would fly, I would get so excited. As I watched the flight attendants work, I would dream that one day I too would do this job.

As a young kid, whenever I would travel on planes, I would make drawings of the crew, and then go to the back galley to give it to them. Aww.

On one flight to Glasgow around the age of 9, I remember handing a drawing I did to one of the flight attendants in the back galley. As I handed her my "artwork" she looked at me, and in a sweet voice said, "do you want to be a flight attendant when you grow up?" I nodded shyly.

One of the older, more grumpy, male flight attendants who was sitting on some kind of metal bin smoking a cigarette (you could smoke on planes back then) said to me, "no you don't sweetie, no you don't!"

That only made me want to do it more!!

I wanted the job so badly; one could say that I was a little obsessed. I used to daydream a lot about the job, and I would even pretend that I was a flight attendant whenever the opportunity would present itself.

One time on a high school bus trip to Quebec City, I brought orange juice, water, snacks, and extra plastic cups, and I walked through the aisle of the coach bus serving drinks and cookies to everyone.

I would also close any overhead bins and tell people to stow their bags properly, as any good "flight attendant" would.

My teacher said, "what on earth are you doing?" I said, "I am going to be a flight attendant one day, so I am practicing."

The bus driver (a nice, older French-Canadian man with a big belly) was so cool and had overheard what I was doing. He looked at me and said, "do you want to make some announcements?"

Without skipping a beat, I said, "OMG YES!" He handed me the microphone...and let's just say I did a pretty good and realistic announcement: "Ladies and gentlemen welcome aboard MacDonald high school airlines. For your comfort and safety, etc."

The whole bus laughed.

(Picture of me on that coach bus
closing overhead bins age 16).

A few years later at the age of 22, I was finally hired by an airline. It was a dream come true. During flight attendant training, we had to make impromptu announcements in front of the instructors. Everyone was so nervous. I picked up the inter-phone on the simulator and did a perfect announcement.

The instructor said, - "you sound like you have been doing that all of your life!"

"Actually, I have," I said as I sashayed out of the simulator confidently. As I walked by the instructor, I noticed he had a very confused look on his face.

What I didn't realize then was that I had actually been practicing The Law of Attraction. The Law of Attraction states that you get in your life, whatever you give your energy, attention and focus to. By pretending and daydreaming, I was actually calling my dream to me.

While I have enjoyed every moment of my job over the past 23 years, I've always believed that once you achieve one dream, it's time to achieve an even bigger dream.

Although I had originally studied acting in college, (something I am now pursuing again later in life), I also have a passion for the healing arts.

Twelve years ago, I decided to go back to school, and I become a certified Life Coach. Shortly after that I attained another certification to teach Law of Attraction workshops, led by Michael Losier.

Michael is the best-selling author of the book, "Law of Attraction" and was even interviewed by Oprah Winfrey a few times. He taught me that it is essential to stretch out of my comfort zone and that it is okay to dream big!

It was around that time when I was learning about the Law of Attraction that I met Jessica De Serre Boissonneault at work. Coincidence? The minute I met her I knew that this woman was someone special. It was like an instant connection, like meeting a soul sister.

After the first service of our flight together, the back galley became like a therapy session (which it often does on long flights), and we talked about the Law of Attraction and life issues and I remember sensing that this woman is a powerhouse! I knew she would go places.

It is not a shock to me that Jessica is now a certified life coach herself, a best-selling author and was recently chosen as one of the Top 50 Most Influential Women in "VIP Global Magazine" in the USA!

As a coach and flight attendant, I find it interesting that flying and reaching your dreams have a lot in common:

- First, you need to know where you want to go.

- You need to take some time and make a "flight plan" to your destination.

- You need to have the right crew to help make the journey easier and more fun.

- You need to avoid turbulence/ storms.

- Very importantly, you always need to put your own oxygen mask on first before helping others with theirs.

Enjoy the journey along the way!

I have learned so much about life from being a flight attendant. It's hard to even explain, but as you read each story in this book, my hunch is that you will fall in love with these amazing authors and our career.

I know their stories of living their dreams and finding resilience during these challenging times will inspire you to become the best version of you!

I am so honored to have written the foreword to this amazing book because flight attendants are the most amazing group of people I have ever met.

May this book inspire you to dream big and own YOUR superpower.

The world needs you more than ever.

So, at this time, I invite you to sit back, relax, and allow these stories to take you to new and exciting destinations.

Love, Jamie Smith, CPC, Law of Attraction Facilitator,
Motivational Entertainer and Flight Attendant.

DEPARTURES

by Jessica De Serre Boissonneault

Let your dreams take flight! - Unknown

Do you have a dream inside of you that is begging to become reality? That urge inside? An idea that just recently surfaced or that you've had for as long as you can remember? I know I did.

First: Dream. Second: Believe. Third: Plan. And Finally: GO!
- jessica dsb

I was once told that we all have a dream inside of us that was uniquely placed there because it **could** be accomplished. I invite you to start dreaming and to believe in your dreams. Believe in the beauty of your own unique dreams that were placed in your heart. It was planted there because it is YOURS to accomplish! And once you believe it, I implore you to take simple daily actions towards it. Protect that dream and share it with those who will help you get closer to achieving it. I'm not saying it will be easy. There will be turbulence along the ride, difficulties that you might encounter while reaching for your dream. But in the end, it will be all worth it. I have been on my share of journeys, and I can tell you that none have been a completely smooth ride.

Over the years of my life, I have had many dreams that I wanted to accomplish. Some of which were planted on my heart many years ago and some just recently surfaced. Some of my dreams are to continue living a happy life, to remain in my beautiful, thriving, loving relationship, to travel with my friends and family more often, and sooner rather than later, to own a nice vacation property somewhere warm. Most importantly, I dream to empower and inspire everyone that I get the chance to connect with. And more specifically, I would love to continue my women empowerment movement by expanding my business in Africa to elevate women and encourage them to become entrepreneurs.

DEPARTURES

What do your dreams look like? What are they? I invite you to not only start dreaming, but also to write about it. These dreams can be monumental or earth-shattering. They can also be simple. The simple dreams are often the most rewarding to achieve. Whatever your dreams may be, nurture them and keep them alive. Everything is a journey in progress!

If you can dream it, you can do it – Walt Disney

The realisation of one's dream has the potential to change the world as humanity knows it. The Wrights Brothers and their dream of building an aircraft, for example! If it were not for their dreams and vision, we would possibly still be on the ground today.

"Just before you break through the sound barrier,
it is when the cockpit shakes the most" – Fearless Soul

Nothing stood in the way of the Wright Brothers' dream, not even the crash that Orville Wright experienced in 1908. Even though he had experienced a trauma and several physical injuries from that unfortunate event, his biggest fear was not flying, but rather the idea of not being able to continue his dream work.

It's kind of fun to do the impossible – Walt Disney

Spearheading this book collaboration is a special dream of mine. There was turbulence along the way. It wasn't always easy and fun. When I was tired, I learned to step away, gain positive perspective, but to never give up. I focused on the vision and our end goal.

The airline industry was one of the most impacted industries due to the pandemic, and for this reason, I am especially delighted to have created a platform to mark this moment in history, to honor and elevate it in all its aspects. I wanted to not only honor our special Superpower job and the Superpower in all jobs, but to honor and elevate all the individuals involved—Flight Attendants, Airline Employees, and passengers alike.

"No one is you and that is your Superpower" - Unknown

DEPARTURES

The theme of Superpower has been chosen with purpose. It is not just a fun, catchy idea. It is true to the magic of the job and represents our wish for all to embrace in their own work of choice. Being a Flight Attendant requires special qualities and attributes, which then develop into unending and exceptional skills and capabilities. Our beloved job of choice furthermore offers dynamics and gifts with which we can truly FLY-HIGH, through all sorts of 'flight conditions'. The personal stories reflect this wonderful alchemy. The true magic!

As such, it is a first of its kind project. It not only relays life chronicles of Flight Attendants, so to raise awareness of the role and its real person; it will also hopefully inspire our readers, the passengers of this book, to attain their particular 'dream job', and as a result, cruise high in the most blissful life possible.

I am grateful for each one of the authors who believed in me, who believed in themselves and who took action towards achieving one of their dreams! As Dr. Myles Munroe would say: "Your attitude will change your altitude". After months of hard work, pouring our souls into this project, here they are, each one of the 21 Flight Attendant authors having succeeded in sharing their stories; a true honor and privilege.

When asked what writing for this book meant to them, the authors have described this collaboration as: opportunity, community, empowerment, pride, unity, devotion, love, passion, strength, courage, and faith. So, let your mind be taken on this beautiful adventure of hope and resiliency. Each page of this book will take you to the beautiful adventure called LIFE!

I would like to invite you to board our **Flight of Empowerment** and to join us on twenty-one unique journeys. But first, we ask that you take in some Pre-Flight entertainment, and accompany us into a deeper look into the history of Flight Attendants.

Flight Attendants Through the Ages
Let's rewind for a minute.

The term 'steward/stewardess' was originally used in reference to the word 'chief steward' in the ship industry. The role of a Flight Attendant is of similar position to that of 'stewards' in passenger ships or trains, however, comes with its own unique criteria.

DEPARTURES

The working environment of a 'steward' in a small metal tube (30 000 feet in the air) consequently requires much more direct involvement with passengers and the level of safety on the vessel.

A man named Heinrich Kubis, considered to be the world's first Flight Attendant, began his career in 1912, tending to passengers on flights within Germany. The United States began hiring male stewards in the mid 1920s purely for flight safety, and in 1929, Pam American World Airways (Pan Am) were the first to hire stewards to serve food. At this time, flights were carried out by a 10 passenger Fokker aircraft that would fly from Key West, Florida to Havana, Cuba, and were targeted towards passengers that loved gambling.

The first female stewardess, Ellen Church, was hired in 1930 by United Airlines. Church was a 25-year-old nurse and was the one who envisioned the hiring of more nurses for this work. Other airlines then followed suit. Back in those days, the job of 'Flight Attendant' was one of the few jobs that were available to women. We have come a long way as a society!

In 1936, male Flight Attendants were quickly replaced by women who were hired for their physical characteristics alongside their knowledge suitability, such as being a nurse. Here is the list of characteristics required to apply for the job in the 1930s: petite, 100 to 118 pounds, 5 feet to 5 feet 4 inches, 20 to 26 in age. Moreover, these women were required to submit to a medical exam four times a year to ensure the continual adherence to these standards. Thirty years later in the 1960s, the characteristics were changed to the following: high school graduate, single, 20 years old, 5 feet 2 inches but no more than 5 feet 9 inches, 105 to 135 pounds that needed to be in proportion with their height, 20/40 vision wearing no glasses.

In the early history of the Flight Attendant career, physical appearance, and consequently the exploitation of female sexuality, was the most important factor when hiring a Flight Attendant. Companies believed that having attractive 'stewardesses' would increase their profit margin. The uniform worn by these women was designed in accordance with this belief. Some of the components of the uniform were high heels, white gloves and formfitting attire.

DEPARTURES

The requirements of having to be a nurse, to not be married, and to be of a certain age meant that a Flight Attendants' career would be quite short; on average 2-3 years. As the years went on, the responsibility of the Flight Attendant increased. From cleaning the cabin, to tossing the garbage out the window, to sometimes even helping to fuel the aircraft!

The transformation of the Flight Attendant uniform over the years has been quite the impressive feat as well. I always remember passing through the San Francisco Airport looking at the colorful display of Flight Attendant uniforms over the years. You can clearly see and trace the evolution of the commercial aviation world. In the book called "Femininity in Flight: A History of Flight Attendants", the author Kathleen M. Barry argues that because of the glamour aspect and image portrayed in the media; the actual labor, skills, and importance of the Flight Attendant role has been obscured. I now have a better understanding as to why we still have a similar issue today. The actual role and most important aspect of the Flight Attendant is the safety of the passengers. As you read the pages of this book, you will notice that this is a common theme. However, as societal rules and norms are often transmitted from generation to generation, it is very clear why many still view the Flight Attendant as a glamourous waitress!

It was in the late 1940s and into the early 1950s when Flight Attendants became unionized and were finally recognized as professionals. Into the 1960s and 1970s Flight Attendants were also some of the first groups of professionals to use the new gender discriminatory laws. One of the biggest fights that was fought was against the airline using slogans such as "fly me" which were extremely prejudiced and chauvinistic.

Finally, in 1971, the courts ruled that both men and women could be hired as Flight Attendants. Moreover, in the 1980's, USA airlines finally lifted the no-marriage ban. Lastly, weight restrictions where relaxed in the 1990's (timelines and conditions vary significantly from airline to airline and especially from country to country).

DEPARTURES

Can you imagine being fired for getting married and becoming a mother, or for simply getting older? As a women empowerment advocate, and as a voice for us female Flight Attendants, it is impressive to see the transformations that took place over the years. I am very grateful for all these Flight Attendants who fought for our rights. It is because of you, and the battles that you have fought, that my colleagues and I have the career that we do today.

*"Dreams can come true, if we have the COURAGE
to pursue them" – Walt Disney*

The airline industry today is built on talent, personality, and fitness for the job rather than on outward appearances. There is still room for growth, but the industry has come a long way. We in this book wear our wings with pride as well as in acknowledgement of those who have come before us.

Let your dreams be your wings and FLY-HIGH,

Always with love,.. 🖤 jessica dsb

"Flight Attendant"
Wikepedia. Wikimedia
Foundation, May 16, 2021
https://en.wikipedia.org/wiki/Flight_attendant

"Wright Brothers"
Wikipedia, Wikimedia
Foundation, May 19, 2021
https://en.wikipedia.org/wiki/Wright_brothers.

IN-FLIGHT CHECKS

FLYING HI, IN LOVE, WITH SUPERPOWERS
Christina Degano (Narayani)

The classic notion of 'Superpower' carries universal meaning: a magical, Superhuman ability or quality, usually reserved for gods or Superheroes.

As humans, we are starting to literally master the phenomena of mythological figures and deities, such as telekinesis, telepathy, super-senses, and other Superhuman powers such as instant healing and regeneration. Incredible personal and physiological evolution due to technological advances and the development of our Quantum and spiritual selves, has made the stuff of Shiva and Thor truly more possible than ever.

As much as this is true and amazing, we are not necessarily referring to these still more elusive Superpowers, but rather to the more practical varieties which are equally as magical, powerful, and arguably even more important for everyday fulfillment and success.

Here we address any type of quality, prowess, ability, or talent—anything that can make us feel omnipotent, and Superhuman in some way.

Our Work as Source and Expression of Superpowers

An important part of our purpose and expression in life is what we do for a living, our daily work.

An awesome livelihood, which has special value (and all potentially do) is a Superpower onto itself. In turn, this 'special' profession usually represents the combination of necessary Superpowers, a culmination, and a repository of all that was required of that individual to attain that position and thereafter to sustain it.

And this manifests through its 'chosen one', the Superhero who brings their own special gifts.

FLYING HI, IN LOVE, WITH SUPERPOWERS

The job of a flight attendant is particularly coveted and competitive, and as such, requires some remarkable attributes and multiple skills, from the get-go.

Being hired as a flight attendant is a result of a competitive battle with hundreds, if not thousands, of counterparts, through several and various stages of selection. The grand finale is typically a very unforgiving training program in which there is extraordinarily little room for error in proving Superhuman suitability.

In the process, these characteristics and abilities are primed, refined, and jet-fueled through the process of competitive scrutiny, so to rise to the occasion of the high standards of the job. Ultimately, they come together to manifest as a Superpower job.

Real & Special, Multi Names & Labels

'Ye of so many names': Flight attendant; Cabin/Crew Member; Air/Sky Host/ess; Steward/ess or 'Stew'; Cabin/Sky attendant; Sky Waiter/Waitress, Trolley Dolly, and even Cart-Tart or Pretzel Pusher (all genders alike, naturally!).

Indeed, the term 'Flight Attendant' holds numerous labels and associated connotations. Characterisations range from being likened to noble and professional ambassadors, and even gods/goddesses of the skies (certainly propagated in the early decades of aviation, when flying was glamorous for all), to other very contrasting, less attractive and inaccurate versions, involving being simple-minded, unpleasant, and wanton.

As objects of simultaneously differing attitudes, ranging between flattering admiration and disrespectful irreverence, the Flight Attendant becomes a well-tempered and grounded species, simultaneously feeling both special and real; confident yet humble.

This results in a special type of maturity or equanimity that becomes a key element for the first signature Superpower: *Service*.

SUPERPOWER OF SERVICE
First Class, Hi-Flying Service

Synonyms of the word 'Attendant' include *helper, assistant,* and *servant.*

FLYING HI, IN LOVE, WITH SUPERPOWERS

Good service is not just about charm and grace, although, when combined with the allure of travel, it can certainly coddle the heart.

Service is at the essence of 'Sky Attendant's' Superpowers and is what makes the job important and meaningful.

In Yoga, Seva is Selfless Service. This type of service is a potent force because its hi-vibe has the potential of transforming everything to the positive.

And the 'Sky god/goddess' who truly practices this higher spirit of service makes their passenger feel as if they were enveloped in the protective and nurturing warmth of a mother's arms.

Not by surprise, most every flight attendant on the planet is the willing and go-to caregiver in their private world as well, moving mountains to nurture and cater to any situation—the more challenging, the better.

And among the excellent ambassadors of flight, this Super Service becomes palpable, bringing comfort, happiness, and peace. This is the special, 'secret sauce' that helps make journeys memorable and Flight Attendant wings truly shine.

SUPERPOWERS of HI-CAPACITY, GENIUS & PERCEPTION

Thermodynamically, Titanium

Super strong, resilient, and efficiently speedy. Like a jet engine. On all levels, Flight Attendants have been tested, tempered, and made *thermodynamic* like the titanium-filled metal chambers they 'attend' and toil within.

The actual job requires real *strength and willful talent:* A snapshot of a typical flight's duties includes pushing a 300-pound trolley (sometimes all on one's own) uphill along a narrow path while managing dozens of passenger needs and problems; serving with professionalism and grace; verifying scores of critical safety items; practicing regulated protocols—all with mandatory speed and efficiency, respecting an unforgiving time slot.

And God forbid, when fate would have it, enacting emergency procedures and first aid, in coordination with multiple colleagues is always a possibility. Your 'Air Attendant' cannot help but become a *super capable, well-oiled, uniformed machine.*

FLYING HI, IN LOVE, WITH SUPERPOWERS

Increasing already existing Herculean demands, work conditions had intensified greatly pre-COVID—an almost trifecta effect of often-times decreased crew compliment, increased workload, and stricter standards. Our limits were pushed beyond maximum capacity, in what was the apex of a tremendously competitive market of 'everyone, everywhere' travel. Yet, we continued to astonishingly adapt to the increasing challenges.

Conditions after landing are sometimes just as unfriendly. As the cliché goes, waking up in different time zones, forgetting where we all are, is true and typical. And even if a Crew Member chooses day trippers as their flight gig of choice, allowing for a same-day return home to sleep in one's bed, it is inevitable that working a 14+ hour duty day of mostly flying, for example, will leave any healthy human feeling zombie-like, no matter how fit or well-accustomed they may be. Pushing through thick and thin, like the Eveready bunny, makes us *efficiently tough and pliable,* able to meet most any challenge, both on and off duty.

In fact, on a lighter and brighter note, we apply this stamina to our playtime as well. Be sure that we can teach you how to find the best shopping deals, eat like a local, and tour a major city in 6 hrs flat. Then we will show you how to successfully juggle many projects and wake up at any time of day or night, super-organised and ready to go.

And when it comes to sheer physiological robustness, we seem to have a bionic type of immunity despite—and daresay, because of—all the continuous and immeasurable toxic, infectious, and unpleasant exposures. Very seriously speaking, considering the central, hi-risk incurred on the job, COVID has not affected our group as seriously as it could have, but we honor all those who have been affected, in one way or another, during this pandemic.

Our great *resilient* capacity is not just physical, but mental as well. COVID proved our mettle when it targeted our industry in bulls eye fashion.

The small percentage that remained tentatively on the job were brave and malleable to increasing risks, ever-changing conditions, and protocols. And for the great majority who were laid off, even after 20+ years on the job, there was little immediate support and no end in sight, after not just losing an income, but a way of life.

Nonetheless, we did not remain in our 'hangars'. The small percentage that remained tentatively on the job were brave and malleable to increasing risks, ever-changing conditions, and protocols. And for the great majority who were laid off, even after 20+ years on the job, there was little immediate support and no end in sight, after not just losing an income, but a way of life. Nonetheless, we did not remain in our 'hangars'. We came together on social media, pooling information, and resources. Most began learning and revising skills, even gaining new or extra certifications and degrees, making the best and maximal use of our long, forced off-duty 'layover'. We got inspired and took to new skies, despite our broken hearts.

'Flying Antennas': Ingeniously Resourceful and Aware

Thomas Edison aptly declared that "Genius is one percent inspiration and 99 percent perspiration". And coupled with Plato, who masterly noted that "the necessity is the mother of invention", together must have been foretelling of the future arrival and story of Flight Attendants on the job.

Confined to a metal chamber in which we have limited resources, creatively thinking 'out of the craft', is often a must. Getting out of tight spots, literally and metaphorically, is our necessary M.O.

Therefore, being resourcefully ingenious is yet another major power. We will find a solution for any problem, individually or as a dynamo team, and follow through to execute it to the best of our abilities.

This special genius is the same one which helps develop the very complimentary gift of 'situational awareness', an actual technical requirement per our Safety Manuals. Trained to be forever alert as the physical eyes and ears of the airplane and programmed to be constantly aware of the many surrounding stimuli, we become extraordinarily perceptive. We can spot an unbuckled seatbelt through a blanket, smell alcohol on someone's breath across a cabin, hear a baby cry from the other side of the aircraft; sense a problem 'hot-spot' before it develops, and foretell an emergency long before it arrives, so to successfully avoid it.

As 'Caveman'—nickname of one of our most well-loved Ramp Agents, now retired—affectionately called us, we are indeed, 'Flying Antennas'!

FLYING HI, IN LOVE, WITH SUPERPOWERS

'All-Inclusive' Capacities

A simple role at first glance yet camouflaging so many different functions and responsibilities. Your 'Sky Servant' has an understated, critical importance and consequent impact on the travelling experience in so many ways.

Viewed from any given passenger seat, the job may seem symbolic and even easy as pie, but do not be fooled. Your Flight Attendant is more than a noble servant of the skies: S/He is a benefic chameleon who needs to potentially wear so many hats and fill so many shoes, with an almost endless list of job descriptions. Possessing a plethora of well-proven and regularly-tested skills and qualities, most well-camouflaged, but ever ready for their critical and life-saving functions, if and when—but preferably never—required.

Your FA must be: As much a Waiter as an EMT; A Counsellor of Hearts and a Negotiator of Terrorists; Both Security officer and Safety inspector; Let us not forget, Fireman and Police Cadet; A Diplomat and in many cases, their Multilingual Interpreter; A graceful diffusor of problems yet a freakishly perceptive detective of them;   An active and assertive doer one minute, and a passive and obedient follower the next A cultured Travel Advisor and generally Excellent Communicator And most importantly, a calm and smiling face during the most stressful of times.
Cabin crew must carry an all-inclusive package of capacities that are both essential and complimentary to your flying experience.

Multipassionately Evolved

By 'day', your Superhero of the skies could easily be a successful and vibrant doctor, lawyer, psychologist/counsellor, yoga teacher, building contractor, artist, YouTube sensation, or teacher to name a few. Far from being simple-minded, and unambitious, one characteristic common to all 'Trolley Dollies' is that of being multi-passionate.

Although they may not be experts in all areas, Crew Members will know a heck of a lot about most things. Generally, the group is in constant movement across borders, dipping quickly, but meaningfully, in and out of countless worldwide hubs and their respective, and varying cultures. This includes perpetual super-sharing with fellow Flight Attendants who all carry the same exponential amounts of 'spark'.

FLYING HI, IN LOVE, WITH SUPERPOWERS

Not surprisingly, flight attendants become *huge consumers and sponges of information and ideas, assimilators of culture,* who are motivated and improved by each new flight of innumerable inspirational contacts and experiences.

The continual interchange with passengers from all walks of life, 'classes of service', demographics, and travel purposes happens easily because they are seen both as approachable and respectable ambassadors, who also hold the good graces of providing sustenance and security.

As a result, the typical 'Air Host/ess' accumulates impressive quantities of *knowledge and savviness.* Being forever energised through friendly, 'up close and personal', continual evergreen contact with real-life models of inspiration makes all possibilities tangible and possible.

'Evolution on steroids', even by the standard of today's fast-paced society.

Moreover, as a natural consequence, 'Sky Hosts/Hostesses' become socially flexible, able to relate and communicate with all different walks of life, demographics, and personalities, equally and comfortably, which further empowers.

SUPERPOWER of FREEDOM
'Freely Cruising Time'

Freedom is a Superpower that Cabin Crew enjoy, at a depth and breath that few traditional professions have the luxury of experiencing. This is because it is freedom that includes the factors of both mobility and time. Our ability to move with freedom is facilitated by the ample time we are granted in which to do it. And more available personal time supports and encourages the privilege of doing more of that which is valued and desired by each one of us. Add to that the special mobility factor, is the gift of travel we are able to take advantage of, oftentimes, even on a shoe-string budget. This in turn helps us evolve further as your 'Air Hosts'.

Freedom of time and movement allows one to entertain other hobbies or activities, express and nurture one's passions, potentially be more productive, and generally enjoy life to the fullest. We unanimously find this to be divine.

FLYING HI, IN LOVE, WITH SUPERPOWERS

ULTIMATE INGREDIENT TO SUPERPOWER: *LOVE*

We are obviously very partial to our jobs as Superheroes of the Skies. *However, it is a fervent wish what you may be inspired to seek out opportunities to achieve similar levels of satisfaction, or greater, within your own activities and jobs!*

Your special Superpower job is possibly or probably completely distinct in nature. It could be a role as a CEO in your favorite industry, a Mental Health professional, a dogwalker, a Social Media influencer, or even, if not especially, a stay-at-home Mom or Dad. Regardless of your special 'cape of choice', if it makes your spirit soar on some level, it will create and sustain an awesome life.

This could certainly be what the Western world refers to as a 'dream job'. Or it could represent what Yoga defines as our 'dharma', pointing to an important mission or purpose. And this inevitably brings copious amounts of hi-flying fulfillment.

In summary, please accept this as your official crew briefing. *Serve the world but let both your work—and you—serve you as well, including lots of enjoyable self-care (remember, your oxygen mask should go on first, so you can then take care of others!). Test and banish your limits. Challenge yourself to go sky high! Work to live well, but do not sacrifice your life to work. Work hard and meaningfully but play hard with just as much devotion. Embrace a job that will give you the time and freedom to fulfill all you wish to do or be! Then, flourish and fly high with gratitude! Find meaning and purpose in your job, big or small. And finally, and most importantly,* **fall in love with your life's work....**

Fall in love with it, in at least some significant way—for what it in-spires, offers, or represents. In this way, it can be *appreciated in the good and the bad, which optimizes our attitude and success in life.* Whether popular or life-changing; deeply meaningful or superficially glamorous; a life-long vocation or a part-time side hustle—in the end, what makes our work a true Superpower is the pure love we feel for it.

When we truly feel this magical connection, our roles have the potential to truly transform our lives. We can blissfully 'live the dream', in lives made exceptional, where we become real-life Superheroes.

CHAPTER 1

LIVE. LAUGH. LOVE

by
Jessica De Serre Boissonneault

" You have your wings; all you have to do is fly."

LIVE. LAUGH. LOVE

The woman you are seeing and hearing from at this moment was not always like this. Some might be looking at me and saying "she's got it all," "it is easy for you," "you are always positive," "she is so beautiful." I would like to say yes to all those four statements. The truth is, I don't have it all. It was never easy and still is not easy. I am not always positive 100% of the time. Guess what?! It took years to finally look at myself in the mirror and say to myself "I am beautiful". I would hear it from others, but I didn't feel like that inside of myself. There is a huge difference between others saying you are beautiful and you truly believing it inside of yourself. Looking at yourself in the mirror and not having to convince yourself that, yes, I am beautiful. Everyone is beautiful in their own unique way. It starts with you believing it. No matter how many people follow you on social media; YOU have to believe it. You have to feel it inside of yourself. And yes, there are days or moments I don't feel as beautiful, but I choose to not stay in that state for too long.

Why am I sharing all of this? What does it have to do with being a flight attendant? Let me ask you this: what is the image you have when you think of a flight attendant? How do we look? What personality traits do we have? It relates to what I just shared above. Some people might look at me and say, "wow she is the luckiest woman in the whole world," "she does have it all," "she travels the world," "she is the happiest," "I could never have what she has". And I tell you, these are perceptions. And perceptions are not facts. There are so many flight attendants in this world. We all have our unique stories, our unique personalities, and our unique baggage. I am here today to share with you my special story. In which I will talk about power, passion, and positivity. Here is what I know now, these are the three elements that I believe to be crucial in living an abundant and purposeful life. Through psychological resilience, I was able to cope with crises and chaos that life can bring by using the power inside me, the passionate woman that I am, and the unbending positivity that I have!

LIVE. LAUGH. LOVE

It was never a childhood dream of mine to be a flight attendant. To be honest, I never knew what a flight attendant really was. I saw them in movies and that was it. My first flight was in 2006 when I booked to travel from Montreal to Paris. I saved up some money, and I traveled alone with my backpack. I had registered with an organization to volunteer for 3 weeks in the west of France. That was my first flight ever. It was my first experience seeing flight attendants. It was my first time seeing them doing their work. At that point, I was not considering becoming one. I never thought of it as a career option. It didn't cross my mind as being available and accessible to me. I was focused on what my mom had always told me "Jessica, you have to go to university no matter what". She told me repeatedly when I was a child that I should become a Psychiatrist or a Lawyer. I listened to her, and I went to university. I studied Sociology at Concordia University and loved it thanks to my Professor in College who was so passionate about being a Sociologist and did such an amazing job at teaching us. I am a lifetime learner and I always love to learn new things. All to say, my studies were going well until I got confused. I felt powerless. I felt as if I was investing all this money and time to study with no exciting ultimate goal. I was going to be proud, especially by making my mom proud for completing my university degree, however, I had no clue which area I was going to work in. My grades were not high enough to pursue a master's degree, and to be honest I didn't care. I cared about having fun in the moment and enjoying life to the fullest! Have you ever found yourself in that rut? That moment where you think to yourself... What are my next moves? A sense of feeling, of being paralyzed. What to do?

Life changed when a friend of mine messaged me on a summer night. I remember it like it happened yesterday. The exact moment of the night. The exact area I was standing, and I remember looking up at my friend with this huge excitement in my eyes. I was at a party on a boat in the Old Port. "Jess, you have to go to the interviews for flight attendants next week! This airline is hiring, and they need people now!" I had such an amazing feeling inside of me when I read her message! Hey, why not?! I have nothing to lose really. I was in university. I had a decent job. I lived with my dad and my stepmom. However, these were not my ultimate goals, nor the fulfilling life circumstances I wanted long-term.

LIVE. LAUGH. LOVE

One of my mentors had taught me to always keep my eyes open and seize opportunities! My mom also always told me to ask myself "what is the worst that can happen?" I went to the interviews and got hired right away. Within 2 weeks I quit my job, quit university, and I was sitting in the training center to start an 8-week special airline training. I still remember the first day I was sitting in that training center. I knew I was in the right place. When people talk about intuition, that urge, that confirmation that you can feel in your body; I had that! It was so present, I was so present to it, and I can still feel it in my stomach when I think about it. Two months later, three other flight attendants and I were sitting in a Uhaul with all of our furniture, moving to Toronto. What a stressful and exciting adventure! This brings me joy as I am writing it. I am filled with gratitude. Working as a flight attendant has brought me so much excitement and such amazing friendships.

Life was good! Life was incredible! Life was amazing! I was flying around the world. Living my life to its fullest. Our first month of flying as flight attendants, six of us roommates (yes, we were nine roommates living together) travelled to Las Vegas for 4 days. What a beautiful memory. We laugh. We visited. We were happy. I then travelled to Florida most of the winter, visiting family. I would go to Florida quite often prior to being a flight attendant. Now with such amazing perks to fly; every chance I could get to escape our Canadian winter, I was gone! I am a sunny, hot weather kind of-gal! I was enjoying every moment of this new, exciting adventure.

Not knowing that shortly after that period of excitement and fulfillment would come one of the hardest, darkest moments of my life. I had to resort to my POWER more than ever as I felt the most powerless in my whole life. I met him at the peak of my career, and before I knew it I got pregnant. My friends and colleagues asked me on multiple occasions "are you sure this is the right relationship for you?" "isn't he a little possessive?" "controlling?". As human beings, we talk about shame often. I felt a lot of shame for many years. I was ashamed because I was telling myself I should have listened to my friends and family. I gave birth to my daughter and I still held on to hope. I hoped he would change. After all, he was the man I married and he was the biological father of my daughter.

LIVE. LAUGH. LOVE

My job as a flight attendant saved me. My maternity leave was coming to an end and I didn't want to leave my baby girl to fly around the world. I did not want to be away from her, I wanted to be close to her so I could protect her. I was in a very crucial moment in my life again; what to do next? How will I manage to go back to work? I asked God for a sign. I asked for an answer. He gave it to me very clearly.

"I had to be broken, to be rebuilt, to be the woman i a m today"
- Jessica De Derre Boissonneault

The moment he hit me and I fell to the floor with my baby girl in my hands, that was it for me. The lioness inside me was unleashed! This was the moment I went from powerless to powerful. There was no way I was going to allow my daughter to experience and grow in that kind of environment. My mom was always my role model; and what kind of role model would I be to my daughter if I stayed? I left and never looked back. Was it easy? No. Not at all. But my daughter made me strong. My daughter allowed me to get through every single day. I was listening to Mr. Les Brown and Dr. Cindy Trimm, and they were saying to always take life one sip at a time! One day at a time. That is exactly what I did. I was asking for energy and strength for that day and would get through it! I also had a very clear vision. I had the vision of not letting my current circumstances define who I was or where my life was going. I went back to university to complete my degree. I held onto the vision of completing my degree no matter how hard it was going to be. I had no money, I had no car. I had two jobs and an extremely variable flying work schedule. I was a full-time university student, a single mom dealing with courts, and I did not have much support. I was physically and emotionally exhausted. I believed my current life circumstances were not defining my future. Let me tell you, that power inside of me, YOU HAVE ALSO! It kept me going forward.

The power you have inside of yourself can be enlightened by the individuals that surround you. Who do you choose to surround yourself with? Being in the aviation industry also exposes you to so many wonderful individuals. Every time I would be at work flying with a new crew, I would get to meet other wonderful human beings! Going to work was free therapy!

LIVE. LAUGH. LOVE

These were truly moments I could never forget. From lending me money because I forgot my wallet at home, to empowering messages, sharing their experiences and wisdom; to even offering to babysit my daughter so I could do my flights! And I give a huge thanks to everyone who supported me, listened to me, guided me, uplifted me during that period of my life. It truly made a difference.

Going from powerless to unleashing that power inside of me exposed me to the second element that transformed my life! An element that was always there inside of me; PASSION. Relying on my power to transform myself and my life circumstances, I found my true desire to help others. I always knew I wanted to help others and I always did so in my own ways. Helping others and being of service is THE ONE quality and skill of being a flight attendant. As a flight attendant, we are THE face. We are THE image of the company. We are THE point of contact compared to other departments that never get to meet the passengers. So, a few years back, I decided to take action and pursue another passion of mine. My passion for writing. This passion allowed me to help others and serve others. I could empower them by sharing my unique stories and empower others to do the same! I had journaled for a major part of my life. Whether it was to keep a dream journal, a gratitude journal, or to express difficult moments. I loved to write. It was a form of self-expression and had a healing effect (still does). There is a great power in writing your ideas down on a piece of paper.

The beauty of being a flight attendant is that I get to journal sitting at a window seat, watching the beautiful clear blue skies or sitting by the ocean somewhere in this world. What I enjoyed so much about being 40,000 feet in the air is that there is no day when the sky is the same. Some days it is partially cloudy, some days it's all clouds, and some days it's clear. When you look down it can be a beautiful Atlantic ocean or a beautiful city around the world. Nature has a magical aspect to unleash your creativity. I am very grateful for that. I had a dream of becoming a published author and thought it would happen much later in my life. I always say, "keep your eyes open for opportunities and life has its ways to send them to you." What you ask for might not always be in the timing you expect, but in the right moment when you least expect it. I was at a women's expo event and the leaders were offering the opportunity to be part of a book collaboration for the attendees. I thought that was my opportunity to become a published author.

LIVE. LAUGH. LOVE

To dip my toe into this exciting world. I became an author in two international best-selling book collaborations which emphasized my passion for writing. Passion is a powerful emotion, barely controllable! As you might know now; I am deeply passionate about creating and writing in this flight attendant book collaboration! Creating this book with all these amazing authors brought me so much joy! It brought us back to the connection we had onboard an aircraft. We are a community. We share our vulnerable stories in the galleys of the airplane, or as we are walking to explore a new city in our beautiful world. We connect. We laugh. We cry. We worry. We share ideas. Most of all, we care for each other. Like we are always ready to help the passengers; we do the same for each other! I am deeply grateful for that.

This brings me to the third element; positivity! Positivity has kept me going this past year. It has kept me sane. Let's face it, I have been a flight attendant for over a decade. I had told myself; I'm set now with 10+ years of seniority! I would never experience a layoff. It is my career. It is our career. It is our choice. It is a lifestyle.

I never thought my last flight would be on February 26th, 2020. Coming back from a two-week vacation in Colombia the airline industry around the world would completely shut down in a week! As many of us would attest to, there was a lot of uncertainty in the following weeks. What was going to happen to our jobs? When would I fly again? Would I be forced to stay home indefinitely? Children out of school, home 24 hours a day; huge adjustments. We are resilient right? I resorted to my psychological resiliency. I leaned into the positive aspect of this pandemic. What was positive at the time? What was positive for me was that I was able to stay home. Being a flight attendant is very tiring for the body. As much as I love the freedom and different flight schedules; it is not easy. Missing nights of sleep, being in different time zones, working night flights, being dehydrated, tired, up on our feet all day, being in a pressurized working environment, being in a tube with 450 jetlagged passengers, etc... Now I got to stay home. I got to sleep normal nights EVERY night. I got to stay home and relax. I gave myself permission to slow down for the first two months. Watching Netflix, learning Spanish, spending time with my daughter, and connecting with friends through Zoom.

LIVE. LAUGH. LOVE

Staying positive was great; I then wanted to share that positivity with others! That's when I became more present on social media and started my own podcast show! Being able to spread positivity in people's lives was very rewarding. Positive energy bounces and it is contagious (the non-life threatening contagious)!

This last year has taught me a lot. It has taught me how life is uncertain. We never know what tomorrow will bring. All we can control is today. All we can control is how we feel about what is happening now. We can control our thoughts. So much of this year has been comprised of circumstances that are outside of our control. I miss flying. I miss my adventurous lifestyle. I miss travelling. I miss my colleagues. I miss my paycheck. I miss my freedom. However, I hold onto my power, passion, and positivity to control today. I want to make the best out of today. I hold onto hope. Hope that we will be back, united again, doing what we love sooner than later.

Saying yes to my friend 11 years ago to go to the flight attendant interviews was one of the best things that has ever happened in my life. It was one of the best decisions of my life. Letting go of your thoughts of worries and 'what if' can prevent you from experiencing the biggest adventures of your lifetime! Remember the woman you are seeing and hearing from at this moment was not always like this. I know now that, leaning into my power inside, my passionate self, and unbending positivity, is crucial to living an abundant and purposeful life. Through psychological resilience, I can cope with the crises and chaos that life can bring. I am inviting you to do the same! Lean into that power you have inside of yourself. It is there. Mr. Les Brown would say you have greatness inside of you! You are unique. You are special.

Always with Love.. 🖤

jessica dsb

My Beautiful Blended Family of Five
Believe in your dreams..

BIOGRAPHY

Jessica De Serre Boissonneault

From small town girl to global inspiration, Jessica has always been known for her positivity and bubbliness! She studied Sociology to follow her passion for helping others and is certified in NLP. She is a lifetime learner with personal growth as an integral part of her daily routine. Following her mission of supporting women, Jessica started her own podcast show and founded the Women Empowerment Wednesday Show. She is the founder of the Take Flight Coaching Academy, serving you as YOUR EMPOWERMENT AGENT. She was nominated for the Top 50 Most Influential Women in the VIP Global Magazine in the United States and is an award-winning author with two International-Best-Selling Books. Her third book being "I am a Flight Attendant and that is my Superpower".

Jessica's real transformation began in 2013 when she made the crucial decision to escape an abusive marriage and start her journey as a single mother. She leaned on her power, passion, and unbending positivity to transform herself, and in doing so, learned how to elevate women just like her. Along with being a flight attendant for the past 11 years, a passionate world traveller, and a philanthropist, today she is happy in love with her beautiful, blended family of 5! Jessica is about to launch her group coaching program to elevate women to live a more purposeful and powerful life. She works with women, entrepreneurs and authors and her motto is: "We rise by lifting each other"! She is dedicated to sharing her contagious energy with everyone fortunate enough to cross her path. Jessica has been featured in multiple media, but you are more likely to see her hiking, doing a family dance party in the living room, enjoying date night with her love, or on a plane for her next adventure exploring this beautiful world!

BRUSSELS, BELGIUM

CONTACT

Jessica De Serre Boissonneault

Always with Love.. 🖤

To schedule a complimentary session;
please text Jessica at 514.824.9402

 ms.jessicadsb

Jessica De Serre Boissonneault

Facebook Group : Women Empowerment by jessica dsb

Websites : jessicadsb.com & www.mysuperpower.world

Email : jessicadsb@live.ca

CHAPTER 2

FROM A MYSTICAL LAND TO UP IN THE AIR …

by Karina V Gonzalez

*"It's the possibility of having a dream come
true that makes life interesting." - Paulo Coelho*

My Birth town

I returned to my city of birth when I was twenty years old. The memories of my infancy and early childhood came back to me instantly. This time however, everything seemed so small: my grandparent's home, the school I attended as a child, the streets…The only things that had not changed in size were the mountains and the lake "Nahuel Huapi."

While I was exploring this land as a young woman, reconnecting with the land that I had left so many years ago; childhood memories started to flood my mind. As a child, I used to play with my younger brother, throwing pebbles into the lake. I remembered my grandfather preparing a delicious "Asado Argentino" (Argentinian grill) and drinking "mate" – just him and I. I started to reconnect to these very special memories from my childhood. I also realized that although I have been able to travel all over the world and have visited some beautiful places, the most beautiful place on this earth, for me, is San Carlos de Bariloche; because it is there where I found the happiest memories of my childhood.

Every time I enter an airplane that takes me to Bariloche, my heart jumps with joy. I know I will soon see so much natural beauty, find so much peace, and find myself reconnecting with this little girl who I was once upon a time. Each time I achieve that goal to go back to that dream place & I connect to the best version of myself, I feel empowered, and I say to myself – "don't quit, never give up on your dreams and love what you do."

FROM A MYSTICAL LAND TO UP IN THE AIR …

I was born in San Carlos, Bariloche, which is located in Argentinian Patagonia. Magnificent mountains surround this mystical land. An old aboriginal legend tells us of a giant monster named "Nahuelito" who lived deep in the "Nahuel Huapi" lake. In the Mapuche language "Nahuel" means "Tiger," and "Huapi" means "Island." Other legends tell us of goblins that also lived in those magical forests surrounded by prehistoric dinosaur fossils.

Every time I return to that magical place, and after having flown for more than fifteen hours - from the far North American continent to the far South American continent, I take a walk to the lake – the famous "Nahuel Huapi."

I pause and sit on the rocks to contemplate those majestic mountains that surround the area from north to south and from east to west. All of a sudden, I find myself dreaming! My creativity is heightened. The beauty that surrounds me inspires me. The wonderful and distinct colors of the sky, the rocks, the trees, the mountains, and the clouds – all that beauty seems to embrace me warmly! It is the place in the world where I feel my best and I am always seeking a way to go back?

The First Time I Left Argentina

By the time of the coup in Chile in September of 1973, my grandfather who was a great believer in justice and freedom for all, was a retired officer of the Air Force. He had decided to leave the Air Force years earlier, searching for a better life for himself and his family. He started a small business that provided well for his family of ten children. When Pinochet came into power, freedom was non-existent, and persecution was rampant. My grandfather was forced to leave the country or suffer imprisonment. He spent three years in Buenos Aires, Argentina hiding from the Chilean government while waiting for asylum. He received asylum for himself, his wife, and his unmarried children to go to Switzerland through Amnesty International in 1976.

FROM A MYSTICAL LAND TO UP IN THE AIR …

A few years later, in 1982, when the war between Argentina and England was declared, my parents decided that it was our turn to leave Argentina and join my grandparents. My father, who was a gendarme and served as a Law Secretary, was told he was next on the list to go to war. In those uncertain times, my maternal grandparents asked us to go join them in Switzerland. A very special person in my life, my aint Rita , who taught me about faith and about how to do the right thing, my mother's youngest sister, flew from Switzerland to Argentina to get my family and bring us to our grandparents.

I was only seven years old when my mother, my brother, and I left my homeland, Argentina. I remember that I was overwhelmed by an immense sadness because I did not want to leave my paternal grandfather nor the gorgeous mountains I was so used to. On top of that, I was also afraid that I wouldn't see my father again, as he had to stay in Argentina for a while longer to finish up some business. As a child, I did not understand why he had to stay at the time– it caused immense sadness, worrying, and fear. Luckily only a few months later, my father joined our family in Switzerland.

From the moment we took that huge, big airplane, I realized we were going to a very far away land. I still have that black and white picture of my mother, little brother, and myself climbing the long airplane stairs to board the plane. In the picture, my fear and discomfort were quite visible. On the other hand, I was happy for my mother who was finally going to reunite with her parents, who she hadn't seen for over 9 years. However, the sadness I felt leaving my hometown was overwhelming.

In Switzerland, I learned to speak German and Italian. I rapidly learned those languages and made new friends. I also got to know my maternal grandparents who were loving people. They shared with me the story of why and how they left their country, Chile. My Grandfather taught me about political issues. I started to understand why my grandfather, who was a nurse in the Air Force, was forced to leave his beloved Chile. One of the saddest parts of his story is that he had to leave his married children behind. Because they had a family of their own, they were unable to join him, their mother, and younger siblings.

FROM A MYSTICAL LAND TO UP IN THE AIR …

About 4 years after arriving in Switzerland, my family and I had to say goodbye to my grandparents, aunts, and uncles. Because of some legal issues we were unable to remain in Switzerland and found ourselves on our way to a new country – Canada. Once again, we were forced to leave family behind and experience the same great sadness I felt when leaving Argentina. My family and I were once again boarding a huge aircraft. I was 12 years old when we landed in Quebec, Canada. Canada became my new home. I was here to stay, for good this time!

Many years later after Pinochet was no longer a dictator, my grandparents were able to return to their home country, Chile. So, at the age of 16 years old, I asked my parents if I could go visit my grandparents in Chile. When I flew to Chile, all by myself, I was so excited! I was finally able to reunite with my grandparents. When I came back, I started planning how I could visit them more often. I felt it was nearly impossible because airline tickets were so expensive. For years I kept looking for solutions, but I could not find an easy one. However, the thought never escaped my mind. Suddenly, I started entertaining the idea of pursuing a career that would allow me to travel more often.

At that age, I had no clue about what I was going to do. I liked the idea of traveling, but I did not know how to incorporate it into my career. My father wanted me to become a lawyer. While still in Argentina, my father had to stop his studies in law, so he could give us a better future. He missed that time of his life and thought he could influence me to follow the same path that interested him.

I chose to study graphic design which I felt was the right career for me as I also had a passion for art and visual arts. He wasn't too happy with my choice of profession. While struggling to find a job opportunity in my field, after a couple of years with no success, I decided to enroll part-time as a law student. It was a total failure for me. I enjoyed the classes; I learned a lot, but the unending hours I spent studying and the extremely long exams, robbed me of my hopes and desires to become a lawyer and satisfy my father.

FROM A MYSTICAL LAND TO UP IN THE AIR ...

I ended up working for big companies in customer service. I even got a job in customer service for a big airline and a big international cruise company. I traveled to Japan, Morocco, Spain, and Egypt! I thought accomplishing those things would make my dad happy – it did not. My dad continued to be unhappy and carry that same look of dissatisfaction on his face. At one point in my life, I became aware that no matter what I would do or not do, I might never make my father happy. And the truth is that I wasn't fully happy either. I felt like something was always missing.

My dream ever since I was a teenager was of being able to travel often to my country of birth. It was a constant reminder of my true deep desire. – "maybe," I thought to myself, "one day, I'll be able to accomplish that goal."

In my early twenties, I applied to become a flight attendant for a Canadian airline. The interview didn't go well. There were hundreds of candidates applying for the same position. At the time, I was not very confident in myself. I was shy and insecure. So, I decided to keep that dream in a very secret place - like a dream. In my dream, I could see myself walking in the airport alongside other Flight Attendants, carrying our luggage, and traveling around the world!

Many years later, I went to work for an medical insurance company. I felt, so numb, so bored, and so dissatisfied. One day, I received a call from a person who mistakenly had called our office. – it was the wrong customer service department. The person explained to me that she was looking for the department that is in charge of the Flight Attendants' insurance. After I transferred the person to the right department, I took a break. Suddenly my mind started dreaming of the idea I had kept secret for so many years. What if I try once again to become a Flight Attendant – I thought! I asked myself why I was waiting to apply again as a Flight Attendant, and decided that I should send my resume once again. Then I thought my dream was just a dream. And then I also thought - what if my dream came true? That same day I sent out my resume to a big international airline company. I told myself I had nothing to lose!

FROM A MYSTICAL LAND TO UP IN THE AIR …

Graduation Day & Receiving My Wings

I will never forget my graduation day. I saw my parents in the lobby of that fancy hotel, arriving to congratulate me on becoming a Flight Attendant! The day I received my wings was one of the happiest moments in my life! Why? Because I was accomplishing one of my greatest dreams! And because, finally I saw that look at my father's face – the look of happiness!!! He was so proud of me and so happy for me! Both my mom and dad had hoped for many years that I would find a profession where I would be happy and fully satisfied! And there I was, looking at them with happy tears in their eyes, celebrating that exciting moment in my life with me! I kept this dream for many years, the dream of being able to become a flight Attendant, to travel the world, to discover new cultures, and also to be able to go back to those magical mountains of my birth town. It took me 8 months to become a Flight Attendant. I failed some exams, but this time, I got right back on my feet and gave it my all. My dream became a reality!

My First Flight to South America
As an International Flight Attendant

I remember my first flight to South America after receiving my wings. I was assigned to be part of the operating crew to Santiago, Chile. To me, it was completely unexpected. That route was coveted and mostly awarded to senior flight attendants. I was on a stand-by schedule, which meant that they could call me at any time of the day to assign me to any flight going anywhere in the world. When I say, anywhere I mean Asia, Europe, Africa, United States, and South America.

This flight to South America happened during my first three months of having received my wings. This was a stressful time in my life because I was still on probation. I still had to wait three more months before becoming a permanent Flight Attendant. I was in the loop! I remember feeling that the process to become a Flight Attendant was so harsh and difficult. We were constantly tested on the job, even though we had successfully received our wings after two long months of boot camp training!

FROM A MYSTICAL LAND TO UP IN THE AIR …

Learning how to evacuate people from an aircraft after a crash, how to extinguish a fire, how to perform first aid for a medical situation onboard, and so many other skills we had to learn and practice over and over.

During those first three months of flying, I was sent to various destinations: India, Germany, Italy, all over Canada, and the United States. But I had not been sent to South America yet!

Then one day! I was in Toronto waiting to receive the call to my next assignment. That day, I had no expectations. Maybe, they will send me on a 4-day assignment with 3 flights per day, I thought!

Suddenly my phone rang. It was the crew scheduling department. They told me, "well, Karina, you have 2 hours and a half to get to the airport; we need you to fly to Santiago, Chile, and to Buenos Aires, Argentina."

"Finally, they chose me to fly to South America!" I thought to myself.

After so many years of wanting to become an international Flight Attendant, I was finally there. I was being assigned that special route that I had dreamed of!

That day while I was heading to the airport in my uniform with my wings displayed proudly on my blazer, I thanked God for this incredible and most desired opportunity.

The crew I was joining was senior in rank and had been holding that route for a long time. I was the most junior on the list and still on probation. To them, it wasn't much of a big deal to fly to South America, but to me, it meant the world!

I remember what it was like, walking through those gates at Pearson international airport - my legs were shaking. My heart was pumping so fast! I felt like laughing and crying at the same time. I was still in shock. I couldn't believe it – I was a real Flight Attendant, and I was going to my homeland.

FROM A MYSTICAL LAND TO UP IN THE AIR ...

Once I met with the other crew members, I tried to keep my cool. I was in uniform; I needed to control my excitement. I knew my exhilaration was apparent, but I tried to act cool and professional. After we received our briefing instructions, there I was, following the 12 other Flight Attendants, boarding the plane with my suitcase, telling myself, remember this moment! Pay attention to where you are! When in a million years would you have thought that this could become real!

The first stop was in Santiago, Chile. I could see the majestic Andes – such majestic mountains as we approached the airport. When the wheels touched the ground, I felt this huge wave of electricity going through my whole body!

I remember talking to my grandparents as if they were there with me. I was greeting them and hoping they could see me! Even though I knew they were dead. I hoped they could see me landing in their land. I thanked them for having taught me to fight for a better future and never give up!

After the crew and I had our 24 hour mandatory rest in Santiago, Chile, we had to take off and operate the flight to Buenos Aires, Argentina – my birth country. And this is when the magic happened for me! While I was still in training, I used to repeatedly practice the welcoming announcements that we say on each flight, in my kitchen. I would say "Ladies & Gentleman, Bienvenidos a Buenos Aires, Argentina!"

That morning when the crew was heading to board the plane, the In-charge Flight Attendant informed me that our colleague who was assigned to make the language announcements would not be flying with us because she felt sick. Therefore, I was in charge of the Spanish announcements. My mind was blown! My first time doing the welcoming announcements with the airline, and I get to do it when we land in Buenos Aires. I could not believe it!

FROM A MYSTICAL LAND TO UP IN THE AIR …

A few minutes before landing, the captain makes the announcements that we are approaching Buenos Aires. "Prepare for landing". There I am, seated in my jump seat, facing the passengers. I am looking out the window. I am listening to the wheels touching the ground. I grab the interphone and start making the Spanish announcements. Again, I felt this electrical energy going through my whole body. I remember looking at the passengers' eyes with a big smile. My hands were wet, and I had tears in my eyes. I started applauding with some of the passengers who were as excited as I was to have landed safely in my beautiful Argentina – it was a jaw-dropping moment! I thought to myself "life continues to surprise me." What an amazing journey!

Here I am! A couple of years later, sharing this remarkable journey of traveling around the world with you. I have met amazing people! I have shared amazing stories with my colleagues while traveling around the world. My uniform is in the closet at the moment. It's been there for over a year now, ever since the pandemic began. I chose to be part of this mind-blowing journey as a co-author with 20 other amazing flight attendants, to send a message of hope, and to share how fascinating it is to work at 30 000 feet up in the air. I wanted to share how this dream of mine, this vision of becoming an international flight attendant, started as a desire that turned into a dream and how that dream then turned into a reality.

My Last Trip to Patagonia Before the Pandemic

February 2020. It was a beautiful sunny day in Patagonia; I was staring at the mountains for the last time before checking-in for my flight back to Canada. Tears were falling down my cheeks because, once again, I would be leaving my beloved country. Every time I leave it, I start to miss it instantaneously. I always say "farewell beautiful mountains; I hope life will allow me to come back home to you."

March 2020. I had recently come back to Montreal from my trip to San Carlos de Bariloche.

FROM A MYSTICAL LAND TO UP IN THE AIR …

I was preparing to be on duty and fly to Rome, Italy. I was usually assigned to travel to Italy once a week for the past 3 years because I speak Italian.

Because the Covid-19 virus had hit Italy severely, I was reassigned to operate on a flight to Brussels, Belgium instead. A couple of days later, I was notified that due to the pandemic, I was being temporarily laid off along with many other of my colleagues.

We all thought this lay-off time would only be for a few weeks, but those few weeks turned into months. It has been extremely hard waiting for the Covid-19 virus to be fully eradicated and for me to return to my normal life. I was able to taste the fulfilling life I enjoyed as a flight attendant. I want to be able to return to that exciting life, to get my wings back, and to wear my uniform.

It's been a year now; I'm still waiting to receive the news that I will be a Flight Attendant once more and be able to return to the skies. In the meantime, I have decided to achieve one of my other dreams. That dream is to become a successful Graphic Designer. I love to create, I love to let my imagination flow, and I love to inspire others.

Life is very much like flying. Sometimes we experience moments of severe turbulence. When the turbulence is high, fear rises, and most often we feel like giving up. However, life has taught me that maybe sometimes we don't achieve the goals we have planned, maybe sometimes we lose, and sometimes we don't feel it is worth the effort. However, there is always a place inside of us that can keep those dreams alive - in secret. There is a place inside of us that connects us to the power of believing in ourselves and our dreams.

Thank you, life, for this amazing teaching journey! I will always continue maintaining those dreams safe in my heart. ♥ I will also continue to hope that one day very soon, I'll be in front of those majestic mountains of San Carlos de Bariloche. That magic place where I connect with myself at a higher level and where I feel that everything is possible!

BIOGRAPHY
Karina V Gonzalez

Inflore DESIGN

Karina was born in Patagonia, Argentina. She is a passionate graphic designer and an international flight attendant. For years, she had a silent dream of becoming a flight attendant and travelling the world. She kept that dream alive until, one day, the opportunity for her to work for an international airline came to her 'Camino'. In this book collaboration, she will share how dreams can come true by sending out real intentions into the universe, by trusting ourselves and life, and by pushing away all limited beliefs. She finds her inspirations, nourishes her imagination, and empowers her creativity through her discoveries around the world. Her imagination was filled with creative ideas stemming from the many countries she has visited... Argentina, Chile, Egypt, Europe, India, Japan and even Morocco. The most special place for her, however, is the town of her birth, San Carlos, the Bariloche. It is at the end of the world, surrounded by magnificent mountains, lakes, and rivers and harbors ancient legends of magical forests protected by dwarfs. Another legend speaks of the monster Nahuelito, a cryptid lake monster who allegedly lives in Nahuel Huapi Lake, Patagonia, a beautiful territory that was once occupied by ancient dinosaurs. She is thrilled to participate in this journey as a co-author where she shares the magic through her travelling adventures and what she found while discovering new cultures and art, all while absorbing the magnificent panoramas filled with history.

Te amo Mama !

With my little brother Mauricio (Wally) & My Mama ...
Departure: from South America to Switzerland

CERRO TRONADOR, SAN CARLOS DE BARILOCHE, ARGENTINA PATAGONIA 2020

CHAPTER 3

FASTEN YOUR SEAT BELT!

by Mélissa Verpaelst

"The future belongs to those who believe in the beauty of their dreams" - Muguette Verpaelst (Née Gendron) 1929-2020

FASTEN YOUR SEAT BELT!

Dear Mélissa,

I am so proud of you. I'm so proud of you for living a life that someone from my generation would have never thought possible. Ever since the first time I held you in my arms, I felt this deep connection between us. I have always known you would achieve anything you put your heart into. You have that purpose of helping other human beings without judgment or hesitation. Through your life's journey, you have encountered numerous great adventures and accumulated so many incredible stories to tell. But nothing can compare to your unbelievable aviation anecdotes! Do you remember that Christmas Eve when you performed CPR on that little 1-year-old girl without any hesitation? Or the very next day, when you bravely managed to go through an abnormal landing while doing your dream job as a Flight Attendant! And I will never forget that day when a passenger physically attacked you at 35 000 feet and still, you found the strength to laugh once you got to the hospital. You pour reassurance and joy wherever you are, and always look for the positive and solution-driven side of a story.

Even after being laid off from that dreamy lifestyle, you managed to find a new purpose through your passion for self-care. Along with that new side gig, came a wonderful community in which you've grown and flourished. You have gained confidence and positive habits which have led you to inspire and empower other people to follow your lead.

Even now that I have passed to the other side, I can see how you have transformed your unfortunate layoff situation into a powerful life-changing series of events. If only you knew how difficult it was for me to see you saddened and in such mental distress for those first few months. I made sure you could feel my presence through your darkest days. I want you to know that I have heard all your prayers.

FASTEN YOUR SEAT BELT!

I understood how you felt disoriented as part of your freedom was taken away from you. I know that being a flight attendant had become such an exciting lifestyle for you, and I knew that it was unimaginable for you to be confined and to feel "imprisoned" at home without a sense of purpose.

It always comes back to your purpose of helping others. You kept on looking for passions that would allow you to keep on inspiring and empowering other people. You have turned hangry people into happy people by delivering food for a while, but you soon discovered that it was not rewarding enough. You have a degree and work experience in Hotel Management, but unfortunately, that was not the most in-demand industry during a global pandemic. You applied to many job postings and went through job interviews, but your heart was not feeling it. You had to slowly go through the process of grieving that lifestyle that had been taken away from you.

As the positive woman you are, you tried to make the best out of the confinement you found yourself locked in. You learned how to play the ukulele with your Samy love, you binge-watched the whole series of the TV show Vikings together, and you spent a lot of time in the kitchen. Oh, how I wished I could have had a piece of that caramel apple crumble cheesecake you baked!

Through all that, I could see that it was once you became a Monat Market Partner that you finally fulfilled your deepest desire of helping people through your passion for self-care. That is when your life shifted towards your greatest journey. You have put together your vision board, became goal-oriented towards your dreams, and achieved the top 3% of the company in only 5 months*. Remember the chills you felt? It was me next to you. I've never stopped being by your side.

Ma chère petite-fille, do not worry. You are on the right track. You have the power to illuminate anyone's day with your contagious laugh and beautiful energy. Your calmness and self-confidence empower the many people who surround you. Keep on taking actions towards your dreams. Never stop spreading your positivity and light. I am so proud of you.

Mamie qui t'adore x x x x

FASTEN YOUR SEAT BELT!

Mamie ♥

FASTEN YOUR SEAT BELT!

I've always been supported and encouraged by my Mamie. She was my role model. She was truly genuine, filled with love, and open-minded. I was easily able to have deep conversations about things that were considered "taboo" for people from her generation. We had many passions in common, and travelling was one of the greatest.

For as long as I could remember, Mamie would tell me stories about her travels with Papi, the love of her life. They have been to many countries, without speaking anything other than French. I've always been inspired by their courage and fearless actions. When I left home at 19 years old and moved four hours away to be able to work in my field of study, she was not surprised. She knew how adventurous and curious I had always been. Even when I left on my own to backpack in Bali for a month, she encouraged me to pursue my dream!

Unfortunately, she passed away on February 27, 2020, at the dawn of her 91st birthday. Grieving my Mamie plus the lay-off of my dream job was devastating. The first few months were very emotional and difficult to get through. I was crying daily at random moments. Even now, I think of her multiple times a day. I feel her presence more than ever and it reassures me. A few months later, I started my own gig and was able to find meaning in my life once again.

From working in hotel management around the province of Quebec, to flying around 5 continents as a Flight Attendant, I have the best stories to tell. Human behaviors have made me speechless, and I was also privileged to see life miracles happen more than once.

When people think of Flight Attendants, they usually imagine an air hostess who serves drinks and chicken or pasta. My purpose in writing this story is to open your mind and help you understand what we actually learn in our initial seven weeks of training. There are a lot of duties and knowledge that go into being a flight attendant that most people don't know about. Safety first, always. As we work at over 30 000 feet in the air, we are trained to handle all sorts of eventual threats. From reassuring a passenger who is going through a panic attack, to evacuating 450 passengers on a full loaded Boeing 777 on fire, we are ready for any kind of situation. I have personally been through a few unbelievable events that have changed my perspective of life on many levels.

FASTEN YOUR SEAT BELT!

First aid on a baby girl

On my first Christmas Eve as a Flight Attendant, I was based in beautiful Vancouver. Surrounded by beaches and mountains, I was living the dream. Being on call, far away from my family who were celebrating on the other side of the country on such a festive night, wasn't easy, but I was manifesting an exciting layover! I was over the moon when crew scheduling assigned me a flight on my roomie's pairing! We got ready together, left home early to grab a Starbucks Coffee prior to our flight, and enjoyed every minute of that special moment. As we were walking through the gates at the airport, we suddenly heard someone yelling for help. As I turned my head, I saw a desperate father holding his baby with breathing difficulties. I dropped my coffee and my suitcase and ran towards them. As my training taught me, I automatically told the man "My name is Melissa, I know first aid, may I help you?". He then quickly handed me his daughter and took a step back with his wife. They were desperate and in shock. I was now holding this little 1-year-old baby's life in my hands. She had foam coming out of her mouth. While my roommate was asking for the airport's Paramedic Bike Squads, I found a safe counter to put the 1-year-old on and examined her state. She could barely breathe and even though the parents didn't see her put anything in her mouth, I couldn't assume that it had not happened. I began the first aid maneuvers, and while it helped at first, she soon completely lost consciousness. I realized she wasn't breathing anymore and proceeded with Cardiopulmonary Resuscitation on that tiny and fragile infant.

Let me tell you, my training kicked in hard because what followed was an automatic series of decisions and actions taken. After a few rounds of CPR, the baby girl regained consciousness and began breathing again. Can you imagine the relief that consumed me at that moment? Meanwhile, as we were waiting for paramedics (which felt endless); she fixed her eyes on mine as I gently talked to her, and I will never forget that special connection I felt. I whispered softly to her how strong and courageous she was to fight for her life. She smiled at me and we kept that connection going until help arrived. They took her from my arms and rushed her away. I often think about that little girl and hope that she is healthy and living a beautiful life filled with love.

FASTEN YOUR SEAT BELT!

Attacked by a disruptive passenger

It all started as passengers were boarding the aircraft. A woman walked up to our boarding door and my colleague asked for her boarding pass. A part of the boarding pass ripped off, and accidentally fell on the doorstep. The woman threw us an impatient look that surprised us. We told ourselves that she may have been having a bad day. She left to go to her seat and passengers continued to board. Once boarding was completed, we finalized our safety procedures and made sure everyone was seated and secured for take-off. It seemed like it would be a smooth late-night flight. There were no signs of agitation that could have predicted the following series of surprising and agitated events...

During the first food and beverage service in economy class, the same lady that had shot us the impatient look during boarding, started behaving irrationally and increasing her level of violence. She was rude to other passengers as well as the flight crew. She first threw her food tray at one of the Flight Attendants. Yes, she literally threw it at her. Afterwards, we heard that she had asked the people sitting beside her to move to another seat during boarding so she could have the whole row to herself. The woman in question didn't appear to be intoxicated. She insisted on having a fresh, hot cup of coffee, but because there was turbulence, and the seat belt sign was on - it was not possible to serve it to her for safety reasons. She requested to speak to a French speaker. I was asked by my colleagues to go to this woman and see if I could calm the situation (I am a qualified French speaker – it is my mother tongue). Once I started interacting with her, I suddenly realized that she was suffering from delusions of grandeur, which was later confirmed by a psychologist who was sitting close by.

Once I got to her seat, I lowered myself to her level and asked calmly and empathetically, what we could do to make her flight more enjoyable. At that point, I simply wanted a better understanding what was going on in her mind. At 35 000 feet, you want to try to defuse any sort of tense situation, not escalate it. To my surprise, she said something about not being able to charge her phone... I offered to charge it for her, and she acted as if everything else was smooth and fine.

FASTEN YOUR SEAT BELT!

At some point during our discussion, the seat belt sign went off, and one of the flight attendants brought her a fresh cup of coffee, just as she had requested. I then told her that her previous behavior and acts were unacceptable and that it was her first official verbal warning. She looked aberrant, then denied everything and asked for a meeting with all the witnesses so we could discuss further. I was speechless. I stared at her, trying to analyze her thoughts and mental distress. She began complaining about the flight attendants, calling them bit***, saying they were uneducated, deaf, and evoking degrading comments towards them in a delusional way.

You know how things happen quickly? Well, this lady looked at me with an empty look and then proceeded to pour her steaming, freshly prepared, hot coffee on the personal belongings of the passenger sitting in the row in front of her. I was flabbergasted. I mean... Why would someone who acts so irrationally be allowed to travel by herself? I calmly tried to reason with her, but then she suddenly poured what was left in her coffee cup directly on the head of the lady sitting in front of her! I could see the steam rising above her head... I was shocked! I gave her a final warning to stop. She then "softly" slapped me on the face and pulled my lips with her fingers! I stood up firmly, my training kicked in, and I was in reaction mode. It was official, this passenger was disruptive! Not only did she physically attack me, but she had physically attacked another passenger as well. It was time to put an end to it. I told a colleague to standby while I went to look for help and the restraint kit.

It was night mode in the cabin and the lights were dimmed. As I came back to her (for translation purposes only), she stood up and came at me in the aisle. I was in a defensive position, with my arms in front of me as protection. She was verbally aggressive and could not look me in the eyes. She seemed to be in a psychotic episode, in a trance. She began to approach me in violent manner and started chasing me. I turned my head to look for help and I yelled, "Someone help me! Aidez-moi!". But every passenger was either looking at their screen or sleeping. And then I blacked out. She punched me in the eye, and I completely lost vision for a few seconds. I was dazed and in shock. Meanwhile, my colleagues managed to restrain her to her seat for the duration of the rest of the flight.

FASTEN YOUR SEAT BELT!

Once we landed, I had to go to the hospital to run tests on my eye. I have to mention that I was lucky and blessed to be surrounded by my amazing colleagues and the destination's airline manager. Thanks to their emotional support and presence, I felt safe, and found a way to laugh throughout the whole hospital procedure. Did you know it was possible to get an ocular ultrasound? Yeah, me neither! LOL!

Step out of your comfort zone

Inspired by my grandmother who, not only taught me many life lessons, but who also taught me to count my blessings, I have written down my thoughts about my mindset as a Woman Entrepreneur. I feel like it is what I want to pass on to my children and grandchildren.

I find power in stepping out of my comfort zone and that's what keeps me going every day. The way you feel after doing so is incredibly life-changing and empowering. Accomplishing something you never thought was possible feels like the next level and it boosts your self-confidence. I've always been someone who empowers people without consciously intending to. It's the little things. Little compliments, seeing the bright side of a story, making them realize their own strengths. Every human being is born with a good heart. Your past experiences have made you, but you can always change your direction and become a better version of yourself! Of course, it takes courage to take action and work on yourself, but it surely is the best gift you can give to yourself for a happier future! Life is about happiness and it begins with self-esteem.

My purpose is to help other humans fulfill their dreams through their passions. I help people who wish to meet their higher self through manifestation, positive thinking, and consistency. I have this deep belief that anything you want, you can obtain. The only thing that will stop you from getting it is your self-talk. By declaring your goals loudly and clearly, by believing in yourself, and by taking daily actions, anything is possible! Also, I highly recommend consulting a psychotherapist to heal your childhood traumas and look forward to a brighter and more conscious future for yourself. Read about self-development (I recently enjoyed the book " The 5 Second Rule by Mel Robbins "), discover parts of your personality through tests (the Enneagram Personality Test was very revealing for me.

FASTEN YOUR SEAT BELT!

I'm a type 7, you?), and most importantly; surround yourself with people you look up to! By doing so, they will inspire you to make the best choices and get you closer to your desires! These are the things that I surround myself with in life as well as through my business.

Good intentioned humans who want to dream bigger! Make a vision board with your biggest dreams on it (family, career, travels, etc.). This helps you to have a clear vision of what to look forward to and also serves as a reminder of what to focus on when days get tougher.

When there's an opportunity offered to you, be courageous, put your fears aside and think about all the good it could bring you! When you say yes to an opportunity, you allow yourself to evolve, grow and learn new things. More often than not, opportunities are sent to you by the Universe, knowing that you can achieve it! The only thing that separates you from your dream are your thoughts. Never underestimate the power of your thoughts. You must have heard about selftalk and self-love? Well, these two notions are crucial when it comes to better selfesteem. Be gentle with yourself and act as your own best friend. Be your biggest supporter and continuously tell yourself that you are capable of achieving anything. Because you ARE! The more often you repeat something positive and powerful to yourself, the more you will end up believing it. That works with negative thoughts too. That's why you should be selective about what you want your introspection to be filled with. Practicing gratitude daily is a way to improve your self-esteem, build strong relationships and enhance your overall health (psychological, physical and habit forming). Gratitude can be felt through every moment of your day. From waking up alive to enjoying an amazing café latte, learn something new, resonate and connect with a new friend, watch a beautiful sunset, or simply enjoy a warm and comfy bed at night. There are tons of reasons to be grateful! By continuously shifting your mindset to look for the good in every situation, you will become happier. It has been proven that if you integrate gratitude into your daily habits, you will be a more content human being.

Anyhoo, I can't wait for another volume of a book collaboration like this one, as I feel I have so many more insights to share with you! Meanwhile, if a part of my story has resonated with you, reach out to me through social media! Let's connect! Xo

BiOGRAPHY
Mélissa Verpaelst

Mélissa has been a flight attendant for the past 5 years. A girl who decided to go for it! She says "yes" to every opportunity that pushes her out of her comfort zone. This has led her to multiple adventures and brought out the best stories to tell. You may see your flight attendants as air hostesses, but the truth is this: they are first aid trained, ready to respond to any kind of emergency situation, and they have amazing social skills. From performing CPR on a baby, to getting punched in the face, you will read the details of some of Mélissa's most personal and unbelievable stories. From living her best life through her dream job, to being laid off and in mourning, she has owned her courage, worked on her mindset, and turned her purpose of helping others into a new passion for self-care. Her goal is to help people feel empowered and beautiful, inside and out. Can you believe she does it with shampoo and face wash?

 melissa.verpaelst

 Melissa Verpaelst

VICTORIA PEAK - HONG KONG

CHAPTER 4

In Difference We Find Unity

by H.K

When I was studying at the university, I never thought that I would choose a career as a flight attendant. Like everybody else, I used to think that being a flight attendant was an easy and simple job. I thought that it only required the person to look a certain way, have a friendly personality, and have a beautiful smile. Shortly after that, however, one of my close friends joined the aviation industry, and through her, I came to know more about the job. It turned out that, yes, it does require those specific criteria, and yes it has that fun side where you literally might have breakfast in one country and dinner in another, but it also requires constant resilience, strength, and a great deal of patience. This knowledge motivated me to apply for the job, to take part in this experience, to feel thrilled whenever I meet new people, and to explore marvelous cultures.

Last year, on the other hand, proved that the universe has bigger plans for everyone. It was a proof that life can be ironic. Life can send you over the edge and then pull you back to be stronger, more open to challenges, and more determined to fight back in any situation. What I am about to share with you in this chapter are stories I have lived and witnessed within the last year that simply made me realize how flight attendants can be resilient in a time of need, and how humanity, in general, can get together and be stronger in dire times.

During the last year, the aviation industry has suffered enormously from the covid 19 pandemic. It is believed to be one of the first sectors to be hugely affected by the drop in travel demand, an impact that will cost years of recovery afterward. Many airlines ceased their operations following government guidelines to contain the spread of the virus until scientists get a better understanding of the situation. During this time, I believe that those of us in the aviation community who were laid off became lost, not knowing what was going to happen in the near future.

In Difference We Find Unity

The concept of travelling has shifted from being a luxury to a necessity. Many people were unfortunately stuck in foreign countries, not knowing how to go back to their loved ones, and as frightening as the situation can be, someone had to step in and help them get home. I do believe that there were very few airlines in the world that took this responsibility to help these people out and to make their return possible. Flights were created hand in hand with governments' efforts to achieve this goal, and as hard as it was, we were proud enough to make it happen. The happiness and gratitude that I felt from those who were able to go home through these flights was worth all the sacrifices and being part of this experience has humbled me enormously.

Now, let me start by pointing out that the airline I am working for is not based in my home country. Most flight attendants come from different backgrounds and cultures and the number of nationalities involved is believed to be in the hundreds. This has been fascinating to me as it broadens my knowledge about the world daily, and every discussion I have with my colleagues about their cultures is simply worth a fortune.

As amazing as it felt to be the ones helping people, it somehow created a dilemma for us. When the virus started to spread, while we were taking people home and connecting them with their families, we ourselves could not go home. Woefully, international regulations at that time did not give us much of an option other than staying in our base and making it a second home. By sticking together as a crew, we got all the support we needed from each other and kept sending positive vibes to our families reassuring them that we were doing fine even in that frightening situation.

There is no doubt that that period was tough on all of us, even if you were not a flight attendant and had a nine am to five pm job, the virus would have affected you in one way or the other. You most probably had to work from home, had to stay indoors all day, and had to create some beneficial activities during your spare time so that you did not get bored and fight the new routine. Same for us, we shared the fear of the unknown, tried to quarantine and social distance as much as we could, avoided any unnecessary contact with others, and created some indoor activities whenever possible.

In Difference We Find Unity

The biggest difference for us, however, was the fact that we were alone, not flying like we used to, and far away from our home countries. Prior to the pandemic, I used to visit my family at least once a month, as my father was going through a health crisis and I had to be there for him at every possible opportunity. Luckily during the last year, he was stable enough and even got better and that has lifted a huge burden off my shoulders because honestly, I would not have been able to be there for him during that critical period if he needed me. Even if I weren't forced to do so, I would most probably have chosen to stay far away from him since I was travelling from time to time and had a huge risk of catching the virus and transmitting it to him. At that time when we were confined to our base, the only family members we had around us were our flatmates. Ironically before covid, we did not meet that much due to the busy schedule that we had, however, the lockdown helped us to get to know each other more. For instance, I had the chance to get to know my flatmate better and to even befriend her during that period.

Another factor I believe affected all flight attendants around the world is that we were never used to staying on the ground for a long time. If I put it metaphorically, it is like you have removed a fish from the water and watched it desperately trying to go back to its ocean. Or you have cut a bird's wings and waited for its reaction. The image might be brutal, but it describes the feeling that we had during that time. Generally, people outside of this job would not understand what we are talking about; the aircraft smell, the briefings, the new set of people that you get to work with each day, the beautiful sunrises and sunsets in the skies, the welcomes and goodbyes of each flight, and the gratitude that we received by the end of the flight from customers who appreciated us taking them to their destination safely. It is an exciting job, and the excitement simply never ends.

It was not like we were forced to stay; we were allowed to leave, take some time off, go home and stay with our families. But for me, taking time off was not an option since I was the one who was support-ing my family and had plenty of commitments back home that simply could not wait. I honestly think that most of my colleagues who chose to stay during that time shared the same responsibilities, whether they were supporting someone or having financial difficulties, or they simply wanted to grab the nearest opportunity to be in the skies.

In Difference We Find Unity

Unfortunately, within three months, things reached their worst. Thousands of cabin crew around the world lost their jobs due to the drop in travel demand. My company was no exception to the rule, due to huge losses they were forced to lay people off for the business to survive. That period was nerve-wrecking as it was ambiguous. I remember that at that time all we had to do was wait. We would meet up to support one another and to mentally prepare for all the possible scenarios we could be facing. Sadly, I lost many close friends during that period, as they had to leave for their home countries. It was quite impactful on everyone. The ones who had to leave lost their jobs and many of them needed that income to support their families. The ones who stayed were heartbroken to say goodbye to their friends and their loved ones. It was the way we came together during those times that made it a bit easier on us, we were gathering at every opportunity to reassure each other that it is going to be okay, that we will survive this pandemic, and that we have one another to rely on.

Before 2020, I used to believe that resilience and strength are terms that human beings, in general, tend to exaggerate. Yes, you can be positive, and yes you can be strong, but it is always only to a certain extent. I believed that when we are overwhelmed, we just cave and decide to build our comfort zone; a place where we usually tend to escape to, and pretend that everything is fine and that if we stay hidden for a while, we will be rescued. Little did I know that last year would be a game-changer. I have since shifted to believe that human beings are the most powerful creatures on earth, that they can change any possible defeat to a winning situation, and that they can adapt themselves to any situation they encounter. For me to explain my point, I will be telling you two beautiful stories.

The law of attraction

The first one was on one of my flights to the United States. I had encountered this flight attendant whom I will always remember. She was very composed; her black hair remained immaculate over the course of the whole flight and her makeup was just flawless. And believe me, it is simply hard to look as fresh as you did when you first came into the aircraft after a long flight like that one. We all loved her positivity. She was super active; she even received a couple of compliments from passengers for her excellent service and hospitality.

In Difference We Find Unity

After landing, and on the way to our hotel, I got to talk to her, and she revealed this shocking factor. It turns out that just before reporting to the flight, she came to know that her father in Japan was not doing well, his health was deteriorating, and he had to undergo surgery. Knowing that, she still decided to show up for the flight and do her best to satisfy her customers all the while keeping only positive thoughts in her mind, was inspiring. She said, and I quote, "there is nothing much I can do if I stay in the house and keep worrying, I need to work and focus on positive things. I need to be surrounded by a familiar environment, to get immersed in something I love and to only think that he is going to be okay".

Her story brought me to tears, thinking of my own father and how if I were in her shoes, I would most probably not be able to pull myself together. It was simply hard to imagine, let alone to experience. I honestly admired her strength and wished to be as strong as she was. She showed me that if you are determined to send positive vibes out in the world, the world will give you those vibes back eventually. Luckily on our way back, she informed me that her father's surgery went smoothly, and that he was in recovery. From the moment that I flew with her, I made it a goal to always keep in mind that people can show something whereas they are struggling with a lot of hardships in their lives, to never judge anyone, and to be more empathetic.

An unbreakable will

The second story is from my dearest friend Veronica. She joined the aviation industry 15 years ago. A tall, blond lady who has a perfect smile that all people, including me, admire her for. In 2018, she got married to the love of her life, Marko, and she was the happiest she had ever been. She even had a beautiful daughter whom she named Isabella. When Isabella was seven months old, Veronica and her husband decided that he should take Isabella to the 'Carnevale di Venezia' for her to see how beautiful that event is, to create some nice memories for her, and to spend some time with her grandparents. Little did they know that Italy would become the center of the pandemic in Europe exactly five days after their arrival in Venice. They did not even know that the situation was that serious and the Carnival still took place. It was quite jammed, thousands of people from around the world came to be part of that event and there was zero space between one person and the other.

In Difference We Find Unity

When the lockdown started to take place, Marko decided to stay with his daughter at his parents' place, to be on the safe side, until things got better. Veronica was devastated, she knew that it was the best option they had at that time, but she could not imagine living without them for a long period of time, not knowing when they will be able to meet again. She didn't know if they were going to be okay without her, and that was just mortifying.

The only solution that she had to keep in touch with them was to communicate via video calls, which was the only option for most of us. She was seeing her daughter grow every day and could not be present for her first steps or even her first word. Her resilience, however, during the whole period was astonishing. Whether when she was talking to her husband and comforting him by showing how strong and well she was doing, or when she had to go for flights putting every little worry she had behind her back. She is an amazing leader; she motivates her team to work better and listens to their problems. She supports them as much as she can because deep down, she knows they have got only each other during those tough times.

Veronica always says to me that life will throw rocks on you, it is how you choose to react that will determine how happy you will be. She believes in the saying "Life doesn't get easier or more forgiving, we get stronger and more resilient." Happily, by the end of 2020, she was able to see her family when things were better in Italy and the travel restrictions were lifted. It is such a relief that she managed to get out of that situation even stronger than before.

Her story has humbled me in a way that I was not able to put into words at first. Let us just say that people are flexible, they have a great amount of endurance they do not think that they have until they are in the middle of a situation that requires all of their strength. I was one of these people, thinking that I could not go more than four months without seeing my family or paying a visit to my hometown, and I certainly thought that I could not live without visiting my friends back home. But here I am, getting back to normality and even creating a new normal kind of life where I am used to the distance for a while in the hope that I will be able to see them soon enough.

In Difference We Find Unity

The troops walk

So, as you can see, people are extraordinarily strong. We may think that we will stand still in the face of a storm, that it is impossible to find the power to fight back. We may think that whenever we fall, there is no way we can get up, stand on our feet again, and fight. But we tend to forget that we are creatures of hope, we keep going and we find solutions along the way until we reach that light at the end of the tunnel. Even if it seems hard and impossible at first, we somehow make it happen.

I believe that last year was a lesson for everyone on this globe. It allowed us to pause for a while and think about everything that has been happening around us. The universe was moving so fast that we did not get the chance to be grateful for those little things that we had. And when it stopped, we finally got the chance to appreciate that walk in the park, the hug from a friend in hard times, and the smile of our family members when we saw them. Last year was a golden opportunity for lots of people, the time that we had helped us to work on our skills and to find new passions. I am not saying that it was not hard and that it did not affect many people, but if you see the positivity out of it you will get what I am aiming for.

For instance, when I look back now, I feel like at that time I had to stay in the house and work on my health a bit more by getting enough sleep, practicing sports, and eating healthily. I learned how to cook, read more books, and even learned a new language. It taught me to call my family and friends more often and to try not to take anything for granted.

Finally, I would like to thank every flight attendant I had the chance to work with as he or she showed me that resilience is not just a word, it is an attitude towards life. An attitude of fighting against all odds and surviving the worst. I would like to keep believing that life will always have its ebbs and flows, and it is the way that we perceive these edges that matters. I will keep the belief that we humans are strong and powerful and that we will defeat this vicious virus and that there will be a day to celebrate going back to the old normal, where there are no quarantines, no social distancing, and DEFINITELY no face masks.

In Difference We Find Unity

To my community of flight attendants, if you are reading this, I would like to thank you for your support, strength, and commitment towards your passengers and your colleagues. You are an example of how difference creates power and how endurance helps you to be the best version of yourself every day. We are indeed united by wings and we will always and forever be.

OSLO, NORWAY

CHAPTER 5

Destination: Real Estate

by Stéphanie Dénommée

The first time I boarded an airplane, I was 18 years old. I knew a little bit about flight attendants, but I was never really curious about it. After flying two or three times in the next couple of years, I started to be impressed by that job where you bring people home or to their next dream vacation. I thought it seemed pretty cool and fun, so on one of my flights, I asked a couple of questions to the flight attendant who happily served my food and drinks. He invited me to sit down with him in the back of the plane and he explained everything to me. Then I felt something pretty strong in my stomach. Something exciting and big started to grow inside of me. Would this be the beginning of a new passion? The answer was a big YES! As soon as I returned home from that trip, I started applying to various airlines. I received one refusal from an airline but got a yes from another. I will always remember the day I received the call. I was having lunch with one of my best friends at a restaurant and I literally screamed with excitement and happiness. Everyone was looking at me, but I did not care. It was the best news I had ever received in my short life: I was about to become a flight attendant! My friend and I ordered a pitcher or two of sangria to celebrate and the rest of my day was about calling everyone I knew and loved to share the good news. A lot of time has passed since that day and it is still a very fresh memory in my mind. It was the beginning of a journey filled with new friendships, awesome places to see, and memories that will last forever...But was I destined to be a flight attendant? Let's go back in time and find out what could have brought me to being paid to travel, and what brought me to my new career as a real estate broker!

When I moved 6 hours away from my birthplace, I was 9 years old and crushed. I had to leave everything I ever knew. Places, friends, and family. But shortly after, I can say that I have pretty good memories of my childhood in my new home. I remember that every weekend or so, my parents took me to visit a new place, a town, or region and we would do a cool activity that the place had to offer. I remember that I really liked to do those little escapades. I discovered so many places and visited so many interesting attractions during that time.

Destination: Real Estate

After I finished high school, I studied tourism in college. I did not know exactly what I wanted to do, but I knew I was in the right place. We learned everything about that big industry. From attractions from all over the world to architecture, Spanish, and how to be a tour guide, it was a really fun field to study. When I finished, I drove to Calgary. I did an internship in a travel agency to learn English and it was really fun, but I did not know if being behind a desk all day was for me. I came back home, and this is when I started to travel. I flew for the first time and discovered the job of flight attendants.

It was in 2011 that I was hired at my first airline. The training was pretty difficult and very demanding. I remembered how stressful it was, but I had the chance to meet a wonderful person, Lisa, who quickly became a close friend of mine. We rented a room together for 4 weeks in the hotel where we received the training, and we helped each other study every night. After the first aid training, the pool survival training day, the firefighting course, and the emergency procedures lessons, it was time for one last final big exam. And I succeeded. The feeling of receiving the diploma is also something that I will never forget. This airline was my first aviation family, and I will never forget them. I worked with them for three amazing winters. Since it was mostly sun destinations, I was laid off every summer, and I always felt super sad each time. I wanted to fly the whole year, I wanted more! And then I saw this ad in 2013 in the local newspapers. A new company, a branch from this airline, was hiring full-time flight attendants. I applied, passed the training, and got it!

I flew with this second airline from 2014 to 2018. They were honestly the most amazing years I have ever had. Since I was hired at the beginning of the creation of this airline, I had the chance to have high seniority and pretty much have all the flights I wanted too. Because yes, in the airline industry, it works by seniority. You submit the schedule you would like to have, and then the crew planning team awards flights from the top of the list to the bottom. I had an incredible chance. Normally it would take 2 years to go to Rome every week, but I had that in my first summer. And it was not only 24 hours at the destination, it was often 48 hours or even 72 hours. My summers basically consisted of leaving on Mondays or Tuesdays to Athens or Barcelona and coming back to Montreal on Friday afternoons.

Destination: Real Estate

I had all my weekends off, which is rare when you start out in aviation. My winters were filled with layovers in Orlando and Las Vegas, so I had a nice tan all year long. All of those layovers with colleagues whom all became friends, and some of whom even became my best friends. How can you not be close to people with whom you visit Europe with every week? With whom you live difficult situations onboard on flights that last up to 10 or 11 hours? Those 4 years were a blast, literally. Even if the working hours were long, the jetlag was brutal, and that I was tired for all those years, it was all worth it. In 2018, I decided to transfer to another airline, mostly because I felt out of breath and I wanted to have a better work structure: fewer hours, better working conditions, etc. I then started a new adventure in September 2018.

And so, in October 2018, I started to fly again after 3 weeks of training. It was exciting! New destinations, new uniforms, new people. The first year was great and I did not regret my choice at all, even though I was missing all my ex-colleagues.

But after the summer of 2019, I began to feel that I needed to learn something new and expand my skills in life. I will always remember a particular flight that I was on. I can't remember the exact date or year, but I had an interesting discussion with a Premium class passenger I was taking care of. We were discussing aviation and why I loved my job. We talked about 9/11, SARS, and other things that had affected the aviation industry. He asked me if I was worried about something else that could happen and affect the industry. I told him that I expected that one day something else will happen. I told him that and I knew that when aviation goes well, it can really go well and that when it goes badly, it can be catastrophic, but that I was at peace with that and that I was enjoying what was happening at the moment. He gave me a piece of advice that stayed in my mind: always have at least two passions in life because you never know what can happen. I agreed with him, but I did not have another passion at that time.

In 2018, my husband and I wanted to sell our condo in Rosemont to buy a house outside of Montreal, and we did not want to deal with a real estate broker, because we wanted to have as much money as possible in our pockets since we did not have that condo for a long time. We tried to sell it by ourselves and after a couple of weeks, nothing.

Destination: Real Estate

We received so many phone calls and letters in the mails during that time, a lot of real estate brokers wanted to sell our condo and we felt quite annoyed by all of that.

Until one day, a real estate broker reached out to us and her approach was different from all the others. We accepted to meet with her since we did not have any success at selling the house ourselves anyway. And this is when I met her and saw how she works, it has changed my perception of real estate brokers. We accepted to sell the condo through her, and she even found the house we were dreaming of. Everything went well and fast and her service and kindness were impeccable. I started to ask her questions about her career. I flew with flight attendants that were also real estate brokers at the same time and they encouraged me to do it. Time passed and after a couple of months, I was still thinking about it and I finally sent my application to a school to take the real estate broker course. I started my course in September 2019 and it was a one-year course. Shortly after, the pandemic arrived. I felt once again lucky that I decided to find another passion. I finished school in September 2020 and by the time I passed all the exams and procedures required to have my license, it was already January of the next year. I then started embracing this very new career in a difficult time for sure, but I was so excited and ready to start something new. I was relieved that I decided to do all of this before the virus appeared and before aviation, unfortunately, crashed, not to make a bad choice of words.

Do not get me wrong, I love aviation. I love flying, the take-off, the landing. I love sitting at a window during my breaks and looking at the storms outside or the northern lights passing in front of my eyes. I loved having dinner on another continent and coming back home the day after.

But I needed something new in my life. A new challenge, being uncomfortable in something that I never did before. And I found that through learning how to be a real estate broker. It is still very new to me, but I can already say how much I love it. I still get to do customer service, but in a long-term way. I used to take care of the same people for only a couple of hours and this time, it is still the same but this time it's for weeks or months.

Destination: Real Estate

I really get to develop a relationship with these people that are about to do some of the most stressful but beautiful steps of their life. Isn't it so exciting though? Visiting all kinds of houses, getting to know them and their taste and mostly being a person they can rely on for all kinds of advice. And I love doing that, and I think a lot of people underestimate the pressure we have on our shoulders to be the person that will help those people whose desire is to sell their house or/and buy a new one. It is emotional and sometimes it is hard not to feel their emotions too. I work hard, long hours, but it does not feel like a 'task'. It is fun, interesting and there is always something new to learn or to see. I always try to remember how I felt during the process of selling and buying a new home and god, it was so stressful and big. I try to take off as much stress from my customer's shoulders as I can to make the process as smooth as possible for them. I love being on the road too, and while I drive, I listen to some music and podcasts. A lot of people warned me that this will be a 7 / 7 job. But I did not mind. I know what it's like to miss some holidays or birthdays. Being in my bed every night was a huge plus for me. As much as I enjoy staying in hotels and not having to worry about cleaning or making the bed, home is home. And I am now the one helping people to find theirs.

It's been one year since I last flew. Already! It seems like flying was in another life. For the first time in years, I saw seasons. Summer 2020 was the first summer in a long time that I was able to enjoy the sun every day. The season passed slower but I was quite ok with that. I finally enjoyed my pool instead of taking naps in the middle of the after-noon to recuperate from my lack of sleep. Fall was amazing because I got to see all the changing colors of the leaves every day. It might sound weird, but I appreciated seeing the slow changes in nature. Being able to take the time to notice it. Winter was so long. So so long for me. I don't mind the snow, but I am not a fan of the cold weather. I was also able to witness all the changes for that season too. Before, I would leave the country with no snow on the ground and come back with a 2 feet snow-drift all around my car. And then the opposite would happen. And other times, all the leaves would disappear from the trees in the 4 days I was gone. It felt like I was missing some part of a puzzle and my brain was confused. Now I have every day to look outside at the same thing, but I can see nature transforming and I like it. Do I miss flying? Yes, I miss the feeling. Being a flight attendant is tattooed on my heart.

Destination: Real Estate

It is a lifestyle, a career that a lot of people dream of and are not able to do. It is something special and very hard to understand for someone that does not swim in it. It is various schedules, night flights, really early morning flights, or afternoon ones all in the same month. It is being able to take care of a lot of nice passengers, helping with medical situations, or holding babies to help mothers or fathers travelling alone. It is being a psychologist, a waiter (sorry!), a person you can count on. It is smiling (or at least trying) all the time, even when we are dealing with something personal at home. Being a flight attendant is a privilege. It is having lunch in the flight deck and chatting with the pilots. It is relying on co-workers that you sometimes don't even know in case of an emergency. It is reassuring scared passengers when there is turbulence. It is being able to see places all over the world, stay in really nice hotels and enjoy a local meal wherever we are. How can I not miss that? We don't know what is next. We don't know when we will be able to fly again as a career but also for pleasure. We don't know how our schedules will be when we will return. I wish I will be able to manage both of my passions like it was my initial plan. But life decided that something needed to happen on our planet. And I think that it took some of us away from great pleasures in life but also made us reconnect with some important things that we forgot were wonderful. Each of us is living through this pandemic differently but I do hope each one of you will at least find something positive out of it. A new habit, a better relationship, or a new passion will stay post-pandemic and bring us good. So many things that we took for granted were taken away, like travelling. Next time I get to travel I will enjoy it a million times more. And maybe take it slower and embrace every moment of the trip even more. Travelling is a privilege, and for me, it will become even more precious than before. The most important thing that I learned in the last year is how to navigate in life being comfortable in the uncomfortable, and I hope everyone will find a way to be happy with their own particular path that 2020 brought on planet earth.

Stéphanie Dénommée; Flight Attendant and a Real Estate Broker.

- I would like to send love, patience, and courage to my sister, brother-in-law, and nieces that live in England and who I miss oh so much.

Stéphanie Dénommée

While being a flight attendant will forever be tattooed on her heart, Stéphanie feels that it is always better to have at least two passions in life (even more if you can!). It was actually one of the passengers in Premium Class, on a flight in 2017, who once gave her this advice "never put all your eggs in the same basket, this life is full of uncertainty". That advice made her decide to search for another career that could become a second passion. After selling her first property and discovering what a real estate broker really was, she felt inspired by the broker who worked with her to sell her condo and buy a house. After going back to school in 2019, she is now embracing her new career as a real estate broker, helping people to find the house of their dreams. Meanwhile, she is also learning Japanese to prepare for when airplanes are back in her life and she can go back to work with her first love: aviation. She is learning a lot about navigating through chaos and being comfortable and positive about the uncomfortable and the unknown. A common point to both of the careers? Customer service for sure, but also being by the side of people throughout the realization of their dreams; either a dream vacation or a dream home!

 Stéphanie Dénommée - Courtier Immobilier Résidentiel

 stephaniedcourtier

OAHU, HAWAII

CHAPTER 6

ABOVE & BEYOND THE SKY

by Geneviève Pagé

"Always Shoot for the moon. Even if you miss, you'll land among the stars..."

The unexpected dream of a lifetime. Learning to feel comfortable in the unknown is probably one of the most empowering states to reach. There were so many times along the way when I had to remind myself of the following quote: Universe please give me the serenity to accept what I cannot change, the courage to change the things I can, and the wisdom to know the difference. This has been my life journey. But where did it all begin...? Is there something more powerful and inspiring than watching a crew walking together at the airport? For as long as I remember, I always had this feeling of freedom, mystery, excitement, and admiration looking at them. Where were they going? Where were they from? Did they all know each other? They were there, walking, with so much confidence in their gorgeous inspiring uniforms, their suitcases, and their airport passes...and I thought: what an amazing life that must be!

That flying seed was planted almost two decades ago. I was probably around 9 years old when I started realizing how lucky I was to grow up in such an incredible family. My father was a very successful lawyer; my family was just like the perfect family of four. Skiing all together, taking classes like there was no tomorrow, we were surrounded by friends, travelling at every opportunity we had. Money was flowing and I did not know anything different at that time. We were in the process of moving into our brand-new house and life was just great and easy for us. In a time when flying was still considered glamorous, I was on my way to Orlando for an incredible family trip, on my very first flight. I still remember that my father looked at me and said: Wouldn't you want to become a stewardess later on? I smiled, enjoyed my flight, and thought it sounded pretty good!

ABOVE & BEYOND THE SKY

I was 17 years old when I told my dad that I wanted to go and learn English in another province. A month later, I was on my way to Banff with some friends. The feeling of freedom and the unknown was so appealing. Then followed a few months of fun, discovering our new town, hitchhiking all summer long, going on road trips, hot springs and skydiving. We came back with an enhanced level of English, and this was just the beginning of a never-ending travelling journey... Two years later, I'm in the middle of my first University session in Montreal when my father's wife calls me to tell me she has some bad news for me. I go home, to the city I grew up in, and learn that he has an irreversible neurodegenerative brain disease and that he will die. He is 44 years old and the strongest man I know. He is my world, my pillar, and with him, I feel secure and protected. I never met someone with such a charismatic personality. Everyone respects and admires him. He is successful, fun, intelligent and I need him. I want to be like him. He is my everything. Without him, I'm lost...

So, for the next year and a half, I stopped school, and despite all my research, there is nothing we can do to avoid what's coming. I have to surrender and accept what I can't change to find some sort of inner peace to face the inevitable. Every day, I watch his condition getting worse and worse. I see the strongest person I know losing every ability he has. His physical ability, his memory, his personality, his capacity of eating on his own, of talking, and eventually of walking. I keep talking to him, and every now and then, there are tears in his eyes, so I know that he understands me. It soon becomes clear to me that the end is fast approaching. I tell him how much I love him and everything I want him to know before he goes away...So at 20 years old, I end up having to learn how to live without him. Almost two decades later, I still feel extremely lucky to have had such an incredible and loving dad.

This experience was such an impactful turning point in my life. I knew and felt that everything was going to be different from that moment on. I wanted to feel alive and to live life to its fullest, as I wasn't sure how much time I had left on this planet. My friends and I came up with a plan. We had heard that someone we knew had gone to Thailand, which at that time, was not a very popular destination. I was intrigued! We had no clue what to expect and THIS was the exciting part!!!

ABOVE & BEYOND THE SKY

So, we took the map, bought our travelling guide, and chose to go to Thailand, Malaysia, and Indonesia. Paper plane tickets in hand, we were on our way on a long journey to get there, but we were happy and full of hope! For the first time in months, I felt like life still had some good things in store for me. We landed in Bangkok and started discovering this vibrant new city. Landing without any plans, on a continent we knew nothing about, was beyond exciting. That first night, we ate our first pad thaï, saw an elephant walking on the street beside us, and ended up bug tasting. Still very jet lagged, this entire scene seemed surreal to us. Over the following two months, we met people from all over the world, learned to scuba dive and rock climb, took an elephant ride (at the time where it was still a good idea to do so), climbed volcanos, and went to the Full Moon Party. We learned to dance with fire sticks, went to "The Beach" from the famous movie, rented scooters, and took boats to explore all the islands we possibly could. We took an extreme bus ride from Thailand to Cambodia just to go see one of the seven wonders of the World: the Angkor Wat temples. It was on that trip to Asia when I suddenly felt something inside me tell me that this was it. This was going to be my life's passion. I felt so lucky to be alive and couldn't wait to see more.

After that trip, I came back to work in Canada for a few months to save money to go back to Asia. We ended up spending seven months travelling all over South-East Asia. That trip made me feel like everything was possible. We looked at the map, pointed to Bali, and chose to cross Indonesia, Malaysia, Thailand and make it all the way to Laos and Vietnam by bus. Our new reality was almost like a dream: horseback riding on the beach, trekking for days in the jungle where the Orangutans live, taking our scooters all around lakes surrounded by beautiful volcanoes. It all felt surreal. We spent countless hours riding in buses, and I always enjoyed that time; that moment where you can just think about life without guilt that you should be doing something else. Going through so many beautiful memories along the way, I had the chance to get my Scuba diving qualification, as well as taking classes in Thai massage and cooking in the North of Thailand. We enjoyed the nightlife of the islands for weeks, jumped on Tarzan ropes, and went tubing in the lakes and rivers of Laos. The sky was the limit.

ABOVE & BEYOND THE SKY

Serendipity kept happening more and more on my path. Indeed, I ended up meeting the most incredible friends along the way. In the smallest village of Sumatra, an island of Indonesia, we came across two Canadian girls. They were probably the first tourists we had seen in two months, as we had been travelling right after the bomb incident in Bali, and the place was almost deserted. We connected right away and traveled with them for two weeks. Soon enough we had to say our goodbyes as there were still a few months left for our trip. We promised to reconnect at some point. Five months later, on an inspiring bus ride, I came to the conclusion that I should go back to school and complete a University degree. So, after long reflection, I chose International development and languages. During my initial test to enter the program, I looked up and saw both of them, the two Canadian girls from my trip to Indonesia! I was blown away, as we never ever spoke about this and we came from different cities. We laughed and soon realized we had the same Thai-written tattoo on the side of our feet, also quite surprising! So, we spent the next three years together.

During the summer breaks, I always had plans to discover new countries. I had a "love at first sight" experience for Asia, so bringing myself to explore another part of the World was not an easy choice. I eventually chose Central America. Whether it was horseback riding in the mountains of Costa Rica, taking in the nightlife of San Jose, trekking and surfing in Nicaragua, discovering the incredible colorful culture or waterfalls of Guatemala, it was an unforgettable experience. That trip culminated beautifully for a few weeks on a small and inspiring island of Honduras named Utila. Scuba diving in pristine blue water followed by a few cocktails and enjoying the nightlife was an everyday reality. Another little paradise was now part of my story.

The following year, I went back for the entire summer as I was working to clock my 60 dives to become a divemaster. Biking beside the Caribbean Ocean on the sand paths to get to work and spending my days on the boat learning the joys of diving were my new passions. Night diving was so impressive with all the plankton shining around. I felt like I was swimming in a galaxy full of stars. Later on that summer, the brand-new boat of our dive shop sunk on a diving trip away from the island that I was hoping to go to.

ABOVE & BEYOND THE SKY

I convinced some friends to go, and despite the Captain's experience, the boat ended up sinking and they were all floating for hours in the middle of the ocean with the gas leaking from the boat that was almost completely immersed in the water. Some of them tried to swim to the shore without a life vest, and almost lost their lives in that attempt. Back on the island, we heard about the tragedy that just happened, but the waves were so strong, no other boats could go rescue them. A small plane was finally sent, and they were spotted just in time before sunset. Thankfully, everyone survived, but it was quite an adventure for everyone.

After my last semester at University, I started looking for a job, but was not quite sure what to do next. A few weeks later, I read in the newspaper that an airline was hiring flight attendants. This was always a lifestyle that appeared so inspiring to me. So, I decided to try and see if it was meant to be. I gave everything I had for this impressive interview process, and a few weeks later, I got THE call. I will always remember the feeling I had when the lady said: "You have been officially hired full time. The training will start in 2 weeks. Do you accept the offer?" Absolutely!!!!!! And this was by far, one of the best choices of my life!!! Seven weeks after the training started, I was officially a flight attendant and ready to fly around the World!!! I still remember my first flight, walking in the cabin, looking at passengers, and pretending like I knew what I was doing. Making the announcements and taking off in my jump seat facing backwards just felt so exciting. I will never forget being invited to the Flight deck for take-off and landing for the first time. I felt so privileged to be there, it was absolutely breathtaking!! I had the earphones on so I could hear the control tower and the pilots communicating with each other; I had tears in my eyes as we took off. I'll never forget that moment. Landing in Vancouver with the ocean and the Rockies was beyond spectacular!!!!! Every time crew scheduling called, I got excited at the idea that maybe this was it, maybe I would be going on my first overseas flight! The unknown was fun. I would wake up in one location and never knew what was going to happen next. Some days you just think "it's time to go to bed," and suddenly the phone rings and the next thing you know, you are on your way to London.

ABOVE & BEYOND THE SKY

I spent the next 14 years flying all over the world, drinking champagne in Paris, eating Schnitzel in Frankfurt, and walking through the streets of London. Layover after layover, I enjoyed every moment of it. I can't even count how many times my crew and I cheered as we realized how lucky we were to be living this dream. Going to Fontana di Trevi in Rome after sipping a Campari with my crew on a patio, smoking shisha in Tel Aviv for Christmas after biking all day along the seaside, eating a Belgium waffle in Brussels or tacos in Mexico City, going to museums, enjoying a 5 à 7 in New York before hitting Central Park: all of this was our life. Of course, in between all this, we had to do countless night flights and less exciting layovers in destinations such as Saskatoon, Regina, Deer Lake, and all the other freezing locations. But even there, most of the time, the crew and I still managed to have fun. Without this job, I don't think I would have discovered beautiful St-John's in Newfoundland and Whitehorse in Yukon. I always loved walking around and finding those new places that would become my go-to places when I went back. Biking in San Francisco, shopping in Los Angeles, running along the beach in Hawaii, going for a massage in Shanghai, eating fresh sushi in front of the temples in Japan, trying a Korean BBQ for the first time with my crew in Seoul, going on a tuk-tuk ride to Old Delhi and finishing the day at the Spa to get my coconut oil hair massage and my eyebrows done, going to the beach in Sydney to end up at the Opera at night: this wasn't a dream; it was our life. We were spoiled and we knew it!

The last year and a half of flying before the pandemic hit, was like a dream come true. I put the time into becoming an In-charge and I waited patiently until my schedule got better. I flew from all bases such as Montreal, Toronto, Calgary, and Vancouver just because I could explore all these options. And finally, I was able to hold dream flights all year long. Every month, I could not believe how amazing my schedule was: Maui, Honolulu, London, Sydney, Tokyo, Shanghai, Seoul, Delhi, Mexico City...This was my new reality, and I absolutely loved it!!!! I appreciated my work so much, it was like I was born for this. I love the effervescence of the airports and seeing people going in all directions. Everyone has a story and I find it fascinating. The lifestyle that goes along with being a flight attendant is absolutely incredible! Of course, I took the opportunity to travel as much as I could during my time off.

ABOVE & BEYOND THE SKY

I loved all the crazy last-minute decisions that brought so much excitement, such as taking my friends and family to China for three days just to see the Great wall, celebrating my birthday in Copenhagen, and going to Paris for a weekend with my daughter and friends. Also, I joined friends in Dubai for four days, enjoyed my maternity leave living in Buenos Aires and discovered Argentina. To top it off, I moved to Havana dividing my time between Cuba and Canada as my two Home bases. Spending two weeks alone with my daughter in Japan, Shanghai, and Hong Kong, waking up in the dunes of India beside my camel, biking down 4000 meters on the gorgeous Death road of Bolivia, there were no limits and I loved it!

We all know what happened next. I did not know that my flight in March 2020 was going to be my last flight for a very long time. I felt as though I had left a small part of myself in Vancouver, thinking I was going to be going back the following month as usual. But usual ended, and we soon realized that days turned into weeks that turned into months that turned into a year. I lost not only a job, but a lifestyle and part of my identity. The first few weeks almost felt like a good thing, a little break to my body from flying and missing nights of sleep. Being home felt like a treat. However, once I realized it was going to be my new reality for a while, it was a huge loss. Yet, I spent the following months redefining who I was and what I liked outside of travelling the world. After all, I spent the last 20 years flying for a living; 52 countries later, it seemed that this was all I knew. Thankfully, I learned to reconnect with my culture by appreciating where I was from, I learned to love winter, something I forgot a while ago. I had the chance to meet an incredible person that showed me a whole new perspective on what our country had to offer. I spent countless hours in the Spa at the Chalet, boating all summer long, and fishing in Hudson Bay. I made fires, rode on 4 wheels, on a skidoo, flew on a Seaplane, and went on a few helicopter rides (a first time for me)!!! So, I've got to say, despite all the challenges 2020 has brought, it's been an incredible and unexpected year full of exciting discoveries!!

Of course, I also had to redefine what I was going to do for work and to reinvent myself along the way. A few years ago, on a trip to Istanbul, I fell in love with Turkish towels. I knew I always wanted to own my own business, and Import Export sounded fun and exciting.

ABOVE & BEYOND THE SKY

So that's where it all began, and I started selling my discoveries to stores in Montreal and other provinces. I imported cushions, lamps and so much more from Morocco, India, and Turkey. That side business was still active in 2020, but when all the stores shut down, my plan B was put on hold as well. Thankfully, I also had a small hotel Boutique in Havana that I could rely on, but again no more tourists were going to Cuba, so plan C was not an option anymore either.

Regardless of the type of emergency, in aviation we are taught to Assess, Adapt and Act, so that's what I did. This summer, after thinking this one through, I decided to bring my import business to another level. I wanted to invest the time and energy to explore the full potential of this project that I love so deeply. I decided to combine all my passions: aviation, travelling, and home decor into creating a beautiful online boutique and blog. In partnership with my incredible designer, we made it happen, and I'm very proud of how this project is evolving every day. One Sky Imports is now my online boutique where people can find my latest World discoveries from Turkey, Japan, Cuba, and Canada. More than ever, I know that encouraging local people is important, so I found Canadian suppliers to work with and I hired people from the airline industry so we could help each other grow and redefine ourselves. This project has been such a positive inspiration, and I feel like angels literally fell from the sky to guide me on this beautiful path.

From my experience, one of the most powerful things we can do when we want to see where life wants to bring us, is to accept what we can't change and surrender to what is. Learning to feel comfortable in the unknown is quite empowering. I imagine myself surfing, and every now and then, you have to let the wave go by until you can breathe again. You know the sun will come back, and the best thing to do is to get in sync in with the wave instead of trying to go against it. So, in moments when life seems more challenging, I love to remember this beautiful quote: "Sometimes you think you have been buried, but actually you have just been planted. " Often, things start to shift for the best and we attract beautiful and positive people and events, and we grow into our next chapter. Let's see what the next one will be for all of us...

Namaste 🖤

BiOGRAPHY
Geneviève Pagé

Geneviève is a passionate and strong woman living life to its fullest and thriving in each new creative project she takes part in. Every choice she made along the way contributed to the incredible life she has built for herself. Starting with an International development degree combined with 14 years of flying, travelling to 52 Countries, speaking 5 languages, and living all over Canada and Cuba, she feels fulfilled. Despite loving her career and the amazing lifestyle it came with, she always knew she wanted to become an entrepreneur. Her hotel boutique in Havana was one of her first business projects, and her latest creation One Sky Imports is now a stunning online boutique combining World discoveries and an inspiring travelling Blog. Her true passions of aviation, home decor and travelling, are now synced together in this dream. Looking for balance in everything she does, she feeds her soul, body, and mind with positive influences in order to attract the best of what life has to offer. Through her writing journey, she also discovered how powerful and inspirational words can be. She lives to create and evolve, and she can't wait to share all her stories with you!

www.oneskyimports.com

 Oneskyimports    One Sky Imports

SALAR DE UYUNI, BOLIVIA

ONE SKY IMPORTS

CHAPTER 7

The Power of Speaking Your Truth

by Karine Boileau

"L'homme qui a le plus vécu n'est pas celui qui a compté le plus d'années, mais celui qui a le plus senti la vie." J.-J. Rousseau, Émilie

I am writing this story while sitting in my sweet childhood home. It's a place that screams love and joy.

I put on my red lipstick to trick my brain. I wanted to get that superpower-flight-attendant vibe as I was typing this dear chapter of mine. It's a big deal. This serves as a beautiful farewell for such an important part of my life. It's a way to honor the past seven years of my existence and all the amazingness that came with it: all the growing, the thinking, the feeling, the living.

One cannot truly understand what it feels like to be a cabin crew member, unless you have walked in those spiky high heels in more airports that you could even recall. It's a world of its own. It is fascinating.

For me, it came with a decision; one to follow my own voice.

How do we know that we are making the right choice?

In a world of endless possibilities, it is so easy to get lost and to lose touch with our mere identity. Too often, we seek for answers outside of ourselves. We survey people, ask for their opinion, and end up following their advice diligently or blindly.

The truth is that we have phenomenal tools inside of ourselves to help us navigate through life. We are gifted with the amazing abilities to think and feel, and we need to trust that we will always be rewarded for listening to our inner wisdom.

I knew ever since I was a kid that something just didn't totally feel right in the way that we live our everyday lives. This big American dream, the race to always make more money and get prestigious titles...

The Power of Speaking Your Truth

It never really made sense to me. I believed in beauty and passion, in kindness and gratefulness. I was always connected to something bigger than myself. As the years went by, I did lose track of it every now and then, as we all do. However, I am here today, finally feeling strong and confident, ready to share my story.

A night out with the folks

I want to tell you about the time I went out for dinner with my parents. For some awkward reason I can no longer remember, my little sister wasn't with us. It is usually always the four of us. We are a strong team, and we never leave a player on the bench. I think it was only me because I had just dumped the guy I was dating at the time. I decided to crash my parents' night out and randomly invited myself out for sushi.

I remember feeling privileged having them all to myself. I had the whole floor, and I wasn't afraid of shining too bright. It felt fantastic hanging out with two of my favorite people on the planet. We had a few glasses of wine and the food was marvelous, as always.

As I had their full attention, I decided to come out and tell them that, even though I was on my way to graduating from university, I did not want a typical nine to five position. I had something better in the back of my mind - I wanted to become a flight attendant, at least until I figured things out. My twenty-three-year-old self strongly believed that there had to be more to life than simply good grades and diplomas.

I wish I could say that they didn't question my aspiration, but it would not add value to my story. They had to challenge me in order for me to be true to myself and to stand strong with my decision. They had to confront me in some ways, for me to be here today telling you that I am so darn happy that I decided to trust my gut feeling. Allowing my intuition to speak for herself was by far, the best thing I could've ever done.

Of course, my dad was concerned, as I believe he would've wanted me to walk in his shoes and have a big and powerful day job, but my mother who always sees the bright side of every situation, laughed and pointed out that they would be entitled to great travelling discounts! And if she was happy, so was my father.

The Power of Speaking Your Truth

I remember feeling loved and supported. I feel so blessed to have them both as role models. They are the best and they have given my sister and I so much; time, energy, free counseling...

Hey, I'm not saying that they are perfect, but they really are awesome people.

The traveller's world of mindfulness.

My family and I have so many beautiful memories on vacation as kids. I remember playing in the sand, chasing seagulls with my sister, while my parents were enjoying a delicious barbecue meal right on the beach. We were in Florida and my mom always knew how to throw a one-of-a-kind picnic. I remember running and feeling the wind against my young skin as I was laughing with my sweet and funny sister. My parents were smiling at each other, enjoying themselves. It felt like pure happiness and freedom. I was perhaps six or seven years old, but I recall the emotions and the greatness of it. It was probably one of my first awakening moments.

In my family, travelling runs in our DNA. It is our escape from reality. It is the moment we drop our baggage and enjoy ourselves. It is the opportunity and the perfect occasion for us to just be. There is no thinking about chores or unpaid bills when you are away. There is just you, your eyes, your breath and basically all your other senses living and experiencing the moment. You are open to receive, to feel, to dream, and it's simply delightful.

I believe that travelling is one of the best ways to experience mindfulness. Peacefully wandering around, with my thoughts on the moment and in the moment, is just so extraordinary and simple at the same time. It is like seeing everything all at once. It is taking time to be present and engaging with our hopes and desires. No wonder I wanted more of that in my life. No wonder I had the urge to so frequently jump on a plane and travel to distant exotic places. Globetrotting, as ironic as it may sound, has always been my path to understanding and loving myself.

The Power of Speaking Your Truth
A whole new chapter

In January of 2014, I finally got the call. I was hired by an airline and the training was starting a little over ten days. I was so thrilled and grateful for the opportunity. I was ready to crush it.

On the first day of training, I was particularly excited. I had been driving around the area since six in the morning, but I still managed to arrive only just on time. I was wearing a fabulous outfit that matched from head-to-toe, and I knew that I was at the right place at the right time. I felt so good within the walls of the center. I loved the refined style of the building and all its aviation pictures, from old planes to crew members of the 1970s. I was so happy to finally be a part of it!

The managers had more surprises in store for us; during our first session we discovered that we were hired for the launch of a new division, and that this would come with great advantages. We were going to cover all the tropical destinations. We were going to operate the European and American routes that had a travelling purpose - destinations like Nice, Barcelona, Athens, Prague, Orlando, Las Vegas, Honolulu and many more! It was simply unbelievable. Since we were all new hires, we were on a brand-new seniority list. That was going to be very significant when building our monthly schedules. We were blessed with so much luck, here we were, all between the age of 20 and 35, given the priceless chance to discover the world while being paid to do so.

Hi, my name is Jeff

Soon enough, we were asked to introduce ourselves one by one with a fun fact. Mine came out naturally; "My name is Karine, and I love red wine!"

His was just as fun; "Hi, my name is Jeff, and I can ride a unicycle."

We laughed and had an instant connection. Something was happening. Jeffrey and I became great friends. Our energy was magnetic. Everything was natural between us. Our conversations were always flowing so easily, and we were there for one another during the ups and downs of the training.

The Power of Speaking Your Truth

He had such a great spirit and a beautiful soul, and it was a charm to be around him all the time.

Little did I know that he was about to become my life partner; better yet the father of my now two-year-old daughter!

Wait a moment! Can you imagine if I had not taken the job? Or, if I had not followed my own dream and stood up to my parents in the first place?

My entire life as I now know it revolves around that empowering decision of trusting myself at age twenty-three!

Isn't it unbelievable?!

As things evolved for us, we moved to Toronto in a hurry and started flying. We got a crash pad with a few other flight attendants. Jeff and I were giving our relationship a romantic twist as we were getting to know each other as roommates, while starting a new job in a different province! Everything happened so fast. I have to admit, it has continued to be that way ever since. Toronto was our honeymoon, and there was much more to come.

Take me on a plane

I always loved going to the airport. It felt like a big teleportation machine! If you have a credit card, you could literally transport yourself to just about anywhere in the world. If you stop and think about it for a moment, it is truly magical.

That was our reality as a flying couple. Showing up in my carefully arranged uniform, with smiling, red lips and my loyal roller bag made me feel so alive! Walking in my heels, crossing security, and slowly heading to my gate was always such a nice moment. I felt powerful, I felt in control of myself. I knew (most of the time) where I was going, and how I could make it extra special for our beloved passengers. I feel like I was always showing up as the best version of myself. I was so in love with the concept of just being on a plane almost every day.

The Power of Speaking Your Truth

It allowed me to exchange and share with people from all over the planet. I knew we had a special job. I was always so grateful for it and all its mind-blowing opportunities.

I'm proud to say that my significant other and I were a great team onboard! It was not always easy working together, but we would both perform our tasks assiduously. We would welcome people with warmth and make them feel at home. We were fantastic hosts! We were great at taking care of passengers, filling their cup in all the possible ways - remember my fun fact!?

Making sure that everybody was safe and comfortable was our priority, but we were always able to transform the whole thing into a wonderful experience. We would get ready, secure the cabin with care and awareness and we would wink at each other from our jump seats before performing our silent review for take-off.

I miss these moments. It feels like they happened a hundred years ago.

Living the good life

As we had control over our schedules, we could choose between spending time on the beach or playing roulette in Vegas! We could go for dinner in Rome once a week if we wanted to. We could meet our friends that were travelling around Europe during their trip. We did it very often! We took every single opportunity and turned it into something so special and remarkable. We visited wineries and canyons. We rented motorbikes and went for hikes. We brought our families on layovers. We met with friends in Vancouver, Athens, Fort Lauderdale...

We knew most of the places we were flying to like home. This has me thinking; being a flight attendant is feeling at home just about anywhere. We have this saying that as long as you have a bathing suit and underwear, you are good to go. Home is where the plane lands.

Learning and growing

When you start a romantic relationship with someone new, you have hopes and expectations, but you can never predict how things will really unfold with time. Jeffrey and I became friends before we could think of anything else. I felt so good around him, like I could be my real self all the time. That is really what made me fall in love with him in the first place.

The Power of Speaking Your Truth

There is also something else that is special to me about us. I feel like I owe him so much in terms of personal growth and development. The sun was in Aries when we were both born, and it truly shows in our personalities. We both have this strong fire inside of us. It is wonderful when everything is going our way, but it can also be very hard when we are facing difficulties. We are two passionate people. We have had our share of ups and downs throughout the years. We have faced many challenges as a couple.

Our relationship and our flight attendant careers happened simultaneously. These two strong influences made me grow exponentially in such a short amount of time. It helped me connect to my true self at the speed of light.

During our years of flying, I learned about forgiveness, compassion, and self-love. I read about taking responsibility, about being in a grateful state of mind. I was introduced to patience, tolerance, and calmness. I had a lot of free time to myself, and I appreciated every single second of it; especially in our beloved hotel rooms! Those are the small moments that I would cherish the most; taking care of my mind and body in my own little sanctuary. Yoga, meditation, healthy foods, workouts... This time was so precious.

Hi, my name is June

In the summer of 2018, I was blessed with a beautiful pregnancy. I felt great even on the plane, so I spent twenty-six weeks flying back and forth to Orlando and Barcelona with a huge smile on my face and a precious light growing inside my womb. We were happy and really looking forward to meeting baby June.

We had a great plan for when she was going to arrive. We wanted to alternate our flights, so that there would always be a parent at home instead of her spending most of her time at the daycare! We were planning on spending our weekends together either at our house or somewhere around the globe. The grandparents were even onboard! They were ready to babysit, or to follow us around the world one flight at the time. Our plan was phenomenal. It felt right and perfect.

The Power of Speaking Your Truth

I know it sounds surreal, but it was our reality. It was the reality we had created for ourselves and we loved it. It was the way we had been living until everything brutally stopped when the boarders closed down. My heart ached when we both got laid off, I felt like it broke into so many tiny pieces and I was truly afraid.

Reconnecting to ourselves and trying new things

I now know that I had many things to learn from this episode. I had to undergo darkness and heaviness to keep on pursuing my journey with brand new eyes and a fierce mind. It took me a while to understand why I had lost my dream job, and what good was going to come out of it. Thankfully, it is clear to me now - even more than ever with this book collaboration. I am, and I have, always been on the right path. I am at peace. I finally mean it again when I quote: "everything happens for a reason".

In the year of 2020, we reinvented ourselves. I got a new job as an English teacher in an elementary school. My better half started working with friends in construction. He gained a lot of skills and is now slowly renovating our home. It's not always rainbows and butterflies, but we make it work. As I said earlier, we are a good team.

I am really looking forward to this summer. I intend to spend lots of time with my charming toddler on the beautiful lake that's sitting in our backyard. I will focus on my writing and wellbeing while working on many more empowering projects.

Whenever I feel like I'm losing faith again, I take out a pen and paper and I start writing to the Universe. I trust that It has big plans for me, and I am ready and willing to welcome it all.

My love for aviation will never truly go away. It is such an important part of my life and it is directly connected to our family's story. I would go back in a heartbeat because it is such a huge part of who I am. Also, because I miss my amazing resourceful coworkers... I miss our galley talks, our eye-opening conversations, and deep connections. Our network and community are a gorgeous blend of so many beautiful energies. I cannot wait to get back to the sky.

In the meantime, I am enjoying the ride.

BIOGRAPHY

Karine Boileau

Karine is a passionate dreamer who loves to spread her light and energy towards positive change. She is a fervid writer and speaker who believes in courage and determination. She has a contagious smile, and she loves to engage with people. She was hired for the start of a new airline at the beginning of 2014 and spent six gorgeous years travelling the world with her better half until they were both laid off in June 2020. She is the founder of Version B, a wellness blog and organization that wishes to empower women to be the best version of themselves by respecting their beautiful bodies, amazing minds, and spirits. They organize powerful and inspiring retreats to allow women to connect, exchange and share. Her bachelor's degree in communication and modern languages is allowing her to temporarily work as an English teacher in an elementary school near her home. It is a new adventure, and she gets to learn from her young students daily. She is also putting together a wide variety of new projects that will soon be leading to more books, blogs, talks and podcasts. Karine is big about living her best life and wishes to empower others to do the same. She lives in a simple house by a beautiful lake with her boyfriend and two-year-old daughter.

 @versionblife + @karinebcommunicatrice

Karine Boileau
Communicatrice Intuitive

 KarineBcommunicatrice

TAMARINDO, COSTA RICA.

CHAPTER 8

Grounded

by Gabrielle Morin

"Travel is the only thing you buy that makes you richer." -Unknown

Grounded

Oh! What a year this has been. It felt like a decade, and I am sure we can all relate to that. If you had told me a year ago that I would now be taking part in a book collaboration about how much I miss being in the sky and how challenging losing my dream job has been, I would've laughed and told you that you were out of your mind. But here we are. So let me tell you a bit more about my story and about how a pandemic made me reconsider my entire life.

Growing up, I wanted to be so many things. From a veterinarian to a lawyer to an accountant (which is funny because if you know me, you know I can't even multiply basic numbers) to a social worker or a therapist. Truth be told, being a flight attendant was never something I ever considered. Some people dream of that job their whole life and I kind of stumbled upon it by chance; by faith, I may say. It was an exceptionally smooth and pleasant redirection. I was actually supposed to be a police officer. Quite the opposite of flying in a metal tube across continents and oceans, I know!

I studied three years in Trois-Rivières, Quebec. It wasn't an easy path. I struggled physically. Although, these three years were the healthiest years of my life, I found myself having a really hard time running, and believe me, there was a lot of running to do. It was always a battle of me against me. I wasn't doing it because I enjoyed it, but because I had to.

After some issues with my legs that stopped me from passing all the physical tests, getting my diploma was delayed a year. During which I kept my part-time job as a dispatch agent for the Quebec Provincial Police. I loved that job. It was the adrenaline without the risk. Guiding officers on calls, knowing I was their ears or eyes when I had someone on the line, was highly rewarding. I was really good at that job. Or so I like to believe.

Grounded

Eventually, I succeeded on the physical aspects of the program, but I couldn't get into police academy, which is an additional 3 months of courses and simulations. This is when things took a turn. I was wondering if this was really meant to be or if it wasn't the Universe's way to tell me that, maybe, I should look into something else. I now call this season of my life the "perfect redirection."

At that point, I had never been on any airline websites. Ever. But something way stronger than me took me there; in the "Careers" section precisely. When I saw they were hiring for the flight attendant position, I didn't think much of it but sent my resumé anyway. "What do I have to lose? They won't hire me anyway!". To my surprise, two weeks later, I was giving my notice at the police station and was on my way to Montreal to start the training. This is when the saying "It was meant to be" took a whole other meaning for me.

The 8 weeks of mandatory training were some of the hardest days of my life. It was wild. I had never put my mind through something so intense. It was physically and mentally draining. We had to know everything by heart. It was army- like but a different army-like. The kind where people rely on you to save their lives in 90 seconds or less in the unlikely event of an emergency evacuation because let's face it, flight attendants are there to make sure you get out of the aircraft alive if it's about to blow up.

I showed up on time, well-dressed every day. I was sharing a room with a stranger that became a friend and then a stranger again. I was one of the oldest in that group and it made me truly impatient at times. Around the end of our training, our trainers would meet with us to give us a performance review. That was one of the most nerve-racking experiences ever. At that time, I was not the most confident. I really felt like I didn't do that well during training and that I would be reminded. What I was told instead were some empowering words I never thought I'd hear because of a lower self-esteem.

Grounded

I was told I would be a Service Director (the lead flight attendant on a flight) one day and that it would be an honor to work with me. It seems really insignificant and, really it was, but I think this was a pivotal moment in my personal life. This is where I started to really believe in myself.

I got my wings in January 2013. That was quite the accomplishment. I was so proud; it felt so glamourous at the time. I was one of the few selected to be a flight attendant. Me? Officially a flight attendant? As I am writing these words, I remember the exact feeling I felt when it happened, and believe me, I don't remember much in my life, but the feeling of pride that ran through my veins that day is something I will remember until the   day I die. I was so excited for what the future had in store for me. This was the perfect new beginning. It was exactly what I needed. My life took a huge turn for the best, and   I've met some of the most amazing people I now call friends.

After the training in Montreal, we had to move to Toronto. The first three years as a flight attendant are the most financially challenging, so we rented a house in the suburbs and at the most, there were 7 of us living under the same roof. That too, was challenging at times. Sharing rooms, waking up at different hours of the day and the night because we were at the mercy of crew scheduling, cooking, cleaning, people not picking up after themselves. It was an interesting time.

During the three years I spent in Toronto, I traveled the world, made and lost friends, was away from family, missed birthdays, Christmases, important life events, fell in love, fell out of love, partied downtown, moved with other friends, drank a lot, spent way more money than I was making, lost myself and found myself again.
I was getting to know myself in ways I didn't before. I was becoming more and more independent in a city that wasn't mine, with a job that was the most exciting thing I had ever done. Times were good and it was only the beginning.

I always adored, even to this day, putting my uniform on, packing my suitcase, knowing with absolute certainty I would meet amazing people that had amazing stories to share, whether they were passengers or crew members. I always felt a sense of glamour doing this job even though it wasn't like that at all times, very rarely actually.

Grounded

I felt like I was making a difference in people's lives. I was taking them to a vacation, a funeral, a reunion with a loved one, a work trip, etc. It was always interesting hearing the stories people had to tell. So many times, I remember crying with passengers in the galley, I remember laughing with them, I remember going on a date with one of them, I remember holding crying babies, making them laugh, making bubbles out of hand soap and water. It was that connection to people that made every day unpredictable and so rewarding. You never knew when you would run into someone with an amazing story or when you would have to use your creativity to come up with ways to entertain tiny humans. This is still the part that I cherish the most to this day. It's the part I miss the most. It's helping that elderly woman with her husband's ashes, it's hugging and taking a mother to the city where her son died of suicide so she could go figure out his funeral details, it's taking that young couple on their honeymoon or that other couple that were bringing back their adopted child to the country, it's meeting celebrities like Chris Hadfield, hockey players or movie stars. It's all these tiny moments of connection, of feeling like we are all together and somehow, linked to one another.

As I am writing these lines, I am actually sitting on a plane to Vancouver. One of my favorite aircrafts, the Boeing 787 Dreamliner, is taking me there. I'm flying for the first time in a little while and I feel heartbroken, shattered, like the love of my life just broke up with me. I honestly didn't think it would be this hard. I have been laid-off for a little more than a year now, and being back in the sky brings back all the things I absolutely loved about being a flight attendant.

I did cry a few times so far today. At this point, I feel like I am grieving the loss of that life I loved so much. I'm at a point in this whole process where it's incredibly hard for me to even talk about it without tearing up or literally bawling. I remember when the pandemic first started in March of 2020. I needed a break, more freedom, and more time with my dog. All these things I was craving that month made me welcome the layoff with open arms, with a sigh of relief that I could finally live life on my own terms. And for the first 6 months of literally being grounded, I did just that. But before I write about this, let me tell you a bit more about where this career took me in 2016 because it's probably the most wonderful thing that happened to me in this life so far.

Grounded

For the first year or two of being a flight attendant, I always heard people telling me how amazing Vancouver was. I had never been before and the way they described it always felt so magical to me. The pictures were dreamy, but it took a while before I got lucky enough to finally have a layover in beautiful British-Columbia, and when I did... it changed me. Have you ever visited a new city or a country and felt like you were at home, like you belonged there without even knowing the place? Because that is how I felt when I first touched down on the west coast. The mountains, the ocean, the fresh air...everything inspired me. I felt at ease, at peace there. And so, in 2016, once again at the most impeccable timing, life gave me a base transfer to the west coast. I packed my car and drove across the country with one of my best childhood friends. A lot of things happened in my first couple of years there, but in 2018 everything changed again.

What provoked it this time is a little Mexican rescue dog I adopted. I picked Bailey up in Los Cabos and we've been inseparable ever since. She is my world. With her, I visited Tofino, on Vancouver Island, numerous times. This is where my manifestation journey started and where I realized that my thoughts held a lot more power than I ever knew before. When I started being aware of my thinking and being grateful for everything in my life, everything changed for the best. I figured out in Tofino that the more I said nice things to myself and the more I envisioned positive and exciting outcomes, the more the Universe would bring positive and exciting things into my life. It's been a way of life ever since and I am so grateful this transition happened in this magical and very spiritual place because I am not sure how I would handle the situation we are facing at the moment if it wasn't for a strong mindset. There is a special place in my heart for the great Pacific North-West. That's why I am so thankful I got to spend four weeks there during the summer after the layoff. It was the best summer of my life. I am so fortunate to have a friend that has parents living there. We both found a lot of comfort there during the summer of 2020. The last time we went, I knew it was the last. I felt it in my bones. I had to come back on the east coast.

Grounded

In September of 2020, I packed everything and moved across the country again, I left the place that felt like home the most, I got a full-time job I basically had no experience in, I reconnected with friends and family, moved back with my mom at 34 years old, and I've been grieving ever since. I am forever thankful for this whole process because feeling things means we are alive, but the contrast between my former life and the new one hasn't been an easy one to digest. Deep down, I know that this is just another redirection and I have faith that this is taking me to the things and experiences that are meant for me. I need to trust. I can't stop trusting. I always had the certainty that everything happens for a reason, and this is just another challenge that is teaching me something. In the grand scheme of things, it's already bringing so much good into my life, and I know it will keep doing just that. Life has a funny way to bring into your life the things that are meant for you even though you wish it were delivered in a different way.

If you had asked me over a year ago, if I was ever going to quit this job or lose it, I would've told you that it was absolutely impossible, that you were crazy for asking such a thing. This career forged the woman I am today. It made me an overall more compassionate human. I believe I always was, but being a flight attendant makes you see people with a completely different outlook. You see people at either their absolute best or absolute worst; something we are not used to seeing on a regular basis. It gives you such a different perspective on behaviors, coping mechanisms, different reactions based on different cultures. It's a weird thing really but also such a blessing to be able to experience this and become more tolerant along the way. With this career came not only the discovery of myself but the discovery of some of my favorite places on earth. I also met my favorite people there and the friendships I gained from this life experience are some that remain to this day.

Grounded

If you have a flight attendant in your life, my biggest advice would be to ask them about their favorite travels, about aircrafts and emergency procedures. Ask them if they preferred taking off or landing. What about their favorite destination or favorite shopping place? What was the most impressive celebrity they had on board? Did they ever have to divert or prepare for an emergency landing? We love to tell our stories. Especially now. It is what keeps a part of this journey alive when everything else seems to have crashed. Our world truly stopped turning in 2020, just like everyone else's, and telling you about the stories and how amazing this adventure was gives us hope that one day, we will be able to collect more memories from around the globe with colleagues that became family for a few days while we were away from our real one.

Now that I've been without wings for over a year, I am craving the sky, I want to be on a plane so badly and do the best I can to make people happy. It's such a precious gift to have found a job I adore with a passion. It is not some- thing a lot of people are fortunate enough to stumble upon. Most of all, I think it's the lifestyle I miss the most. To get to fly with friends and have fun layovers in cities I would've never been to if it wasn't for this job, to take my mom on trips to Europe, to go trav-el South-East Asia by myself, to sit in business class and just enjoy the ride, to work 6 months a year and to have all the flexibility and freedom of making my own schedule. This career brought me some of my best memories and sitting on this plane is like watching the movie of my own life. I can literally see myself walking down the aisle and I truly hope to be back one day to add some clips to this film. It is not so much about the job itself. It's about the memories we collect along the way. I hope you have something in your life that lights you up like this. It's probably the thing that helps you carry on with everything going on.

Keep doing the things that *i n s p i r e   y o u*. Keep positive and high vibe thinking. Keep dreaming and believing that someday, this will be all behind us and life will be able to resume. Then maybe I can tell you: - *"Hello! Bonjour! Welcome aboard! Bienvenue à bord!"* on the way to the place you've been dreaming to go this whole time.

BIOGRAPHY

Gabrielle Morin

Gabrielle was born and raised in a small town in the province of Quebec. At an early age, she knew she was destined to accomplish great things. She took matters into her own hands because she always knew she was the only one in charge of her own happiness. In 2013, she became a flight attendant, and her life took a turn for the best. The job not only brought her all around the world, but also took her to her favourite place, the great Pacific North West where she met her people and lived for 4 years. The fresh air of the West Coast brought clarity into her life and that's when her conscious manifestation journey started. She is a positive woman with a big vision and an even bigger mindset. She is ambitious and has big dreams. During the pandemic, she really focused on her side business which has been a true blessing in her life and the lives of so many others. Gabrielle's love language is quality time. She aims to make the best memories with her family and friends, her dog, and her own self. She is independent, loves to get out of her comfort zone and wants every woman out there to know they are capable of achieving anything they put their minds to. She believes we all deserve the best of what life has to offer as long as we are willing to put our fears to a stop and just go for whatever it is we desire.

 Gabrielle Morin

 gab_morin

PHUKET, THAILAND

CHAPTER 9

"The job that saved my life"

by Nadia Lepage

*"Let your light shine and share it with the world,
Igniting light in others"*

You may think my story isn't special, but it is colorful and unique just like me. Just like your story is to you. I hope you will see and understand how becoming a flight attendant and being part of the aviation family, saved my life. I also really wish, from the bottom of my heart, that you'll find hope, light, and maybe some guidance in my story. This is a simple one but, who knows, maybe you'll even recognize yourself a little bit in me and my story.

As I am writing this story, I am so happy, grateful, and fulfilled in my life. I have an amazing partner, and we are expecting our first child in August. I have family and friends by my side. I even had the chance to start my own business where I have the opportunity to create with my heart. I help women find balance in their lives and learn how to love themself despite the strong societal pressure we all face. I connect with amazing people and I work on creating a community that works to raise each other up! I am so grateful to be where I am. Even if life is not always a walk in the park, it's an amazing, fun, and creative adventure and I love it. BUT, I have to tell you, that wasn't always the case.

In this chapter, I decided to tell you my story along with its vulnerability, and about the time when I was at the lowest point in my life. I put my power in someone else's hands, and at the time, I didn't even realize it. For that story, let's call that someone, Matthew. I was in a toxic relationship for a while, 5 years to be exact. I was unhappy, unhealthy, empty, and I almost lost everything and everybody in my life. When I first met him, I didn't even know if he was my type! I didn't know that we would end up being together for 5 years. I remember him being a good talker, an intelligent guy, a charmer with a nice look and smile. He was a confident guy and he made me feel like a special woman. Early in the relationship, I realised that we were only together to make each other feel better in our own lives, and I knew that wasn't healthy.

The job that saved my life

Matthew was jealous, but at the same time, I felt like he didn't care about me. I think that he loved having control over me and my thoughts. Not too long into the relationship, I found myself about to be unemployed, isolated with nobody left around me, and in a really bad place mentally. Abused at every level, without even knowing it at first (violence, drugs, manipulation, and bad choices), I was stuck in my little world. When I think about it today, I don't even recognize myself from that period of time. I could have chosen a different path, yes, but knowing what I know now, I had no choice but to go through with that relationship and learn some lessons the hard way.

When I was young, I never thought it would happen to me. I dreamt with an open heart and open eyes. I gave my all to everyone and put my whole heart into everything I did. I was a big sister, an athlete, a coach, a friend who was always there. I was a hard worker. I think I was a good little girl. At one point, one day, I started to realize that everything I did, every choice I made, was for everyone except myself. I forgot about what I wanted, and I proved myself to others by doing everything they needed instead. I had a lot of baggage and I was far from being perfect (and I'm still not perfect to this day!). So, I started a process of personal growth, but I was still fragile. That's when I met Matthew. I forgot everything that I had learned about changing and living a life that aligned with my core values. Prior to Matthew, when challenges arose, I was more in control of my choices, more in control of my inner power to "fight back". When that event happened, I realized I was just looking for acceptance, for recognition, for love without even having it for myself.

When it all changed...

Two years into that relationship, that's when, without knowing much about the job, I applied to be a flight attendant! Being a flight attendant was never my dream when I was growing up, but I always loved travelling and human connection. So, when I was 28 and the opportunity presented itself, I said why not, and I just sent in my resume! I was in Kelowna at the time. I love the Okanagan Valley. I remember working in a beautiful winery. I was able to find some happiness at that time, the people, the views, the fresh air, it was amazing.

The job that saved my life

Just a couple of days after I sent my application in (the timing couldn't have been more perfect!), I got a call from the airline: they wanted to do a phone interview with me. I even remember running out of minutes on my flip phone on that call! I called back, too excited not to, and they told me they wanted to do a second interview in person, two weeks later in Toronto! OMG! I couldn't believe it. So, Matthew and I drove back East. We were coming back to Montreal a couple of days later anyway, so we just left a little bit early. Then, on the road, I realized that he wasn't too happy about me becoming a flight attendant, even though he was the one who kind of gave me the idea to apply in the first place. Afterward, I realized that he didn't believe in me nor did he want me to get the job. Maybe it was because of his jealousy, or the fact that he was scared that he would lose some of his control over me when I become more independent. To this day, I am still unsure of the exact reason.

At the interview, everything was amazing! I realized I was one of the oldest candidates, but I didn't care, I felt like a little girl; so excited and so nervous at the same time. I met beautiful people who I'm still in touch with to this day. During the long process, in between interviews (we had different kinds of interviews to go through that day), the gossip was that if we got a medical appointment, the chances were that we got the job. I got the medical exam, and I got an email telling me I was hired not long after those tests! I trained in Montreal, but I was based out of Toronto. No surprise here, Matt wasn't too happy about this either. To be honest, I almost didn't accept the job at the time. Can you imagine? I remember being at my mom's house when I got the email and Matt and I had a huge fight. It might have been jealousy, frustration, or anger on his part, but my heart was loud and clear: I had to do this. That's how the adventure began! I am so happy I made that choice. It has completely changed my life. Please, if you find yourself in a similar situation, always believe in yourself, and don't make the mistake of living your life for somebody else. This opportunity, this amazing job saved my life in so many ways and I'm so thankful for it. I was away from home from time to time and living by myself in a crash pad (not exactly a five-star hotel, but I had a good time!). I wasn't always thinking about all of the bad things, I wasn't scared all the time, just taking care of myself and nobody else.

The job that saved my life

I'm not going to lie, that relationship was a long and difficult road, and after three more years, I had finally had enough. I respected myself and said: "That's enough!". I should have called it quits long before that. Probably around the time when I missed my first flight EVER because I couldn't physically do it and because the police had to get involved. But that's not my story; I had to go deeper and become stronger before I could see it.

That job and the people I met working as a FA reminded me that there is beauty and happiness wherever you look. I didn't have to feel like I was being judged, sad, scared, and not myself all the time. I always wanted (and still want) to help people to be happy, balanced, and to see how beautiful they are inside & out, but, for so long, I forgot about the most important person of all: ME. Listen to your heart even if it hurts sometimes. Believing in yourself and being brave are the best gifts you could ever give yourself, even when it's scary.

I have to be honest; I don't regret that phase of my life because I'm at peace with it now. I learned so much about myself and others. I'm not angry, scared, or sad anymore. I know now that I was also trying to save someone who didn't want to be saved at the time and who was hurting too. I know now that I was paying attention to someone else because I didn't want to look at my own personal scars. Ever since I was a little girl, I had always been trying to be the savior for everyone else, that was my only purpose, that is, until I faced my fears. That's why I was doing everything for everyone, to please them, to feel useful, needed and special. I know some people stay in that phase forever, but I remember being determined to create and do more. I also remember thinking about how it's so much easier to tell your friend to be careful and "wake up" when she's in a bad situation than to realize it for yourself when it is happening in your own life! That's why it sometimes takes longer than you wish to get out of there.

When you are in the center of the storm, it's weird to say, but you don't always see it or realize it. You concentrate your energy on the little happy moments, the things that keep you going and make you forget about the storm going on around you.

The job that saved my life

You kind of put a mask on for others and also for yourself because you don't always want to suffer and see the negative side of your life. If you ever get to that point, try not to push everyone away because you think you are in control and are strong enough to deal with it alone. From my humble experience, it's harder to come back afterward if you do so. I have to tell you that, amazingly, a lot of good happened after all that. All the stars aligned because I decided to change.

On a plane, you realize that your crew and you are the most important people to keep safe, and that it is a necessity to take care of each other. They are your family in the sky! To do so, you have to open up and trust them. That's what reminded me of that feeling in my life. The feeling of being important, to trust others, to be listened to, to be part of a team. Flying around the world with amazing colleagues who became friends, discovering amazing places and people around the globe, being in charge of a team like I used to do before, having time for myself; just being with the crew was my lifesaver. My crew reminded me what it felt like to be loved unconditionally, to be loved for who I was without any guilt or asking for anything in return. I wish for everyone to feel this way in their own life: in control of their happiness and wellbeing inside & out.

I didn't change in a blink! I had to change my perception, ask for help, face my fears, and be honest with myself. I built a wall around myself during those years and I had to face it and tear it down. I had to remember that, like everyone else, I had my place in this world and it was my responsibility to grab it and/or create it. I was the savior for a while, yes, but I also realized that I was playing the role of the victim and the executioner. I had to connect with myself, for real. It's a lifetime job, sure, but I had to start somewhere. I don't regret my past for a second. It's a part of who I am. I am proud of the person I am today, the road I took, and everything that surrounded me. This story happened a long time ago, but it made me the woman I am today. Writing my story down for you was another personal proof (and challenge!) that I am at peace with my past, and that I can use it to give you hope if you ever feel trapped in your present situation. I hope you also feel at peace with your past so that you can make space for the new you and create your dream life step by step. You deserve it.

The job that saved my life

A year ago, layoffs happened. Easy to say, but not that easy to live through. Some flight attendants had been doing this job for over 20 years! Can you imagine the feeling of losing a job that you had done and loved for so long? To be honest, it was a really hard truth for all of us to digest. In the blink of an eye, we all had to figure out different paths for ourselves. As I'm writing these lines, it's already been over a year since my last flight. I think I was one of the lucky ones. I have a partner who is there for me, who loves me, who supports me, who encourages me to follow my dreams, and who helps me realize that I can do anything. A sensible man who cares for people around him, and I'm the lucky one who gets to share a life with him. I am far from being alone. I also know that some of my colleagues weren't necessarily in the same kind of situation. It's a different story for everyone. Aviation is one of the industries that suffered the most during this pandemic. A lot has changed, and a lot more is going to change in the future. I hopefully wish that the fear, the limitation, and the anxiety won't refrain us from doing our job forever. I remember the feeling I used to get before a flight, I was always so excited for the next adventure ahead. Even when I was doing a turn (flight to a destination and back) on the same day, I knew I was going to meet new crew members and have new passengers with awesome stories to share with me. From a passenger's perspective it may look like we do the same thing on every flight, but in reality, every day was different. I learned so much while I was on a plane. I also know that most of the passengers I had on a flight had preconceptions of what my job was. "Oh, you are a waitress in the sky, right?". I was always telling them that they weren't wrong. If the flight happens to be a calm one, that's mostly what I am, but your safety is always my priority. Don't forget that if something happens on a flight you will be more than happy that my crew and I are onboard. Emergencies happen. Probably more than you know. I don't want to scare you; I just want you to see that we do so much more than you may think. I'm not just talking about emergency landings here, but all sorts of emergencies and/or fulfilling individual passenger needs. It was always so satisfying when a passenger noticed the hard work that we do, when they thanked me for my help, my smile, my support, etc. It was one of my favorite things! They recognized my work, they liked my personality, and I had the chance to help. Everyone is special, and onboard, it was my job to make you feel that way whoever you are.

The job that saved my life

I had the chance to have my family and my friends onboard my flights when they were going on vacations. I even brought my partner on layovers with me. Sharing is caring! But in addition to these blessings, I had many other difficult situations happen as well. I had a passenger who was scared to death to fly. She was crying before even setting a foot onboard. I had to talk to her for quite some time before she got on. I even asked another passenger to help keep her distracted during the flight, and in the end, she had an amazing time. Another time I had a family with a kid who had psychological challenges, who also fought and cried as he was boarding the aircraft. This family had to be separated on 2 different planes, but they got to their destination safe and sound. I had them on their way back also and they were so thankful that we had helped them deal with this situation Another time, on a 10 hour flight, I helped a really sick gentleman and his girlfriend who was stressed out and scared. I had sick people, dangerous people, anxious people and so many other kinds of people on my flights over the years. I have also had mechanical problems, delays, and emergency landings, all of which we dealt with like champions because this is what we do, and it's our job to keep our passengers safe. I hope you can see this more now than ever.

With the pandemic and the layoff last year, as I mentioned, I had to reinvent myself. I always dreamed of having my own business, to start my own project. So, I took this time off from flying to do so. But I never imagined that I would be grounded for more than a year and still counting!

Every day, I cherish those memories. I feel so lucky to have had the chance to enjoy these little, magical moments for 7 years. I'm dreaming of being on a sailboat in Greece, of eating tapas in Barcelona, of walking around beautiful Lisbon, of visiting and eating in a local restaurant in Rome with my crew, of renting a car and going on adventures finding new and special places to explore everywhere we went. I even miss having my little routine on a 24-hour layover in Athens, because that felt like home! I could go on and on and on! I miss meeting amazing people onboard and discussing life and travels with them. I miss flying!

The job that saved my life

By now, I guess, you understand why I'm so grateful for this job and for the way it changed my life forever. I'm so happy with the way it turned out. We all have a turning and deciding point/moment in our life, and it's our responsibility to make it worth it. I don't know where I would have been or how I would have turned my life around without this opportunity. That was my safety net for a while. I'm so proud of myself for listening to my heart, for making some changes, and for accepting help. I hope you do too because you never know where it would lead you.

Today, I am so happy, healthy, lucky, supported, loved, and so humbled to be a part of this amazing project with these amazing FA's I discovered along the way. I always keep myself and my heart open to new opportunities. I push myself to get out of my comfort zone, to be comfortable in a new zone! I suggest you do the same and take back your power along the way. Always find hope in every situation and follow your inner light. Everything you need is already inside of you. Give yourself a chance and believe in the amazing and unique person you are. Treat yourself as if you were your best friend and don't be shy to reach out if you ever feel the need to. Be proud of who you are no matter what.

This job has and always will have a special place in my heart. I don't know when I'll be back in the sky, but all these memories will follow me forever. Hopefully, I will see you onboard soon!

BiOGRAPHY
Nadia Lepage

Nadia is passionate about people and wants to make a difference in their overall well-being. She dreams of sharing her experiences and learning with others. She truly believes that everyone should shine by being who they are: unique. Nadia started her career as a flight attendant at the beginning of the launch of a new airline and had the chance to see the world for 7 wonderful years before she was laid off in June 2020. She was lucky enough to start her own business in the field of well-being during that time. She has created a program for women who put too much stress on their shoulders, has given talks, workshops and participated at wellness events as well. She wishes to continue building a strong community that rises together and connects to all the possibilities that life offers. She is living a simple life in the Laurentides area with her partner, and they are expecting their first child in August 2021.

 nadia_lepage

 Nad.lepage

www.nadlepage.com

Courriel: projectsinsideandout@gmail.com

HYDRA, GREECE

CHAPTER 10

Until you spread your wings you have no idea how far you'll fly

by Chantal Perron

*" Power Is given only to him who dares to stop and take It …
one must have the courage to dare." — Fyodor Dostoevsky*

Practice What You Preach

I am here, ready to board and share my story with you; my journey as a Flying-Therapist-Mom. Through sunshine and storms, it has made me the woman I am today.

To some, I might appear to be confident, someone who holds it all together. However, let me tell you that behind the scenes, that is not always the case. I must confess that I had mixed feelings about embarking on this beautiful book project. Never having participated in the writing of a book, and with English not being my first language, I doubted myself and my abilities to write the lines that will follow. I felt like an impostor. The challenge came from the anxiety associated with being outside of my comfort zone.

On that note, taking my attention deficit disorder into account, I decided to embrace the adventure as it gave me the possibility to grow, and it allowed me to overcome my discomfort. I felt like I owed it to myself to at least try, no matter what the outcome might be. This was an opportunity to try something new, by daring to discover all the unexplored emotions that went with it. What has always allowed me to move forward in life, is having faith that there is a reason as to why situations and experiences present themselves. They are all opportunities to gain wisdom through facing my fears. This is what I invite my clients, family, and friends to do, now it's my turn to practice what I preach.

**Until you spread your wings
you have no idea how far you'll fly**

Serendipity

During my teenage years, I was inspired by a TV show, and became interested in the life of a stewardess, (that's what Flight Attendants were called back then). Even though I had never been on a flight, something inside me was steering me in the direction of travel.

I finished the 11th grade at the age of 17 and I wanted to apply for the airlines, but I wasn't old enough. Therefore, the school counselor suggested I study Hospitality instead of going to college. He believed it would be an asset for me when the time would come to apply for my dream job. I followed his advice, and I am so happy that I did. To this day I am not sure what drew me towards the airline industry aside from the feeling that it was, and still is, simply meant to be.

Just after turning 20, my boyfriend's mother called me to let me know that an airline was hiring. She knew how much it meant to me. I applied to that airline and that's how it all started. Life was just delightful, being a young adult with no other responsibilities but to be able to embrace life, travel the world, and do my dream job. I will always remember my first day wearing my crew uniform and toting my luggage. How great I felt as I climbed the airstairs to enter the airplane. I can picture it perfectly as I am writing these lines. It was simply one of the proudest moments of my life. Sadly, the company went bankrupt two years later.

Destiny

I then decided to apply to university to study Human Resources. Not having attended college first, I regretted (at the time) not having studied further, for I felt unprepared. I also tried different jobs, however, nothing made me feel as blissful as flying did. After four years of job hunting, I curiously applied to a nationwide airline, the airline where I have now been employed for the last 24 years. Presently, I am on temporary layoff status due to the COVID-19 pandemic and the severe impact it has had on the travel industry.

Until you spread your wings
you have no idea how far you'll fly

An incredibly sad, unpleasant phase for many of my colleagues, as it has been a period of great uncertainty. In all honesty, for me, it have me a chance to delve deeper, to have the time to take care of myself like doing more yoga, meditation, fasting, and other things that feed my soul. Putting in place healthy habits that I hope will stay when I return to the skies.

Going back to applying for this company at the age of 26. At first, I hesitated, I wasn't sure then, that I wanted to go back to flying. Perhaps, there was another career I should be looking into instead. I wrestled with the negative ideas and the inconveniences the job would bring. My list of cons was greater than my list of pros. Moving to another city, commuting for an undetermined period of time, being at the bottom of the seniority list of thousands of crew members, and consequently having little to no choices of schedules, days off, and vacation allotments. Not to mention a salary that was not very appealing! I found all of it to be very daunting indeed. Thanks to my mom's wisdom, however, she convinced me that even if there was doubt in my mind, I had to give it a try. This way I could make an informed decision instead of regretting my choice further down the road. I didn't want to wonder "what if...". If this profession was no longer for me, it would be clear, and I could then put it behind me and focus on something else.

Sure enough, on my first flight back as a flight attendant, it was apparent that the aviation world was where I belonged.

Strength Through Resilience

Since then, many enriching and educational experiences have arisen. They have given me the chance to surpass myself. I am grateful for these experiences in parallel with personal therapy. I discovered more about my personality, who I was with my fears, my strengths, and my weaknesses. It is a big part of what has made me evolve and become the woman that I proudly am today.

Until you spread your wings
you have no idea how far you'll fly

One of those opportunities was to be part of the recruiting team of the In-flight department to recruit other aspiring flight attendants. It was a very gratifying and enriching assignment. It made me realize, even more, that I was where I belonged, and that being a flight attendant was part of my identity. The objectives reflected my beliefs, which were to actively seek people with a desire to help the public while always maintaining the highest degree of safety standards set by the airline. I have a lot of admiration for my team members who supported one another to succeed as a group to achieve a common goal. Amongst many other skills that I acquired, two managers in particular, who led by example, mentored our group and taught us the essence of teamwork. I cherish the friendships that I made as a result of this assignment.

Another experience unfamiliar to me was becoming an instructor. A temporary assignment in which I was interested. A friend suggested it and I applied. Without putting much thought into it, I submitted my resume. After preliminary interviews, I was not selected. But that did not stop me from applying again. I was selected and I proudly joined the In-Flight Service Training Department.

Once again, I felt completely out of my element by becoming an instructor. In conjunction with personal therapy, it became one of the most important periods of self-growth in my life. Some people are quite at ease standing before an audience. For me, however, it was quite the opposite. I must admit that after the selection process, I did have second thoughts of withdrawing my candidacy. I reflected on why I would put myself in an uncomfortable position when I already had a job that I loved and could do with ease. What made me dive into the adventure, was the opportunity to face my fears, learn something different, and follow through with what life presented to me. Faith and gratitude have been great companions in my life, and I have always relied on them to keep myself moving forward through thick and thin.

In the first lesson that I facilitated, I was so nervous that my hands shook, and my voice cracked. I felt vulnerable standing in front of a class filled with adults, whether they were new flight attendants participating in the initial training, or more experienced colleagues doing their annual recurrent training.

Until you spread your wings
you have no idea how far you'll fly

The feeling that I would appear to be insufficiently prepared, and my ego would be bruised, was a fear that I had to overcome. I had to swallow my vanity and go with the flow. There were also a lot of adjustments to be made, like balancing the new work schedule with my family life, which was already very busy with raising two teenage stepdaughters and my two-year-old son. I realized all too soon that flying with irregular hours allowed me to have more time at home than an office schedule of working 5 days a week, 8:00 am to 4:00 pm and driving in horrendous traffic. My new assignment, as fulfilling as it was, meant less time for me.

Facing My Fears

During that period, I also had to deal with a co-worker who was harassing me. The aggressive tone, disapproving remarks, and confrontation made my work environment extremely unpleasant. I was afraid of this person. My only respite was when she was not at work. Thankfully, I had started therapy, and my therapist helped me face this matter instead of avoiding it which, at the time, was my defense mechanism. It took all the courage that I had just to approach her and to discuss our differences. After a few conversations and sharing how we felt, the outcome was phenomenal. We were able to reach a mutual understanding and resolve our differences. She even apologized for her behavior. This resolution of conflict made me evolve, be stronger at standing my ground, and helped me learn how to defend myself better. I am thankful for the experience because my co-worker and I have since created a healthy working relationship. Through the storm we have bonded, she now holds a place in my heart. We both taught each other about mutual respect, communication, and relationships. A lesson in life I would have missed had I not faced my fear.

So, through all this teaching experience, I have learned to stand my ground, speak my truth, and give feedback in a way that is genuine and responsible. I faced the fear of being judged and not accepted. Yes, there were moments of despair, my pride did take a beating from time to time. But it was all worth it because I was then able to enjoy the reward of being a stronger version of myself and having a better working knowledge of who I was.

Until you spread your wings
you have no idea how far you'll fly

Looking back, I would do it all over again. It is incredible how much I have learned about myself. By not taking on this challenge, I would not have evolved as much as I did. Through training sessions upon training sessions, I have built confidence and a better sense of self. The experience has been invaluable, and I am thankful for all the encouragement that I have received. I never realized that I would have such a passion for teaching.

One Thing Leads To Another

As I mentioned previously, with the training experience, I simultaneously started personal therapy to help me through a difficult divorce. I must say, it was one of the best gifts that I could have ever given myself. It began by simply reaching out for help and ended in being impressed by how much I was discovering. I was getting a better understanding of my emotions, my reactions, and where they were coming from. My curiosity regarding behavioral psychology peaked and I decided to enroll in a course at The Quebec School of Human Relations and Behavioral Studies (École Des Relations Humaines et Études Comportementales du Québec) in order to have a better comprehension of interpersonal relationships. As you can see, my path has been all about one thing leading to another, nothing was planned, and I just following through with what the universe had to offer.

That is how I embarked on another journey towards getting to know Chantal Perron better. In my first three years as a student, I participated in personal and group therapy sessions. It was not all fun and games. I was forced to revisit a lot of fears, anger, sadness, and despair. I delved into painful areas of my life, things that I had been carrying from the time I was born, or possibly even before, depending on your beliefs. Following those three years, I did a two-year internship, and aside from the present COVID-19 confinement, I have never stopped attending classes. I graduated five years ago, and still feel that I have much more to learn. I believe that there is always room for improvement, and so, as a way to master my skills, I assist my teacher and other interns. This helps me to thrive and nurtures my soul. It is part of who I have become. Every day I have opportunities to evolve by acquiring new knowledge and awareness.

Until you spread your wings
you have no idea how far you'll fly

Not being a natural go-getter, it was an effort to attend those classes after a long day of teaching or flying. Most nights I dragged myself to class. Going through a divorce also meant I had to rely on family and friends to take care of my son on some evenings and some weekends. My work schedule revolved around my course. However, for every single session, once I was there, it all made sense; I was exactly where I needed to be. Being a therapist had not crossed my mind on the road to enlightenment. It was entirely for personal growth.

One day my friend, Caroline called me up and asked me for some help. Caroline's friend was going through a rough time and Caroline wanted her to speak to someone objective and compassionate and asked if I wouldn't mind conducting a therapy session. At first, I was reluctant because I felt that I lacked experience. I had never done anything outside the classroom environment before and I was uncomfortable with the idea. She insisted and told me she was convinced I could be of help. After some thought, I agreed, and I embraced the opportunity wholeheartedly. To be of guidance and comfort to someone in distress gave me a great sense of satisfaction. Our session flowed quite naturally and Caroline's friend left feeling reassured and less troubled. She even booked a second session. From there, my practice flourished. It made me realize that this is something I already do every day with family, friends, and colleagues. I felt as if I had found my niche. All the hurdles on my path have led me to the accomplishments of where I am today. Along with the tools I have gathered over the last fifty years of my life, I am now better equipped to accompany others in their struggles with fear, anxiety, and depression. What might have been judgment at a certain point has now definitely transformed into love and compassion for everyone's unique story. I am proud to be a therapist and will continue to offer my services while pursuing my passion for flying.

**Until you spread your wings
you have no idea how far you'll fly**

Dare to regain Your Power Through Adversity

All the experiences I have lived through made me go beyond who I thought I could be. I am very proud of the strengths I have acquired. I believe that life is about daring....

Daring to make mistakes, that's how you learn.

Daring to be true to yourself, by respecting who you are, you teach others to respect you.

Daring to face your fears, you will develop wisdom and have a clear view of what is real versus what isn't.

Daring to be out of your comfort zone, you will become more resilient.

Have faith in the process.

It is the path to a feeling of enlightenment, freedom, and mostly of life and LOVE. It does take strength, courage, and faith to face the unknown. We never know where life will take us. You may fail a few times or fall down from time to time but get up on your feet, spread your wings, and fly like you have never flown before. Believe that everything has a purpose. Simply board the plane and let the adventure begin. If you don't try, you will never know what you are capable of achieving. Let life happen, and one day the pieces will come together, the journey will all make sense. It Is how I have become the Flying-Therapist-Mom that I proudly am today.

Who knows where this beautiful book project will travel, and the impact it will have on the rest of my journey ... looking forward to maybe sharing it with you one day.

BiOGRAPHY
Chantal Perron

A proud mother of a young boy, Chantal Perron at fifty, defines herself as a Compassionate Flying Therapist Mom. Travelling being her first passion, she has been employed with a nationwide airline for over twenty-four years. Most of her flying experience is as a Service Director. Through her career she also had the opportunity to do special assignments within the In-Flight Service Department. She proudly joined the recruiting team for eleven years in addition to her seven years of being an instructor in the airline's training center. Following her path and being open to what life has to offer, she went from participating in personal therapy, which was a turning point in her life, to becoming a therapist herself. Her mission is to help others reveal their inner strengths and courage to face their fears and challenges. She does this by developing cognitive and emotional knowledge in order to allow her clients to have better relationships with themselves and others. She believes that love, truth, faith, and gratitude are food for the soul. She uses yoga and meditation to help her achieve a state of mindfulness.

Thérapeute en approche corporelle et relation d'aide
Tel: 514.924.3995 - E-mail: cperron26@hotmail.com

ROME ITALY

CHAPTER 11

Tragic to Magic

by Dwayne Mightley

"Don't let your past hold you hostage to your future."
- Byron Nelson

Chapter One

You Inspire Me

Despite life's ups and downs you inspire me, you inspire me to get up no matter how many times I fall.

You inspire me.

No one ever said this would be easy, no one ever said that my biggest battle would be with me. You inspire me.

It's not about the money and fancy cars, it's not about the woman and caviar. See a lot of people have champagne tastes But only hold Coke Cola money.

You inspire me.

You inspire me to think outside the box of what could be, "it's just work," "Go beast mode." How bad do you want the things you say you do? Because it's just work, what are you willing to give up to get what you want? Because it's just work, you say you want to eat but you can't, you want a steak but only have Burger King-type money. It's just work, You can walk at first but when you get it, sprint like hell, you say you workout but if at the end your muscles don't hurt, then you didn't workout, cause It's just work.
You Inspire Me

You may have to drop some people off to move forward, you can read a book but if you don't implement what it is you are reading then you missed the boat. Because it's just work !

You Inspire Me

To fall down is to be expected, to stay down when the only way to go is up is failure,

It's only work, pick yourself up, dust yourself off and keep going, cause it's just work,

You inspire me !

Written by: Dwayne Mightley

Tragic to Magic

It was my senior year of elementary school, I was a couple of months away from graduating and I was illiterate. Though I was in 6th grade, my reading and writing was that of a 3rd grader. I thought I didn't care that I couldn't read or write; I mean I was planning on being a pro soccer player, making a lot of money, and living The High Life. Never once did I not think I wasn't going to make it... but I did care.

Though I told my dream to many, the response in return was always, "you'll never be as good as your older brothers.". I would constantly be heard repeating Ali's famous rhyme, "fly like a butterfly and sting like a bee, you know Muhammad Ali, he looks just like me"! Oh, I was going to sting some folks all right!

Miss Ramos and Mr. Olympia, if there were two people that saw something special in me when no one else could, it was definitely those two.. They were every students beloved teacher's at Hampstead Elementary School. I was fortunate to have both of them in 4th and again in 6th grade! If I said I was over the moon, that would have been an understatement. Every kid in their lifetime had a teacher crush... it was Miss Ramos for me! To show my love, every year, I would bake her a cake and ask my mother to decorate it for me. To make Miss Ramos happy was my life's mission!

It was lunchtime when I was in the yard playing like every other kid. Out of the blue, I heard "Dwayne come here !" It was Mr. Olympia. Millions of thoughts raced through my head! "Did I miss detention? (not that I ever really got detention) Had I forgotten to hand in an assignment?" I was led into the gym. Mr. Olympia had locked the door behind me and asked... "Want to play 21 ?" After I let out the hugest sigh, I thought, "You know I'm a black man right and you're asking ME to play basketball? (I thought it but didn't really say it to him) Hahaha...sure !?" Leaving the playground it was all "ooooh's" and "aaah's" and "you're in trouble!" If they only knew I was in the gym representing. I did get my ass handed to me a couple of times, but I sure did get my licks in too. When I did whoop butt, I always knew there would be call for a rematch. A teacher couldn't have his student beat him in a one-on-one game!

Tragic to Magic

Miss Ramos and Mr. Olympia were meant to be teachers, even more so, my teachers. They provided me with confidence in an indirect way. Even though I was illiterate, I felt I could conquer the world. I have them to thank for this! They saw my strengths and helped me build on them. They also saw my weaknesses and helped me there too aka reading and writing and now I'm writing my first project. It could have gone in a very different direction, easily.

Although Mr. Olympia and I loved to play some 1-1 basketball during Lunch hour, my true passion was soccer. This is where I felt alive! I was good at it; better yet, I was great at it! I knew I had so much potential. It felt so different from the classroom, and I needed that. There was only one problem. When making Nationals or wanting to move to the professional league, I had to fly...in an airplane....

In 1987, the movie La Bamba came out. Ritchie Valens, who was played by Lou Diamond Phillips, had to get to Philadelphia for his next show. The snow was falling; and there was only one spot left on the plane, but there were two of them: Richie and Tommy. They were forced to flip for it. It was between a 45-minute flight or 6-hour bus ride; Richie won the toss. He chose the 45-minute plane ride. That was the last time he was ever seen. The plane crashed, nobody made it. That was the day I swore I'd never get on a plane ever again.

Going back to my love of soccer and having to travel, I was in quite the dilemma...

God sees, God knows, & God hears all.

God has blessed her with an amazing gift
she is unique in her ways, that when
she talks everyone listens.

She is unique in her ways, she is a master
of her domain, she is a fountain that pours
forever onto them
she opens the minds of many, she is nor
 the dream maker, or dream seeker, yet she
 is the dream helper,.... revealer!

When they came to her for the first time she
caught and opened their eyes to the infinite

power of one's mind, that all could be achieved
if you work for it, all could be achieved if your
soul desires it!

She came to them as the moon but ended up
Their star
She came to them as a prophet, she is of God's
children sent here to do God's work, heal all
those whose minds are lost, guide those who's
heart is open

Pour onto them the knowledge that yes they can,
 Pour onto them that you're only in their lives for a
short time, but will forever remain in their minds

Remind them you are like sand, and the tighter they
squeeze the more you'll fall through the cracks of
their fingers; yet if they cup their hand you remain
like the never ending mountain, forever they can
climb!

Teacher

Written By; Dwayne

Tragic to Magic

Chapter 2

"I found myself chasing my goals and dreams and thinking I had to leave here to achieve it." KRS1

It was the summer of 1992 and our team, NDG (Notre-Dame de Grace), was doing extremely well. We knew we had a very big chance to make it to the Nationals! The finals were being played in Québec City and we were to play against our nemesis: the Sporting Patriots. The culture and history of the city are an international draw. At that time, I could not have cared less, to be honest, where we were playing. I was going there with one thing in mind and that was: to win! This rivalry was tangible. It felt like that of the Chicago Bulls vs Detroit Pistons or Montreal Canadiens vs. Quebec Nordiques. Or even, New York Yankees vs the Boston Red Sox! We were down 2-nothing and came back to win the game 4-3 on penalties. I still remember fans of the Patriots (mostly parents) chanting "We're going to Winnipeg! We're going to Winnipeg!" during the game. That was where the Nationals were taking place that year. After winning, I took it upon myself to run by them after the game to chant, "You're not going to Winnipeg! You're not going to Winnipeg!".

Once in the changeroom, my first question to the guys was, "how long is the drive to Winnipeg?" They all laughed and said, "We're not driving, we're flying!" Oh shit! Now what? Panic set in... I had told myself that I was never going to fly again after watching that movie but, was I going to miss the Nationals, one of the biggest stages for an adolescent, and close the door on my dream? There was no way! Needless to say, on that fateful day in October 1992, I was on a plane to Winnipeg. That was the true beginning for me. As I overcame my fear of flying (thanks to my passion for the love of soccer), I willingly got on a plane for a commercial shoot, a serving job at Disney, and the chance to play professionally in Italy. These were experiences I am so very thankful for as they have helped shape who I am today and prepared me for my next huge move!

Tragic to Magic

I cannot move onto the next chapter without giving some attention to Audrey. Audrey was a fellow student in Miss Ramos and Mr. Olympia's class. She was also of African American descent, like myself, and a great student. One day the whole class was seated in a circle on the red carpet. This is where we did most of our reading assignments. Miss Ramos was sitting in her usual brown leather chair and led the way. We each took turns reading, and once a person made a mistake, that was the cue for the next person to take over. Out of 28 students, I was sitting almost 4th to 5th position from the last reader...and that was intentional. As it was getting closer to my turn, my nerves were getting the best of me. This time, we were reading Charlotte's Web. Audrey was seated to my immediate left and Karen was to my right. Karen had just started reading when there was a sudden knock at the door. It was the break I was waiting for. As Miss Ramos went to answer the door, I got up and moved two spots over. Audrey looked at me in utter disgust. The look in her eyes spoke volumes as to say, "It would have been better to try and fail than not try at all!" That look, those unspoken words, cut me like a knife. She was right and I was being a coward. I learned a huge lesson that day and I took it with me everywhere (and still do!). Whether it was on the soccer field or facing my fear of flying, I needed to try.

Many people say, "The Lord works in mysterious ways". As for me, I believe he just works and that there is no mystery at all. Sometimes, when speaking your truth to the universe, one must be careful because she is always listening. I had mentioned earlier that I was never going to fly again. I also stated that I'd made a huge move. Well, the irony would have it that the universe had some huge plans for me that I had no idea about!

Words put to paper speak an unspeakable thought

The message song, the words move

Like a ripple in the ocean

(Sing) Can you see what I see?

Blue skies like grey ones the rain must fall as the sun must shine

The seeds planted, blossom & grow

As he the body and we his limbs an extension of his love, life,

laughter, strength, stretch to no earths limit

Like hands meets glove, tongue meets cheek we are one

The horizon in plain view of what is and what will always be

He who walks the walk and talks the talk is LEADER

Not all readers are leaders but all leaders do read

Tall dark complexion, rich baritone voice all muscle & bustle

impossible to be missed and ditched

All 42 white pearls shine bright like a diamond

(Sing) Can you see what I see,

Morpheous!

Written By; Dwayne Mightley

Chapter 3

"When written in Chinese, the word Crisis is composed of two characters; one represents Danger and the other represents Opportunity". John F Kennedy

After telling the universe I would never fly again, I was on a plane twice in the space of four months. I can't say that my fear had completely disappeared, but I no longer held onto that promise I made myself years ago. I was no longer held hostage to a fear that had held its grip on me for so long.

Fast forward to a few years later, and I was in a place in my life where change was needed. I was like a dog chasing his own tail and not getting ahead or reaching goals that I had set out for myself. I needed a new plan, new goals, new...everything. Do you know that feeling? It's deep in your gut. It's like a push or a pull towards something. Surprisingly, the thought of becoming a flight attendant popped into my mind. I knew from my experience as a server and manager that I had some pretty good people skills, and to see the world (and get paid for it), sounded like a pretty good deal to me! So, surprisingly, I applied for a position.

Seth Godin once said "The feeling that everything is about to fall apart, that panic is precisely what growth feels like. You want to escape that terrifying feeling as fast as possible. Your brain thinks that your body is in danger, and the most important thing is to get rid of that danger, to end the tension. You want to run away, call mama... That's the critical moment when most people lose. The key is to recognize when you feel this way, and to lean even deeper into those moments.

To say that I was in panic mode, would definitely be an understatement. I was in full-on anxiety-filled mode. This was huge growth for me, and I KNEW it!"

Tragic to Magic

My journey into the flight industry started off with a small company. I was responsible for checking in passengers at the check-in counters. Flying wasn't part of this, and I was quite comfortable with that. Then, that feeling in my gut returned. I couldn't believe what I was doing! I literally applied for a job doing something that I feared so much...but that pull was strong. Not only was I going to be entering a career where flying was "what you do" but I was also having to relocate to a completely new city for this career move. To be honest, though, I was more ready than I had ever been!

When I took the position as a flight attendant, I saw it as a way of conquering my fears. As a kid growing up I wouldn't even dare jump off the low diving board let alone the high diving board; I was that scared of heights. Anything worth dreaming about, anything worth fighting for, will have growing pain attached to it. No one is exempted from the trials and tribulations that come along with success. Some might say they knew from a very early age that they always wanted to do this job. I said I would never get on a plane after 1987, but yet, here I am. Playing sports gave me that taste of travel, seeing and experiencing different places around the world, and allowed me to dream. Becoming a flight attendant was one of the best decisions I've ever made in my life. The people I've met, the relationships I've made; I wouldn't trade for the world. "Tragedy hits every 5 to 10 years." The real question is, "when the next one hits, will you be ready?"

If 2020, the year of perfect vision, taught me anything, it was that I wasn't ready for what God had planned for me; spiritually, financially, or emotionally. This was the year that people showed up, showed out, and showed their true colors and, to some extent, I wasn't ready for that either. If 2020 genuinely was the year of perfect vision and people displayed who they truly are, do I believe it or do I try to rationalize their behavior? It is forever pounded in our heads that we can't make excuses and money at the same time. Paraphrasing Mr. Byron Nelson, "Either you buy into their lies or they buy into your reasoning, so you must choose powerfully". Above all, 2020 has taught me to open my eyes. Open them to the beauty of life: the ups, downs, excitements, and disappointments as they all lead us to the lesson we are meant to learn... the universe, God, is speaking to us and our only job is to listen.

Tragic to Magic

It reminds me a little of the story of Old Yeller. I had to "hurt enough" to want to make a change. Comfort is both a gift and a curse. In order to want to make a change, grow, move up in life, we must move out of our comfort zone. Our comfort zone has us just that, comfortable, so to speak. I never realized that I wasn't growing in my comfort zone... until 2020. That is the year I realized I was yelling but due to my own doing.

The year 2020 was, admittedly, tough; there were many ups and downs. For the majority of people, it has appeared as though there were a lot more downs than there were ups. For me, truthfully speaking, this had to be one of the most blessed years I've ever had. It was the first time in 25 years that I actually experienced summer. Our world moves & grooves to the hustle and bustle of everyday life. We daydream of vacations where we can just put our feet up and relax. This was a time for people to do just that, stand still and breathe. Take it in, enjoy life, enjoy family time, enjoy kids, get fresh air, exercise, get healthy and eat healthy! How many of us actually took time to learn a new craft or pick up a new skill? How many of us took the time to call an old friend just to say "I miss you"? How many of us took the time to mend broken friendships, relationships, or family affairs? This was the time! There will eventually be a new normal and some of us may look back fondly at the beauty of life when we had the opportunity to enjoy it at its pace. I'm not going to lie, it was a little scary at the outset but I also saw it as a challenge. To challenge myself and not just sit, wait and ponder "what if ?". This was the time to take control of my life and live my best life yet. No one is promised tomorrow! There are no guarantees that when one goes to bed at night that they're going to wake up the next morning. Live every day as though it's your last. I've always loved the saying, "Live full, die empty".

Tragic to Magic

I made a promise to myself in 2020, "the next time I will be ready, financially, emotionally, spiritually!" Starting a home-based business during a pandemic definitely tested one's nerves. Everything was a learning curve but becoming an entrepreneur has been an absolute blessing. It gave me the opportunity to set and change the direction of my family tree. There's a saying I've learned in business, "those that you think will, won't and those that you think won't, will". It's amazing how many people call themselves your friends and when you ask them to support you or to join you on your journey, they simply won't. Some wait to see if you're going to make it, some wait and hope to see failure... friends...ha! I'm wise enough to know that an opportunity for me is not an opportunity for everyone. I've had drive my whole life and have had to push through many obstacles to reach some of my goals. One thing stayed constant throughout though... I never gave up! Some of my biggest supporters and my biggest fans turned out to be people I don't even know; strangers I've met off the street. I know what it's like to be full of fear and I also know what it's like to be poor but, let me break down what those two words actually mean to me.

P.O.O.R= Passing Over Opportunities Repeatedly

F.E.A.R= False Evidence Appearing Real.

2020 was a year of letting go and releasing fear and stop being poor!

Every job I've ever held, I'd bust my butt to get to the management role. I also came to the stark realization, why not bust my butt for myself and build my own dreams as I work for somebody else busting my butt and building theirs!??

Though this past year has been the toughest in Canadian Aviation history. The Archer must pull the string of the Bow and Arrow as far back as possible to fly as high and far forward as possible. We've been pulled way back and down, stepped on and kicked in the teeth, but every winner had to lose first to know what it would take to win.

'Till we fly again,

It's not bye, but, see you later.

BiOGRAPHY

Dwayne Mightley

After Dwayne saw La Bamba in the summer of 87' and said he'd never fly ever again, so much for that! His dream was to be a professional soccer player, and maybe one day, own his own restaurant. Life got in the way, distractions occurred, and he became a Flight Attendant and a Poet.

Not bad for a black kid who was just supposed to be another statistic. Dwayne never let anyone's opinion of him become his reality. Hard work and determination always pay off. One must go through the mud in order to see the light on the other side. It comes down to making a decision, and Dwayne did just that. He bet on himself when no one else would, and today he can call himself an author.

 Milky7231

 Dwayne Mightley

PUNTA CANA, DOMINICAN REPUBLIC

CHAPTER 12

After the earthquake, rebuild.

by Kristen McGirr

"Happiness can be found, even in the darkest of time,
if one only remembers to turn on the light." - Albus Dumbledore

After the earthquake, rebuild.

Being brought up in a half Italian, half Irish home, you can just imagine the strong, powerful mentors I had to look up to. Good values, kind-hearted, traditional, honorable and respectful. These were not just words to my family, they were who we were meant to be, as individuals, in this lifetime. My mother has always been a force to be reckoned with. This beautiful green-eyed woman with puffy-yet-styled black hair is kind and gentle, unless she feels threatened. I do not believe she has ever lost a battle in her life, because she knows what she is worth and so, she fights for it. She taught me to be the same way. My mother raised me and my sister, who is two years younger than me. I was brought up to be my sister's protector, the person who would always defend her no matter what. As I grew up, this trait became a big part of my life. I am considered by so many as the "Mama bear".

We had an activity in our annual recurrent flight attendant training, where we all had to write a word that best described us on a post-it. They distributed different colored ones, but I remember mine was yellow. On it, I wrote "Mama bear" with a purple sharpie. Our instructor then took our thirty some post-its and placed them across the board. She read them out loud, and we had to guess which person it belonged to. Many notes on the board were difficult to determine who its owner was, but when it came time for mine, everyone...and I mean everyone in the classroom shouted out my name. I honestly had shivers run down my spine. I felt honored to be known as the mama bear in our aviation family. Everyone knows that if you approach a sow and her cubs, she will be as ferocious as they come. Her babies are her life, so consequently, she will become vicious and will not hesitate to give up her own life for the safety of her youngsters. That is what best describes me today. I would give up my own life to protect my family and my friends. My loved ones are everything to me. If one of them is hurt, I am hurt too. I bring it upon myself to heal them or, at the very least, keep them safe. The same situation applies with my colleagues. In any flight I have operated, if a passenger demonstrated aggressiveness towards myself, it was no big deal. If, however, that same passenger went on to threaten one of my colleagues, I became very defensive.

I have a presence that does not go unnoticed, because I believe in my principles and the equality of every other living being. Unfortunately, my type of personality has been misunderstood by many throughout the years.

After the earthquake, rebuild.

I have often had targets on my back because I have had a voice for many who were too afraid to express their thoughts. I have defended people in situations that I believed merited an ally. I have protected my team and gotten the heat for it countless times. Being this mama bear made people see one side of me. A fearless woman who is so strong that she can handle anything that comes her way. A leader who is not easily affected by what others say or think of her, because she can put up that solid steel armor and protect not only herself, but everyone around her shield. What many people do not take the time to see, when it comes to my nature, is the same aspect that many of us forget about the sow. Once she goes back into that cave with her cubs, she puts down her guard and becomes the affectionate and vulnerable creature that she is. She is filled with love and is so proud that she has done her duty and that her little ones are safe. She has many wounds that ache, but her heart is so pure and well intentioned, that she does not allow those wounds to bring her down. I have gone my entire life being that very sow, even if I do not have children of my own. That is why it came as a shock to all my loved ones, that I just got out of a toxic and abusive relationship.

When we first met, it was memorable. We both knew there was something there and it did not take long for both of us to fall madly in love. Our entire relationship seemed to have unforgettable moments. The night we met, all my friends could see that there was an undeniable chemistry forming. Within a month of us dating, he started travelling with me on the flights I operated. It was magical. I had the opportunity to have three-to-five-day layovers at the destinations I was flying into. Being so fortunate to have accommodations and transportation paid by my company, I would operate my flight to and from these beautiful foreign countries, and then we had all these spare days in between flights to go explore together. From our evenings eating the most flavorful pizzas and gelatos in Italy, to visiting ancient gothic cathedrals in Spain, sunbathing on the beaches of France, climbing waterfalls in Morocco, doing wine tasting tours in Saint-Emilion, our life was like a fairy tale. We were living the dream. Even the first time he told me he loved me was like a scene from a princess movie. We were in Eze France, a breath-taking commune off the famous Provence-Alpes-Cote d'Azur.

After the earthquake, rebuild.

While visiting this charming medieval village, we made our way to the hilltop of its spectacular castle, overlooking the Mediterranean Sea. He looked over at me, placed both his hands gently on each side of my face, and told me there was no better time to express that he was in love with me. He could not travel with me every time I worked of course, but he was lucky enough to have a flexible work schedule at the time, so he joined me countless times for new adventures.

Our story just got even sweeter when we decided to move in together. For our one-year anniversary, we bought our first house together. Yet again, the way we found the house was remarkable. We had been looking at houses with an agent, and we were very unimpressed. Nothing was speaking to us and we could not imagine ourselves living in any of these places. One day, we had visited two houses and they were probably the worst we had seen thus far. We had gone to the visits with both our vehicles, as I met him after landing from Athens, Greece. We were about to go back to our duplex, where we were currently living together with two other roommates, when I told him I had to make a pit stop first. I am a noticeably big fan of anything that is an antiquity. Both my parents are big collectors, so the apple did not fall far from the tree. I was in the process of building a small collection of vintage cameras that I was going to display on an antique ladder. I had found a great 1959 Olympus Pen camera that a lady was selling for only ten dollars. I went over to her house to purchase it, while my boyfriend went back home to start dinner. When I arrived at her home, I could not believe how connected I felt with it. It had such charm and character, with a warm cottage feel. It was built in 1972 and the current owners were the original ones. They could not have been more precious. In their late seventies, the lady greeted me at the door while her husband rocked back and forth on his rocking chair in the living room. I expressed how much I loved their home, that was not for sale, and that I would feel so blessed to be able to find one just like it. We got to talking for several hours, and long story short, they sold their home directly to me. We lived there for three of our four years together.

I had my doubts about moving in together so soon, but it just felt right. We had countless amazing moments together and as much as our new home was one of them, I also believe that it is where our problems truly began.

After the earthquake, rebuild.

I had seen some red flags before we purchased the house, but nothing I concerned myself with. As any couple out there, we had our disagreements. Some of them were valid arguments and some were silly now that I recall them. We both got caught up in wanting to be right, instead of just letting go and focusing on being happy together.

Between all the wars we had, we were genuinely happy, or so I thought. It was like being on a rollercoaster. We would live through such memorable highs, but then plumet into such awful lows. I tried to be there for him when he was hurting, but it proved to be an impossible task for me. I always did it wrong, no matter what I did. He had an anger inside of him that he could not control when I was present, and he crossed boundaries that should never have been crossed. I am not even certain I could tell you about the first time it happened. It all started and ended so quickly; I think I was in shock with what had just occurred. I was always so strong, how could I, in the blink of an eye, end up being one of these abused women you hear about? My answer in that moment was simple; I was not one of those women. It only happened once, and it was no big deal. It would not happen again because I told him I would leave him, and since we were meant to be, he would never allow that to happen. But, like any true narcissist, his exaggerated sense of self-importance dominated any disagreement we had. I could not share my thoughts or feelings about a disagreement, because in his eyes, the conclusion was always the same. I was the only problem. He would blame me for his words and actions every time it happened. Constantly reminding me that I was the fuel to his fire. I was the only one he spoke to that way, the only one that made him so uncontrollably furious. He would tell me he never spoke to his friends or family members that way; it was always me who pushed his buttons. Honestly, I did have many faults in these situations. After all, you cannot fight with yourself, right? I wanted to be heard and respected, so I did not let the many disputes go, back then. I just could not believe that the person I loved most on this entire planet, was treating me so poorly in his moments of anger. His lack of empathy was shocking, it was like I did not know the man standing in front of me. His heart turned colder than ice, and he just wanted to hurt me. We all say things we regret in moments of anger, but nothing as brutal as the words that came out of his mouth. They hurt a thousand times more than any bruise I ever had, as a result of his loss of control.

After the earthquake, rebuild.

My mother kept telling me to never put up with all this, and my sister was warning me about the dangers that laid ahead. I knew what I was going through was not normal, but I thought I could save us. After all, that is what I am trained to do. Us flight attendants are everything on board the aircraft. We are the doctors, the nurses, the psychologists, the firefighters, the police, the babysitters, the cooks, the cleaners. You name it, we do it! But above all that, we are trained to save the lives of our passengers, in case of any emergency. Safety is our top priority. So, why wasn't my own safety my top priority? Well, we had our house, we had a fully planned wedding for October 10th, 2020, and we had picked out the names for our future children. We never officially settled on a boy's name, but we knew that if it were a girl, it would have been Abigail. So, how could I just walk away from that entire future? I did not at first. I started reading anger management books, to try understanding what he was going through. He would often tell me I was not there for him in his moments of anger, so when he was calm, I discussed with him what he needed from me. I wrote down tools to help us stay in the present moment, so that we would not get caught up in our emotions when triggered. When none of that worked, we went to couple therapy. I was so happy that he was doing this for me, but as I just said, he was doing it for me. He did not believe in therapy, so he was never going to truly try. You cannot force someone to see something they are not ready to accept, and in the end, he could not accept what he had become.

If he were telling this story, he would be telling it very differently, and I would most definitely be the worst villain to ever walk this earth. No matter what he would have to say about me, and I know he would have many cruel thoughts to express, I also know he will always have to carry with him the truth and burden of his actions towards me.

The year 2020 was when I hit rock bottom. With the pandemic majorly affecting the aviation industry, I was temporarily laid off. You know the saying "You don't know what you have until it's gone?" Well, I knew what I had. Being a flight attendant was not just a career, it was who I was as a person. Traveling was the way I expressed myself, it made my heart whole. It was also the best way for me to escape the hectic life I had back home. Even if I left for a 24-hour layover, those 24 hours were mine. I felt like I could breathe when I was away.

After the earthquake, rebuild.

I always thought it was related to my love of travel, which a huge part of it was, but I soon realized it was also a way to break free from my toxic relationship. When that weekly getaway was taken from me, I had no choice but to come to terms with what was right in front of me. The universe was trying to tell me something, and I finally listened.

Change must start somewhere, and although it is terrifying at first, if the change is for your best interest, you owe it to yourself to acknowledge that it is worth it. So, a cancelled wedding, a sold house, and a fiancé out of the picture, I had found myself suffering like I had never suffered before. If a broken heart could kill you, I would not be here telling you this story. It was like my life had just been devastated by a major 7.0 earthquake on the Richter scale. My entire world, as I knew it, came crashing down. My career and the person who I thought I was going to spend the rest of my life with, were gone. Things only got worse after that. I was diagnosed with a genetic kidney disease and was told that, by the age of 50, I would go into total kidney failure. "Never two without three" they say, so I almost felt some sort of relief in thinking that was my third and final piece of dreadful news. Well, it was not. I lost my absolute best friend just a few months after all this devastation, my grandfather, at the age of 92. He meant the world to me and when I got that call, I had honestly lost all hope in life. I did not even know what to cry about anymore. The loss of my beloved career, the failure of my relationship, selling the house I loved so much, cancelling our fully planned wedding, being told I would be sick with my kidney disease in 18 years, or not being able to talk to my grandpa anymore. It was all just too much to handle. I was calling my father every single night, barely breathing through all the tears. My dad has a way of calming me down, that no one else has the power to do. He was reminding me that I was still young and that I had a lifetime ahead of me to be happy again. The way my mother, father, sister, and friends handled everything I went through with me, is the reason I am alive today. They all carried me while I was too weak to walk. The day before beginning a new chapter in my life and moving into my new house, by myself, devastation hit one more time. During the night of November 27th, 2020, my father suffered a massive heart attack, and the doctors told us there was a big chance he would not survive his open-heart surgery. I was praying like I have never prayed before.

After the earthquake, rebuild.

I was asking my grandfather to come take me instead. I was begging him not to take my father and I was telling him I was ready to go. I felt there was nothing left for me to fight for anymore. I guess my grandfather did not appreciate hearing that. He not only did not listen to me, but he gave us my father back, just in time for Christmas. He was our miracle, and he gave me hope.

Kintsugi is the Japanese art of putting broken pottery pieces back together with gold. This is built on the idea that, in embracing flaws and imperfections, you can create an even stronger, more beautiful piece of art. Today, I am rebuilding that broken vase that represents my very life. My friends and family have been the gold keeping me together, strong and safe. Their love and support for me has given me the courage to keep moving forward. I am working on one piece of me at a time and evolving into someone so much stronger than I ever was. Letting go of what I could no longer control was the best gift I could have ever given myself. That, and fighting through the pain I went through instead of giving up, because it is all leading me towards a path of enlightenment. The memories I hold in my heart, good and bad, will make me wiser for the years to come. I have made a beautiful and safe new home for myself, and I found a new career in interior designing. Flying will always be my life though, so as I patiently await to be called back as a flight attendant, I have begun my pilot courses to obtain my license. I am still in the air doing what I love most, being one with the sky and now knowing that I can achieve anything I set my mind to. So, sit back with me, relax and enjoy the flight of life!

BIOGRAPHY
Kristen McGirr

Kristen McGirr currently works in interior designing. She became the manager of a prestigious 120-year-old store shortly after she was hired. Kristen is a people person, and that is what makes her stand out in the customer service field. Compassion and kindness are everything to her. She puts herself in other people's shoes and treats them all equally. At the age of 23, she set sail with Carnival cruise line to work at the front desk of a 3000-passenger ship for 9 months. Upon her return home, she wanted to pursue a career in aviation. She worked for her first airline, as a flight attendant, for 2 years. She then got the call of her dreams and was hired for one of the biggest North American Airlines. Eight years later, her aviation career was put on hold, like so many others in her field, after the industry was majorly impacted in 2020. No matter what, travelling is and always will be her passion. Her parents travelled with her and her younger sister since she was born, opening Kristen's eyes to all the wonders that she had yet to discover. Today, she has begun her flying courses to become a pilot. When she sets her mind to something, Kristen becomes unstoppable. A true inspiration for all to believe in the beauty of their dreams.

 krism30

 Kristen McGirr

TAJ MAHAL, AGRA, INDIA
ONE OF THE 7 WONDERS OF THE WORLD.

CHAPTER 13

Grounded and Grateful

by Amber McCreight

Grounded and Grateful

What do you want to be when you grow up? The answer to this question had always eluded me. The first time I heard the phrase "Jack of all trades, master of none," I immediately identified with it. My interests were so plentiful and varied that I had a hard time committing to and mastering just one thing. Nonetheless, upon graduating from high school, I decided to pursue a career in the sciences. After completing my undergraduate degree, I dabbled in the idea of becoming a dentist, a pharmacist, even a paleontologist. Recognizing that I didn't have a clear path in front of me, I chose to take some time off before committing to a next step. While searching for a job, an acquaintance of mine, a pilot, informed me that his airline was hiring and encouraged me to apply. I went for it, and I sent in my resume. After a successful interview and a rigorous five weeks of training, I received my wings, and began my new adventure. I entered this incredibly fascinating and unique field, and since then, I have experienced so many things that I could never have imagined. There have been good flights and there have been bad flights. I have walked off the aircraft laughing, and I have walked off crying. And while every flight in the past seven years has been memorable in its own way, there is one flight that defined my career and helped me to define myself in the process.

It was January 6th, 2017. I stepped out of my apartment, uniform on and baggage in hand. The crisp morning air filled my lungs as I made my way to my car. I placed my suitcase in the trunk and drove towards the Montreal airport. By the time my car was parked, the sun had begun to rise, and a warm glow lit the sky as I waited for the shuttlebus. Ten minutes later, I made my way through the revolving door of the airport entrance and was submerged into the large crowd of commuters heading in every direction. I fought my way onto the escalator and headed towards the crew resting area. There, I found a subset of my colleagues who I would be flying to Fort Lauderdale with that day. We chitchatted about who was laying over and who was scheduled to work the return flight.

Grounded and Grateful

I had been one of the lucky three that would be escaping the Canadian winter and spending the next twenty-four hours in the Floridian sunshine. I looked down at my watch and realized it was time to head to our gate to prepare for boarding. We made our way through the airport, through customs and security, and as we walked, we talked about how easy the flight would be given that the projected passenger count put our plane at half capacity. This, however, was a short-lived moment of excitement.

The five of us approached our gate, and instantly noticed that all available seating in the waiting area was full. The gate agent pulled us aside into a huddle and told us that the Miami flight had been cancelled. There had been a mechanical issue with that aircraft and, since our flight wasn't full, those passengers who were travelling to Miami were going to be placed on our flight and shuttled to their final destination via ground transportation. We broke from the huddle, grabbed our things, and made our way onto the aircraft. The air was brisk as we stepped into the aircraft indicating that the doors had recently been open. We frantically opened the trolleys and, much to our dismay, discovered that catering had already passed. This was a problem because the news of the Miami flight cancellation would not have been passed on to the catering team and, as we suspected, we had only been stocked with enough food for the expected half-capacity flight. We made the necessary calls to ask for more supplies. Between waiting for an answer from catering and booking/re-routing the Miami passengers and their luggage, our flight departing from Montreal to Fort Lauderdale was delayed by an hour.

The flight itself went well. Less people ordered food than anticipated and shortly after finishing our drink service the overhead chimes rang informing us that it was time to land. We performed our safety duties and made our way to our jump seats. The plane touched down and began to taxi down the runway. Suddenly, the aircraft stopped. We were motionless on the tarmac. I gazed out the window and noticed something peculiar. There were civilians walking around outside the terminal building. Under normal circumstances these areas are only to be occupied by trained crew members wearing appropriate fluorescent vests. I turned in my seat and asked my crewmates if they had any idea what was going on. They did not.

Grounded and Grateful

The lead flight attendant called the captain, and we were told to standby while he and the first officer made the call to request information. While the flight crew made their inquiries the seatbelt sign was kept on, but we were given permission to move about the cabin. My colleagues and I walked through the aircraft, ensuring that passengers remained in their seats. As I made my way down the aisle, I made sure to keep my everything-is-ok smile plastered on my face. Every few rows someone would raise their hand or press their call-button to get my attention. And each time I would explain that, while we didn't know what the exact situation was yet, we would know soon, and the captain would be making an announcement shortly. However, before the captain had that chance, some passengers, having access to their phones and internet, revealed what was happening. There was an active shooter in the baggage area. Only moments prior to our touchdown, someone had fired shots in the terminal building. At this point there was no information on fatalities or injuries. My smile faded as the information began to sink in. Everything was not ok. I promised the passengers that I would let them know if we received any more news and I made my way to the back of the aircraft. As I walked down the aisle, it hit me; if we had left on time, the passengers, myself and the two other crew members joining me on layover would have likely been exactly in that spot at this exact moment. Our lives may have been saved by that one-hour delay.

My fellow flight attendants and I met in the forward of the plane. We drew the curtains and began discussing how to proceed. The phone rang. The captain made the decision to extinguish the seatbelt sign, allowing passengers to use the lavatory and move about the aircraft. We didn't know what was happening outside the plane, but we knew this; there was no way to know how long it would be until disembarkation was possible and there were approximately 270 passengers aboard. In an attempt to be proactive, we first decided to make an announcement asking passengers to divulge any pre-existing medical conditions. Two chimes went off. One woman sitting mid-cabin near the emergency exit disclosed that she was diabetic and one man sitting near the back of the aircraft informed us he was prone to anxiety attacks. We banked this information and made sure to check in on those two passengers every time we went into the aisle. Next, we decided to do an inventory of our food supplies. We counted 150 perishables and 400 non-perishables.

Grounded and Grateful

Knowing full well that we may be there for a few hours, we decided to hold off on handing out this limited supply of food. Instead, we began with a drink service. Now, under normal circumstances, we would perform a drink service with the four bar trolleys that the plane is equipped with. However, we were on the ground and those trolleys could have posed a blocking hazard if an emergency arose, and we suddenly needed to deplane. Instead, we awkwardly struggled to carry drawers of pop cans, each weighing twenty pounds, through the aisle. As I returned with the last drawer filled with the left-over club soda and tonic water that no one wanted, the captain called us to say that we may be getting clearance to fly to an alternate airport. We grabbed garbage bags and rushed to pick up the trash as quickly as we could. We made an announcement asking people to be seated, anticipating an imminent push back. Alas, nearly thirty minutes later, we were told by flight dispatch that this plan was no longer possible. There were rumors of a second shooter in the adjacent terminal building and there was to be no aircraft movement. Up until this point, passengers had been calm. They too understood how differently their day could have been if we had landed on time. However, we were three hours in, and people were beginning to feel restless.

We decided it was time to hand out the non-perishable snacks. There were enough snacks to go around, but the variety had greatly decreased by the time we reached those passengers sitting in the back-most rows. This was met with some frustration. One man began to raise his voice in exasperation. He had not had a chance to eat before boarding and was disappointed that his first meal of the day would be a bag of Twizzlers. I apologized and told him that I would let him have first pick of the next meal.

During the first few services, I felt calm. I felt grateful that we were safe within the confines of the aircraft. It wasn't until a colleague of mine offered to let me borrow his phone to call my family that my emotions got the best of me. I dialed my mom's phone number and, as the four rings rang, I felt fine, but when her outgoing voicemail message began to play, a lump in my throat began to form. My voice cracked as I tried to explain the situation.

Grounded and Grateful

I began to think about how fragile our lives are and how unpredictable these random acts of violence can be. I hung up and handed the phone back to my colleague. I went to the lavatory, composed myself and continued on with another water service.

The sun was still high in the sky, and consequently we asked people to close their window shades to prevent the cabin from getting too hot. The sound of the flight-attendant call button rang in the galley and I made my way through the aisle to row 14. A deeply religious couple in their early forties informed me that it was Shabbat and voiced their concern about getting off the aircraft before sundown. They stated that, after sundown, they would not be permitted to use public transportation and were anxious about having to stay at the airport where the availability of Kosher food would most likely be scarce or possibly non-existent. I spoke with the captain many times throughout the next few hours, constantly seeking updates and hoping to be able to give this couple some good news. However, we learned that we were now at the mercy of the FBI, as this matter had fallen under federal jurisdiction. There was nothing we could do but wait.

We were over five hours in when we decided it was time to hand out the fresh food. We made an announcement asking families with young children to come and choose what they wanted before we handed out the rest to the masses. We explained in the announcement that we did not have enough food to go around and asked that they please share amongst themselves. Surprisingly, there were no complaints. People understood that we had no other choice than to be grateful for what we did have available. As we were handing out the food, a voice came over the intercom and everyone let out a sigh of relief when we received word that the rumors of the second shooter were false.

The next few hours went by with little to report. We passed with water every half an hour. We let those passengers who were feeling overwhelmed by the energy in the cabin join us in the galley for a bit of privacy. We checked in on those passengers who had disclosed their medical history. And mostly, we did what we could to keep pushing through the exhaustion we felt. Around hour seven, we noticed that the waste and water indicators were showing that we were low on water and high on waste.

Grounded and Grateful

We still had no indication of how much longer we would be stuck in the aircraft and thus decided to shut off the water to the lavatories. We wanted to preserve as much drinking water as possible. Thankfully, the airport maintenance staff had begun servicing the twenty-two planes that were still on the tarmac, and we were up next. Hearing this news, we immediately turned the water back on. No one wants to clean a lavatory with no running water.

Moments after our plane was serviced, we received news that we would also be getting some food from the airport. I could feel the excitement in the cabin as people's spirits began to rise. Not everyone was able to eat during the last meal service and were famished. I asked the captain if we would be opening a door to allow catering to enter the aircraft, but as it turned out, that wouldn't be possible. Opening a door would have been a security threat, so instead, boxes of cookies were handed to us through the cockpit window. I could see the enthusiasm in the passengers' eyes fade as we began passing out these tiny cookie packages. I felt embarrassed that this was all we could offer, and I wished that we would be able to give these people some good news soon. My wishes were met a little while later. The first officer's voice echoed through the plane as he announced that we had received clearance to move our aircraft to the gate. Cheers erupted and people clapped their hands furiously. We ushered everyone back in their seats, prepared the aircraft for movement, and a few minutes later, we arrived at the gate.

A low chime sounded indicating that the seatbelt sign had been extinguished. People began to stand up and collect their luggage. Then, the phone rang. The lead flight attendant informed us that the FBI was only letting one plane deplane at a time, and since we were one of twenty-two, it may be a while before we could open the doors. This last hour was probably the worst of the whole day. We were so close yet so far from being free of this flight. One man began to have a panic attack. The excitement of being able to leave, followed by the crushing disappointment of being told otherwise, was too much for him. We brought him into the galley and had him sit on the floor with his head between his knees as we placed cold washcloths on his neck.

Grounded and Grateful

We asked him to try to match his breathing to ours and just as he began to calm down, the announcement we had all been waiting for came over the intercom. We were ready to deplane.

After deplaning the passengers, we finally exited the plane ourselves and entered the terminal. There wasn't a soul to be seen. As we walked through the halls, I could hear only the sounds of our feet hitting the ground and our luggage rolling along behind us. An eerie feeling filled the hall and it sent shivers down my spine. There were abandoned pieces of luggage strewn about haphazardly and I could feel the panic that filled these rooms earlier. I shook it off and kept walking. We made our way down the stairs, through the doors, and outside into the arrivals area. It felt phenomenal to breathe in fresh air, however, while we were finally free of the aircraft, we were still stuck at the airport. There with thousands of people waiting for the shuttles that would transport them to a secondary location where they could make their travel plans.

The sky was dark, and the moonlight danced across the waves of the ocean as our taxis pulled up to our hotel. The clock had stuck midnight, and it was a new day. As I sat on my bed, I pulled out my phone and looked up the articles about the shooting. Five people had been killed. We had spent over eleven hours in that plane and, while that had its own difficulties, we were here, we were alive, and we were safe.

It has been four years since I stepped off that flight, and yet, I can replay the whole day in my mind as if it were yesterday. That flight tested me on so many levels. It tested my patience, my flexibility, my resilience, and my imagination. It was after that flight that I realized that I had finally found a career where being a "jack of all trades" was required and revered. As a flight attendant I could be so many things all once, a caregiver, a nurse, a manager, a concerned friend, and so much more. I finally felt like I was where I was meant to be and doing what I was meant to be doing. I had grown up; I was a flight attendant and I felt masterful.

BiOGRAPHY
Amber McCreight

Shortly after completing her Bachelor of Science degree at McGill University, McCreight made the decision to enter the workforce before continuing her education. She was hired as a flight attendant for a Montreal base a few months later and quickly fell in love with the world of aviation. During her six years as a flight attendant, she travelled to many countries including Iceland, France, Greece, Spain, Portugal, Peru, Morocco, and Chili. Her many hobbies include various types of crafts such as quilling, painting, and drawing. She is a proud vegan as well as a caregiver to her two kitties, Gideon and Kevin. Over the past year, McCreight, like the rest of the world, has had to reimagine her career goals and re-envision what she wants her future to look like. Currently, she is taking classes to expand her creative skill set and is in the midst of writing her first fictional novel.

DUBROVNIK, CROATIA

CHAPTER 14

Love At First Flight
By Arianna Di Fruscia

*" It is during our darkest moments that
we must focus to see the light. " Aristotle*

Love At First Flight

It all started when I was a little girl, my obsession for planes and flying that is. When I was only two years old, I would look up to the sky and say "aereo," which is Italian for plane. Yes, I was born to first and second generation Italian parents. That's where that comes from. As I got older, I started to name every airline and plane that passed over our family home (taught to me by none other than my grandfather). Flying was a dream to me but for some reason or another seemed unattainable. Wow, how lucky were the people in that plane? I wonder where they are coming from, having seen different cultures, all having had different adventures and experiences. I wonder what the crew is like. How they are feeling at this point, what are they doing right now? I later learned they were probably very highly concentrated in their final approach, but we'll get to that later.

LET'S FAST FORWARD...to my teen years, I knew for sure that customer/public service was definitely my calling. I was eager, very eager may I say, to work and be independent. At the age of 14 I scored my first part-time job at a shoe store that turned into me becoming a barista at a Café, and by my last year in high school I was working at a hair salon, banquet hall, and clothing store. My passion was always to serve the customer and to work hard. A work ethic I picked up from my father. After completing high school, I had no clue what I wanted to do or who I wanted to be. Ideas ranged from fashion marketing to hairdressing and cosmetics to a veterinarian (as I love animals), etc. I thought of it all. Coming from a very traditional Italian background, I had this pressure of having to have my life figured out by 18. Having older siblings and cousins who took the college and university route didn't help. I just didn't see it being the route for me. Everyone seemed to have it all figured out, was I really the black sheep who couldn't?

WELL I DID IT....Well, I thought I did. Having it all figured out. I went out and got my diploma in hairdressing and make up artistry. Yup, that's what I was going to do. I decided. I was determined. I was working at a hair salon, I'm good at doing this, I'm doing this. I loved the salon, I loved the people, I loved the clients. However, I felt like something was always missing. I had this urge for adventure, this taste for flight. I just couldn't shake it off. A part of me felt content, and then there was this part of me that felt unfulfilled, like a void.

Love At First Flight

I was always looking up at the sky as if I was in the moon or had my head in the clouds. What I was actually looking at where the airplanes passing by. One day it just hit me, I got my computer out and started looking up flight attendant jobs. That's where my next question comes to play.

SHOULD I STAY OR SHOULD I GO? This became a big question. I ended up applying for a job at a small airline. Here it was. I was taking my big leap of faith. I went through a few interviews, and all seemed great. My boss kept making airplane sounds every time he walked by me. It felt good, it felt real. A month or so went by and I hadn't heard back from them. I just thought maybe it wasn't meant to be. This was about the same time the 2010 winter Olympics in Vancouver were happening. I decided to take an adventure since I guess the whole flight attendant thing wasn't working out. I got on a plane and went to work for the Olympics.

   I started working for a building maintenance company which serviced all homes rented out for police and search and rescue teams. I was having the experience of a lifetime. Two weeks in, my phone rings, and it's a number from Montreal. I answer. I hear "Hello is this Arianna?" my voice which awkwardly replied "yessss this is she". Well, you guessed it, here we have it. It was the airline I applied for. She introduced herself and said, "we loved you and would like to offer you a temporary seasonal position in Montreal". I remember that moment like it was yesterday. I knew exactly where I was standing in the heart of Whistler village. My brain completely froze like I ate an ice cream too fast, but at the same time it flooded with emotions. If I can tell you every emotion, it was every emotion. Just to name a few.. here we go! From excitement, like I wanted to start breaking out the Carleton dance (you know the one from fresh prince of bel air), to omg Girl you prayed for this, it's happening, it's here, go get it. To "wait, what do I do? I'm not in Montreal, I'm in Whistler living this completely amazing opportunity my boyfriend and I had just gotten a fifth wheel camper to live in".

I committed to this. It seemed like forever in my mind, but it was 30 seconds to a minute tops. Ok Arianna, think fast, you need to say something. All of a sudden, the word "No" spit out of my mouth.

Love At First Flight

I couldn't help it. It just overcame me. "I thank you for the opportunity, but I will have to decline." We hung up. There was this moment thereafter where I thought "did I make the right decision? Did I really just refuse the opportunity to do something I always wanted to do?" UUGHHHH. Self talk came into play "Ok, no girl, pull yourself together, you refused because you're here living this once-in-a-lifetime opportunity in your own country. When will you get the opportunity to be on an Olympic assignment again and feel this energy again? Probably never." I told myself if I'm meant to be a flight attendant, I will be one for a big carrier, and it will be a permanent position. I went about my life and lived that adventure to the fullest. My parents would beg to differ as I was always told I should regret it and living in a fifth wheel camper, as it was so shameful for their Italian daughter to be breaking the traditional rules of life. but hey it was honestly till this day, one of the best experiences of my life. I met the most amazing people. I lived the most amazing things.

June came around. I came back to Montreal and got a temporary job for a car dealership as a receptionist. I was not used to sitting that much, being a girl who's always on the move. But hey, it was cool. I was surrounded by nice cars, and I met friends who I still cherish till this day. I started talking to the receptionist who sat next to me. She was always telling me about her husband who worked at an airline. I told her about my big dream of one day working for the same (we'll call it big airline). She came to work the next day and says "Hey my husband told me they're interviewing for flight attendants, but you have to be willing to move, as they don't have openings in Montreal. Want to go with me?" 5 min later my brother sends me a message with the picture of the add in the paper for the same job. I felt it was a sign. I said, "sure let's go, let's do it." Plus, I was totally down to move at that point.

The day came. We met up and went to the interview together, we wanted to be one of the first people there. We went in and did our interviews. I was asked to come back the next day, I happily agreed and left. The moment I opened the door to leave the room, there was a line up. A flood of people wrapped all the way down the staircase - you know what you see American idol looking like - well picture that. I said to myself, "omg what are the chances that out of all of these amazing candidates they will pick me." The next day I went for my interview.

Love At First Flight

This one consisted of a one-on-one and a group interview where we were given different scenarios and had to come up with solutions. They called all the other members of the group except me and this other girl. We looked at each other and were like "that's weird, we didn't stop talking, you think we didn't get it?" Those girls seemed like they walked out of the room happy as can be. Then we get called. They asked us to take appointments for medicals the next day. I thought "alright cool it's part of the process I guess". We get in the elevator and the girl just yells out a huge "AHHHHHHHH." I looked at her like she was insane. She looks at me and says "girl if you pass this next part, we're in. You're going to be flight attendant." Wait what? At that moment I felt compelled to meet her in her excitement and yelled out my own AAHHHHHHH in this hotel elevator. I went for my last interview the next day which consisted of a medical exam, and a few weeks later, I got an email saying I got the job WOO HOO!!! I was going to be based in Toronto, although something in my heart really wanted to go back to Vancouver. I told myself "hey Toronto it shall be". I accepted my fate and started looking at apartments. I was willing to accept being a Blue Jays fan. Hockey on the other hand - absolutely not. I'm a true Montreal Canadiens girl at heart.

The first week into the most intense training of life, I knew without a doubt - this was my true calling. Everything about it felt right. It felt good from the simulators to the colleagues. Yeah, remember that girl - we ended up becoming the best of friends. Day by day pouring my heart and soul into studying till the early hours of the morning. We had an exam practically everyday on something different: a different aircraft, a different procedure, and you can't make more than a few mistakes without getting kicked out. So naturally, becoming a perfectionist was my new thing.

When you wish upon a star

About - I would say 3 weeks in - one of my friends came to visit from Vancouver and I remember we went to hang out and watch the stars at a local park, and for the for first time in my life I had seen a shooting star. I was beyond excited. Oh wait wasn't I supposed to make a wish? Ok here it goes - eyes closed… "I wish I would be based in Vancouver, I miss it so much". I went back home, went to sleep, and forgot about it. It was more like I put it out there and let it go. My classes started in the early afternoon. We started with a home room and then got into our course plan for the day. Well let me tell you, that wish didn't take long!

Love At First Flight

Our instructor came in the next day and says "hey guys does anyone want to go to Vancouver? They sent us a message this morning. They're looking for bilingual flight attendants and want to know if anyone from this class wants to go." I literally felt like the world stopped. Is it just a coincidence or are shooting stars really what they've always been let out to be? A powerful attraction from the universe – whatever it was - I couldn't believe what had just happened. I raised my hand and of course said "me! I want to go." I got my dream job in my dream city. Pinch. Me. Now.

We graduated training after two months, we had our celebration, got our wings, and off we went. I packed up, moved across the country into a ground level apartment in Richmond, BC to start my new life. I started off being on call. I remember it was so slow at first. I would call scheduling to make sure they had the right number. I know, insane!! I came from being a girl who worked 2-3 jobs at once to being on call 18 days a month sitting and waiting.... Patiently waiting. About a few weeks later I had my first flight and as you could've guessed it was love at first flight. From the boarding to the take off role to the service. Everything about the job made me feel alive. I had a vision board of every place I wanted to go, places I wanted to travel to, ones I wanted to see and – slowly - I was attracting them all. I somehow even managed to get back to Montreal for my friend's wedding when I had told her I was on call and couldn't go.

I was based in Vancouver for about 5 years until I transferred to Toronto as I wasn't able to be based In Montreal. I went back and forth between Toronto and Montreal. In 2016 I decided to take on a new challenge and applied to be an inflight service director. It was a big year for me, I started a new position and got my first house. Which ignited my passion for real estate and interior design. We'll get back to that. I got the position in Toronto till about one year later - after over 7 years of being away - I finally held my base in Montreal.

I can tell you countless of travel stories about trips I've shared with colleagues, all the late-night galley talks - no one gets each other like flight attendants do. We understand our tired jetlagged moods. We have our little galley buffets when one cooks something from home and wants to share it with the crew or we stumbled upon this awesome bakery on our layover and want to share some treats with each other.

Love At First Flight

The part I love most about the job is the journey leading to the destination - you meet so many passengers from all different walks of life with different stories and backgrounds. They may be going to see long lost family members they haven't seen in years, taking trips around the world trying to complete some bucket list items with their partner or even travelling solo. The one that marked me the most was seeing this lady who was in her 80's - spunky little women who dressed so well - and after a few hours of serving her I asked her "mam, where are you coming from?" She said "a cruise dear" I said "oh you joined some friends" as she seemed to be travelling alone. She said to me "oh no dear I travel alone. My husband passed away a few years back and no one wanted to go with me so I now decided to live on my own terms and take every trip I want. You only live once you know, and I don't know how much time I have left. Plus, you make wonderful friends along the way. Who wouldn't want to befriend an old girl like me." I loved her attitude - her zest - she impressed me. I saw a part of myself in her. A part of myself that I had been supressing for a long time. I always thought of her. Quite some time later in 2018 I made the painful yet crucial decision to leave a very abusive and manipulative 5-year relationship. It was the hardest thing I ever had to do, but I knew in my heart it was the right decision. I decided I was going to find myself, be true to myself, and find the confidence I lost to travel and to live my life on my own terms again. I bought a house, I took a course in interior design, and pursued a career in real estate. Between school and work I didn't stop that summer, but I loved it. I was running on adrenaline. I worked hard, studied every chance I got, and passed my big real estate exam on the first shot. Woo hoo accomplishments!! My first big project was a complete home renovation - designing the layout, choosing the floors tiles, cabinetry, and everything else down to the paint colour. Once it was complete, I felt this sense of pride of being part of a journey of taking a home that was falling apart and watching it beautifully fall into place.

The TV shows I had watched for years on DIY'S were now becoming my reality. I absolutely fell in love with the process of being manual and that of creation. I felt like the world was my oyster - and then the pandemic hit. I lost my job in aviation and I literally felt like a bird with its wings clipped. I was meant to fly, and now I couldn't, and I had no control over it. I was such an extroverted person - always on the go - if it wasn't for one thing it was for another. I loved people, I loved my yoga classes, I loved working out with my gym fam - and it all got stripped away.

Love At First Flight

I knew I wasn't the only one dealing with this. We were a whole world going through the same thing together. Despite all that, I started to realize that I never did the inner work I needed - I was just always so concentrated on everything else and everyone else, making sure everyone else was happy and taken care of - I forgot about myself. I always wanted to make everyone happy. I had started this path of making myself happy - I did all these great things, but I never did the emotional work - it was just a façade. Being less busy and on the go, I realized there's way more to growth then just that. I started to finally process the emotional side of growth. You know the part where you look back - see everything you've gone through, been through, and you find this simplicity in just letting it all go - not storing it. I found a place of peace and forgiveness. I realized everything, every moment - good or bad - leads you exactly on the path of where you were meant to be and where you needed to be at that time. Everything truly does happen for a reason.

As much as the pandemic hit aviation the most, it allowed me to truly find myself and put myself first. It gave me a chance to dive into real estate and follow other passions such as baking. I would bring the goods I made to the local hospitals and give them away to family and friends. Let's be honest - a girl can't eat all those treats. I would get lost in my baking creations. My home reno creations. I pursued becoming a foster parent for a local animal shelter - which I had wanted to do for years - and it led me to the most precious cat. I never thought I'd be a cat mom but Yes - I foster failed and adopted her. We never know what life will throw our way, but one thing that it has taught me is to live with passion, grace, in the moment, and to know that the universe always has a bigger plan - you just got to trust the process, but most importantly trust yourself and that little voice within you. Always remember that perseverance is power and with power you can do anything.

BIOGRAPHY

Arianna Di Fruscia

Arianna is someone who truly believes that energy is contagious. She loves sharing her warmth and kindness with anyone who crosses her path. "Everybody should feel important" is her motto. Her life has always led her to believe in the power of perseverance. She believes that what defines us is how well we rise after falling. As a young girl, she would always look up to the sky and name every airline of each plane that would fly over her family home with a burning desire to one day be living the jet setters' life herself. In 2010 that dream became a reality when she landed her job in the aviation industry. She knew from that point on, her heart was finally at home, in the sky. In 2018 she made the painful yet crucial decision to leave a toxic abusive relationship where she felt like she had completely lost herself. On her path to self-discovery and regaining her power, she made the decision to follow her second passion: real estate and interior design. She is an entrepreneur, animal lover, avid world traveller, a yoga and fitness aficionado as well as a passionate baker. She is the example that perseverance is power, and with power you can do anything.

f Arianna Di Fruscia Residential Real Estate Broker

SAN FRANCISCO, CALIFORNIA

CHAPTER 15

Leaps of Faith Will Bring You Miracles

by Sarah Delagrave Bourget

Don't die with your music still in you! - Wayne Dyer

I chose to tell you my story to inspire you. To inspire you that life can be wonderful, surprising, and fluid when you trust it!

There's nothing exceptional about me. Like many people, I was very unhappy with my job, but I stayed there for the security it brought me, while spending my time whining and dreaming of a life where I would be free to do whatever I wanted, whenever I wanted! Basically, I wanted to feel the way people do when they travel! You know, when everything is possible? When we are free to choose what we are going to do at any moment! When we take the time to be amazed by every detail! And above all, when we let ourselves be guided by the opportunities that come our way without really knowing where they will lead us!

One day, I decided to live my life this way, even when I wasn't traveling. I remember that day very well!

I was 29 years old, sitting at a table with about 15 people. I had been getting to know them for the past 5 days at a seaside yoga retreat in a beautiful protected national park in Merida, Mexico. We were sharing an excellent meal of fish, freshly caught by the cook!

Leaps of Faith Will Bring You Miracles

Since the beginning of the retreat, I had been complaining about my job and all the heavy casework I had to deal with the day before I left for my vacation. Then I was saying how I was confident that it would change one day, and I talked about all my biggest dreams, from which I often felt so far away.

All of my hopes, at that time, were in the network marketing company that I had been working for over the past 2 years.

My plan was to become a millionaire selling creams with my awesome team, and then, have all the time and money I needed to do what I was really passionate about: traveling as much as I wanted and helping people by making a real impact in their lives!

The problem was that my job as a psychoeducator was taking up so much of my energy that I didn't have any left to work on my business at night.

Now, back to that day in Mexico which changed my life forever!

So, I was whining and elaborating on all of this during that amazing gathering, when one of my new friends said to me: "but Sarah, why are you waiting to be a millionaire to quit that job that's making you miserable? Why don't you follow your dreams? What's stopping you from doing it now?"

It should be noted that at that time I was making an average of $500 a month with my business. So, I answered in a cocky way as though he had just asked me the most stupid question ever: "well, I have to pay my bills!" But in fact, it turned out to be the most relevant question of my life! Ha ha!

He answered me with a beautiful, serene smile: "If you take the risk to follow the path of your soul, your intuition, what brings you joy, life will always bring you exactly what you need, whenever you need it. It will support you on that journey."

Leaps of Faith Will Bring You Miracles

Wow, that got me thinking! I meditated on this for the rest of my trip. I knew deep down that it was true, but my god it was scary to apply it to my reality! It was like jumping into the void and hoping that something would catch me! But despite the fear, I was getting more and more excited about taking this leap of faith!

Within 15 minutes after getting back to work, I was in my supervisor's office to tell her that I was quitting.

It was the best decision of my life! Yes, I went into debt, but I also experienced lots of little miracles that made money fall from unexpected sources and that brought me great opportunities. I never felt more alive and haven't lacked anything since!

My network marketing company was the springboard that gave me the courage to jump at that decision and I will be forever grateful for this beautiful experience.

After spending a wonderful spring and summer of pure freedom, meeting many lovely people, and learning more about entrepreneurship, I realized that it wasn't for me either. There was something else calling me: I wanted to work with children!

Two days later, I had referred all of my clients to someone I trusted and was hired at a daycare center to stimulate special needs children through play. For a year, I brought my inner child to life every day by playing and giving lots of love to those kids. Obviously, I got back a hundredfold of what I put into that job, and it filled me with joy. One morning in July, one of my educator friends, whom I was working with and who knew how much I loved to travel, asked me the second most important question of my life: "Sarah, have you ever thought about being a flight attendant?" I answered no and said that it never appealed to me because I felt that flight attendants were always tired, never home, and that it probably didn't pay very well.

Leaps of Faith Will Bring You Miracles

When I asked her why she had asked me this question, she said that a friend of hers had told her that an airline was hiring. She explained to me that she had dreamt of being a flight attendant and had always wished to travel the world since she was a little girl. But it wasn't realistic for her since she had two kids, and when you start with an airline, you usually have to move to Toronto or Vancouver, which would have been problematic.

Vancouver? A year ago, I visited a friend there and I fell in love with the sea, the mountains, and the Zen atmosphere. I had thrown the idea out into the universe, without really believing it, that I would live there one day.

This really sparked my curiosity. That same day I contacted my only flight attendant friend to ask her about her job; all of the pros and cons. Here's the summary: you're either on call, still get paid and can do whatever you want at home, or you work half the month and have the other half to do as you please! Like traveling or working on a personal business! All the destinations the company flies to cost us between 75$ and 150$ round trip! When we work, we have a minimum of 24 hours of layover in overseas destinations, a nice private hotel room, and we have plenty of money for expenses that we can either use to spoil ourselves during the layover, or use to save money (and pay off our debts). The flights are sometimes tiring, but we have breaks to sleep on the long flights (those more than 8 hours) and it's so worth it when we get there. On each flight, we meet new crew members, and often we go out together to eat local food or do a special excursion!

OMG!!! Why didn't she tell me about this before! This was my dream job! So, I did everything I could to convince my educator friend to apply along with me, but she chose not to. I had another friend who I was able to convince, but she didn't go through with it either.

During the airline training, I met many young mothers who had to sacrifice time with their families to realize their dream of being a flight attendant, but they knew that the best gift they could offer their children was a happy mother who knew the importance of following their dreams.

Leaps of Faith Will Bring You Miracles

It doesn't matter that my friends had made the decision not to apply because life doesn't let us down, it always has something else to offer us. We just have to be brave and daring enough to jump into the uncertainty and follow our joy and inspiration. We will then be rewarded by a reality we never dared imagine. It is never too late!

So obviously, you can guess, I applied the next day! Ha ha! You are starting to get to know me, aren't you?

At the end of September, on a Friday afternoon, my boss at the daycare informed me that it was my last day of work. I had been filling in at the nursery for the past two months since the daycare no longer had the budget for the special needs program.

She had just realized that legally, I could not be an educator because I was two courses short of the equivalence between my master's degree in psychoeducation and the training required to be a daycare educator.

At that point, I had only done a short phone interview with the airline and still had to complete the psychological and reflex tests, the in-person group interview, the individual interview, and the medical test.

I had heard a rumor from my flight attendant friend that if I were hired, the paid training program would probably start in January. Assuming this was true, what was I going to do for the next 3 months?

I must admit that I panicked for a few days! I was $20,000 in debt, had an apartment in Montreal and a car to pay off, and I couldn't see myself looking for another job knowing that I would be quitting three months later. Even if I wanted to, I'm really not a good enough liar to be able to do that. I'm so passion driven that I couldn't have convinced an employer to hire me while having another job in mind.

Leaps of Faith Will Bring You Miracles

So, my mind was spinning for two days trying to figure out what to do. I was about to go crazy! So, I decided to give my mind two days off during which I completely let go of trying to seek a solution and just took care of myself. I took a bath, played ukulele in my hammock, watched a good movie, went out with friends, etc. On the second day, I had a great idea. I had managed to keep my mind silent and was then able to hear the incredibly wise voice of my intuition!

Here is the plan that my intuition shared with me: since I wanted to start the training in January and move to Vancouver; I was going to take advantage of the whole month of October to sell my furniture, rent out my super nice apartment, sort through my stuff to get rid of as much as possible, and move the essentials to my mother's house. Then from November to mid-December I would find a place in the world where I could do work-exchange (meaning I would work for about 20 hours a week in exchange for accommodation and food), then come back just in time to spend the holidays with my family before moving to Vancouver and starting my training two weeks later.

So that's what I joyfully did! Well, I thought I was a little crazy, and so did everyone around me, but I knew I could trust my intuition. Remember, I had not even done my in-person interview at this point, the idea that the training would start in January was only hearsay, and I had no idea if the company would decide to base me out of Vancouver... but I decided to jump into the void of uncertainty once again! Life had my back and helped me to fly!

I was called to do my in-person interview and the medical test in October, which was the perfect timing. I found a fruit farm in Hawaii where I worked 4 hours a day, 5 days a week, cooking one meal a day for the staff and cleaning the rooms that were rented out on Airbnb. They fed me plenty of delicious fresh fruits and vegetables and whatever else I asked for. I had all the remaining time to enjoy the pool, the sauna, the spa, the sacred cave on the property as well as the many nearby beaches, waterfalls and volcanoes on the island.

Leaps of Faith Will Bring You Miracles

Then on December 2nd, with about 10 days left in Hawaii, the airline called to let me know that I had been hired in Vancouver and that the training would start on January 3rd. That was so awesome!

Everything went perfectly and as planned. Life and my intuition guided me to this reality that seemed disastrous at the beginning. By surrendering to life and by fully trusting my intuition, things turned into a reality more magnificent than my wildest dreams!

After my training, I lived in beautiful Vancouver for two years, right between the beach and the mountains. Then I decided to return to my roots and move closer to my family back in Montreal. During my time as a flight attendant, I gave my love and shared the joy of freedom with excited travelers, met many beautiful people, and experienced great moments during layovers (Great Walls of China, hiking in Australia, walking through the Champs-Elysées while drinking a glass of wine with a few colleagues, shopping in London, eating the best gelato in Rome, meditating by a small creek in Japan, shopping in the souks in Casablanca while eating the best clementine, drinking a hot alcoholic beverage in a Christmas market in Zurich, etc.).

But what was even more delightful was that this dream job, and all of the spare time that came with it, allowed me to build my online coaching business on the side. So, for two years, I was coaching women around the world and helping them with their relationships. Then in December 2019, just before I had to stop flying because of the Covid pandemic, I had an extraordinarily strong intuition telling me to launch an online program. Which I obviously did! This program was conceived to help women manifest the relationship of their dreams by first healing their past wounds, showing them how to love themselves fully, how to stand up for themselves, and reconnect to their sacred feminine energy! And of course, it would show them how to follow their intuition and fully trust the beauty of life! It has been a really successful experience, and 2020 was my best financial year so far!

Leaps of Faith Will Bring You Miracles

I'm looking forward to flying again, to continue mixing my two passions: traveling and helping people by making a real difference in their lives! And in the meantime, I'm taking advantage of this little break to create a beautiful baby boy.

As I told you at the beginning, there's nothing exceptional about me, I have nothing more in me than you have in you. And don't get me wrong, my life isn't always perfect, but most of the time I feel like I am exactly where I should be. I have a lot of gratitude for the life I have created for myself.

An inspired life that makes you feel vibrant, where you feel free, happy and fulfilled, where you don't need a vacation because you feel free to choose what you are going to do at any given moment, and you feel that anything is possible. This is accessible to EVERYONE!

All we have to do is follow our joy and inspiration wherever it leads us. When we are confused or having a hard time, we just need to let go and trust that everything happens for a reason and that there is something wonderful behind this challenge! Life always has our back!

The universe and life have wisdom that our minds cannot grasp. Our connection to that wisdom is our intuition, our inner voice, our joy.

I really wish you'll follow this path inside of you, so it will lead you to a reality beyond your wildest dreams, beyond the limits of the sky!

BIOGRAPHY

Sarah Delagrave Bourget

Sarah Delagrave Bourget is a 35-year-old free soul spirit from Montreal! She's the perfect mix between a therapist and a witch, and her biggest passions in life are travelling and helping people. Her longest trip was spending 10 months in Asia by herself. It was on this trip that she truly discovered the joy of travelling : discovering amazing scenery, trying new food and sharing experiences with people from around the world. For as long as she can remember, she has always been really curious about how relationships work. Consequently, that's why she studied psychoeducation at Sherbrooke University (bachelor and master) and completed 3 years of training to become a couple and relationship therapist. She worked as a psychoeducator for 5 years, helping families in crisis in Montreal's CLSC (social services). Then, in 2017, she became a flight attendant while also building her relationship coaching business on the side. Sarah helps women learn how to follow their intuition to then manifest the life and the relationship of their dreams. She does so by helping them to heal wounds from their past relationships, get rid of their limiting beliefs, fully love themselves, reconnect to their divine femininity and learn to communicate their truth easily. Sarah can't wait to go back to flying and to continue to fulfill her two biggest passions once more: travelling and helping people.

 @ deesses.de.lamour

 @Sarah Delagrave Bourget

Facebook group "Manifeste ton âme soeur: Les déesses de l'amour"

PARiS

CHAPTER 16

Kindness

by Pinar Tahirbegi Esfandiari

"Be a rainbow in someone else's cloud" Unknown

Kindness

Sitting on a bench one beautiful summer afternoon with my dear friend, waiting for our kids to go on their rides in Toronto Islands and chatting, she asked me a question that changed my life forever. "Pinar, why don't you come and join us at this airline and become a flight attendant? They are always looking for people who can speak Japanese." Up to that point in my life, I had never even considered becoming a flight attendant. For me, my family and their wants and needs were everything. I already had a job as a realtor, and I was being paid fairly well. After I had my kids, I always found a way to be there when they needed me. Whether it was for their drop offs or pick-ups from school, homework routines, after school programs, you name it, I was there. I didn't want anything to interfere with that. They had never experienced day cares or babysitters, that's just how I was, I didn't want to miss anything as a mother. However, they were also coming to an age where they could be more independent and responsible. For me this was a perfect opportunity to put all my experiences and knowledge of languages to good use and have some fun at the same time. The idea of getting paid to travel definitely appealed to me. All these thoughts in my head going back and forth, I eventually made the impulsive decision to give it a try, and before I knew it, I found myself sitting in a classroom filled with people half my age, listening to emergency exit drills in a multitude of different types of aircrafts.

I must say, I have been through many challenges in my lifetime, but the training to become a flight attendant made it to the top of my list in a noticeably short time. It was a slow torture that drains you, and brings on a level of mental fatigue that is hard to imagine. My training sessions began in the afternoon at 3:00 pm, and we didn't leave that building until past midnight for the duration of two whole months. So, before I even started flying, I only saw my kids and my husband in the mornings before they went to school or work.

Kindness

All the stress of being able to pass the daily exams with no room for failure, took a toll on everyone. I also never imagined that I would get so close to the people I trained with; we practically became a family in a short time. Tears, laughter, exhaustion, and of course the aircrafts became a part of our daily lives, and it didn't take long for me to realize that becoming a flight attendant was much more than just serving people drinks on planes. During the training, I met a ton of new and wonderful people and I felt a sense of belonging. In fact, what I learned throughout this process ended up became the most memorable part my experience.

After our training was over, I was stationed in Montreal because of my language skills which of course made my journey even more adventurous. I didn`t have a place to stay in Montreal, nor did I have access to an easy way to get there for my first three months, and I had no desire to move my whole family from Toronto. However, my many experiences in the great city of Montreal were something, to say the least. I flew with the best crews I could ask for, the most fun-loving people, and I enjoyed the sense of stepping out of my comfort zone, discovering all these new friendships, and going through all these wonderful experiences. One of my colleagues helped me with my accommodations, if I ever needed to stay in Montreal, and I am forever grateful for her help. Many of my flights were to Japan, which made my commute somewhat easier, as I knew my schedule ahead of time.

My very first flight was a true eye-opener for me. Everything we learned throughout our training was finally coming into play, and the pieces were all coming together as I watched my colleagues doing everything so effortlessly and wondering if I would ever achieve that level of effortlessness one day. There were so many new experiences that needed to be learned, which was a bit overwhelming at first. We sat in a class for two months and went through every single scenario that could possibly go wrong in an airplane, but not much emphasis was given on the day-to-day working experiences I'd come to endure. I remember one of the passengers had made me an origami crane, she must have felt my nervousness or sensed that I was a bit tense, and that little bird, which I still have to this day, made my very first experience so beautiful.

Kindness

Going back to Japan again after all these years, even only for 24 hours, was full of different emotions. It did however, made me realize once again that I had made the right decision. I genuinely enjoyed being there, shopping like a local, eating all sorts of delicious food that Japanese cuisine had to offer, and visiting temples and their beautiful gardens. Believe me, you can get used to this routine extremely fast if you enjoy travelling as much as I do. Over the years I came to believe that somewhere in my bloodline, I had some Japanese in me and as I kept flying back and forth, it only made me believe it even more.

Working two jobs while juggling my household had its own challenges. I remember trying to write up offers for my real estate job and making phone calls just before getting on the aircraft because I was going to be disconnected from the rest of the world for the next 12 hours. The time differences, depending on where I was flying into, didn't help either. As I mostly flew to Japan, my days turned upside down, literally. I did however always manage to figure out a way to fit everything together.

Like everything else in life that you get used to, my travelling became a part of my family's routine, and everyone got used to me disappearing for few days. I purchased a stuffy for my daughter who was 7 years old at the time, and we named it 'mama' so she can have a cuddle with it when I was gone, and she would always make sure to pack a little stuffy bear for me in my suitcase for me to cuddle with when I was away.

From the many commutes I have done, there was one of them that stuck with me the most. I needed to go to my daughter's parent-teacher interview in the morning and make my way to Montreal the same day for my flight to Japan. I had made it to the airport just in time to successfully get on the 10:00 a.m. flight, which was very comforting for me knowing I would be able to make my flight to Japan just in time. It was a very cold and icy day in Toronto, and after the aircraft doors closed, we were the 30th in queue for the de-icing process. We sat inside the airplane for around an hour and a half, which felt like an eternity. Eventually when we finally took off, it was clear to me that I would be late for my flight to Japan, but there was no possible way to get in touch with anybody to let them know.

Kindness

As soon as we landed in Montreal and we were approaching the gate, my phone started to ring. It was a call from crew scheduling, wondering just where in the hell I was. I don't remember a time in my life where I was under that much stress, and also didn't realize I could run that fast. Needless to say, when I finally made it to the aircraft, I was welcomed by a wonderful crew who made my stress disappear into the air as we took off. After that day and throughout my commutes, I really started to think more and more about getting my transfer to Toronto, and how much that would only enhance my already wonderful experience with the airline.

When I finally received the email that my transfer to Toronto was approved, I couldn't even begin to describe the instant relief I felt. I could finally land, jump in my car, and drive home right away instead of waiting to catch another flight to get there. I could also be home a bit longer before my flights. Oh, what a relief! My experience in Toronto was completely a game changer for me. With the stress of commuting taken out of the equation, the way I looked at this job was completely transformed. It was clear to me that I would be a flight attendant for the rest of my life because this job only kept getting better and better for me.

My happiness didn't last very long though. Soon after my transfer, we were all hit with the unexpected. Covid-19. Everything we had worked for as flight attendants was suddenly taken away, with little to no notice or time to prepare. Who could have imagined that a virus could affect so many lives? Many of us had to face the inevitable, layoffs. Even though I was just a newbie, I felt the emptiness in my life almost immediately, and I couldn't help but think of my dear colleagues who had been working for 20-30 years losing what they valued the most, it truly broke my heart. Reflecting upon this pandemic, I think we all realized how little control we have over the things happening in our lives, to an extent anyways. This realization though has only allowed us the opportunity to learn, to be more grateful for the present moment, and to not spend too much time stressing over the things that don't deserve to be stressed about, or that we just can't control. As the dear Dalai Lama said, "there are only two days in the year that nothing can be done. One is called yesterday, and the other is called tomorrow, so TODAY is the right day to love, believe, do, and mostly live." How wonderfully said!

Kindness

Through this past year, I have witnessed my airline family coming together in these very unprecedented times and helping one another as much as possible. This proved to me that as long as there are people with a common purpose to achieve a clear goal, we are able to harness the absolute best in ourselves and able to address the multiple challenges we face on a daily basis. So, let's keep up what we've been doing, stay united, and check on one another.

The reason behind my participation in this book is to show that there's always more to people than what simply meets the eye, and that goes for everything. There is a deeper meaning to everything you lay your eyes on, whether it is the environment around you, the people around you, or our world as a whole. If everyone can take the time to deeply look at one another and try to see the most in each other, I genuinely believe, the world would be a different and better place. There's always a reason, or an explanation as to why we behave a certain way. There's more to that flight attendant who is serving you your drink, or that realtor helping you sell your house. Anywhere I find myself in life, I always believe in the power of being me and being comfortable with who I am and with everything I do, and I want people to feel the same way. It's ok to make mistakes, to laugh at yourself, to cry, be sad, or not to show any emotion at all, it's all a part of this big learning process we call life. But whatever forces are holding us down, we need to learn to let go of them and whenever our lives turn upside down, we just need to adjust our view and keep going.

If I can be an inspiration for someone, even just for one person, and show that stepping out of your comfort zone opens a whole new world, it was worth to share my story. There's no limit to what we can achieve within ourselves, and with working together. It's always a great joy and a true gift to rediscover the little details that we push aside along the way and to go back and rediscover what life presented you with. I am a true believer that everything happens for a reason, and all our experiences, winding paths, frustrations, and confusions give us a true chance to become someone better and stronger. My experiences throughout this process definitely gave me a chance to deeply appreciate things in my life. Whatever our next journey may be, wherever we may find ourselves next, our love for the skies will never leave us.

BiOGRAPHY

Pinar Tahirbegi Esfandiari

Pinar Tahirbegi was born in Ankara Turkey. She has a bachelor's degree on Linguistics and language Sciences, and she majored in Japanese from The University of Ankara in Turkey. During her university years, she worked on multiple projects in Turkey as a translator and taught Japanese at a language school. Her long journey then brought her to Canada, where she started her family. She's a mom of 2 beautiful children, Deryn and Ayla, and she has devoted herself as a mother and guided them through their childhood journeys, while working part time at a local restaurant. This gave her the motivation to open up her own restaurant which she ran together with her husband for a few years. She then started a pottery studio with her friend, which eventually led to an after-school program for kids. This decision was driven by the fact that she wanted to be with her kids while at the same time enhancing other children's creativity and social skills. In 2017, she started her journey as a realtor, and joined Royal LePage, which she is still a part of today. Then in 2019, a bit of persuasion from her friend mixed with her passion in travel and customer service led her to become a flight attendant. Pinar loves to sing and has been a part of a jazz ensemble called "The Ambiance Singers", for the last 11 years. She loves animals, cooking and baking, and is still eagerly waiting for her next possible adventure coming her way.

Pinar Tahirbegi
Sales Representative Direct. 416-801-5308

Office. 905-568-2121

E-mail pinar@royallepage.ca

f pinar.tahirbegiesfandiari

www.pinarrealtydreams.com
pinartahirbegi.royallepage.ca
Empowering Your Realty Dreams

30 Eglinton Ave.West, Suite 201 Mississauga, Ont L5R 3E7

KAMAKURA, JAPAN

CHAPTER 17

Breaking Isolation Through Writing

by Isabelle Rioux

"Always put yourself in their shoes. Give up your opinions and judgments for a while in order to understand them."
– Dalai Lama

It was never my dream to become a flight attendant but rather, it was my mother's. I agreed to accompany her to the interview process hoping that my presence would help her overcome her own fears towards getting the job she so desired. I found myself sitting beside my mother during the final group interview. I was happy to see my mother put herself out there and highlight her value during the group exercise. It suited her. The nervousness that she displayed in the interview process was an emotion that she had never let me see before. I felt privileged to experience this moment with her and to see her in this new light.

One night when I was studying for an exam at my parents' house, I heard the dining room rotary phone ring. My mother answered, but the call was for me. She looked at me with a beautiful and proud smile as she handed me the phone. While I was happy for myself, I was disappointed for her. I felt like I was somehow taking her spot, taking her dream! I was still a student at the time, and I was planning to become a teacher. In the end, I accepted the job offer. I was convinced by my inner voice repeating my mother's favored sentence: "Let them say no to you!"

I had no idea what I was getting myself into. The intense training, many hours of studying and many exams. I was scared! Everything was in English! I broke down in tears on day one! My mother put her hands on my shoulders, and that's when I understood that I wouldn't be going through this alone. I had a strong and formidable ally. Sentence by sentence, she made sure I understood. She would translate every word, correct my pronunciation and my writing errors. I wanted to succeed, I needed to succeed, for her. This is how I obtained my wings. I was so proud to be part of the new flight attendant cohort and to wear the world-renowned uniform. I was ready for Take Off!

Breaking Isolation Through Writing

I quickly fell in love with my new job. The luxurious hotels, dinners with colleagues on layovers, free time to visit new places, many days off, breathtaking views from aircraft windows. It was perfect. Moreover, I had a career that allowed me to spread my wings further, realize my dreams, and improve myself all around. The sky was no longer the limit, but rather, it was my office.

So, it was... then one day, I started brooding. I wanted to build a family. I was ready to start on a new path – the path of maternity. I had a growing desire to give life. I was convinced that all would be well. There was no other alternative! While pregnant, I ate organic, did yoga, stopped drinking coffee, stopped eating sushi, I meditated in the evenings, listened to Mozart, and watched my big belly grow! I was zealous and feeling Zen. Life was beautiful!

Without knowing it, I had created expectations and was building preconceived images of what my family life would be like. My reality was nowhere near what I had predicted. Rejected Take Off! Please Standby!

My son was only 2 years old when he received a diagnosis of autism. The doctor's announcement turned my life around, despite my deepest wishes, and made me land on another planet. This was a new world. One that I didn't know much about, and that terrified me. I had to tell my friends and family the news knowing that, more than ever, I would need their support. I made the calls. My voice was hardly audible. It seemed that the words didn't want to come out of my mouth, afraid of making it all too real. My heart was crying. My body was trembling. I was mourning the life I have envisioned for myself, and all the while, pregnant again! What if the next baby also had autism? Could I cope? MAYDAY MAYDAY MAYDAY!

My son has autism. Yes. My son, my little boy, has autism. It was sinking in, but it didn't end there. He also received a second diagnosis – a muscular weakness. His challenges would be gargantuan, and so would mine. I was ready for anything. I couldn't turn a blind eye. I had to become knowledgeable and do away with my own prejudice and fears that were built in my mind. I had to roll up my sleeves and take the necessary steps to acquire the necessary knowledge to pull through for a successful future.

Breaking Isolation Through Writing

I wanted to be there for him, I wanted to help him with his needs, and most importantly, I wanted to do what I needed to do to understand him.

I started reading about the subject – I read a lot. I wanted to know everything. To learn everything. I was attracted to everything everywhere and for every purpose. I acquired information on all possible interventions provided by a large spectrum of professionals. The options were dizzying, and it was quite easy to get lost in the sea of pamphlets, documentation and offers. During this period of searching and researching, I had wonderful encounters with people who helped me on my quest. I slowly drew the path to the road I would travel.

I was successful in building a good team of professionals who were a good fit for my son. The matches were perfect. Depending on my son's needs and the objectives he needed to attain, I would determine which team professional would have the best tools to help him reach his goals. His schedule was overwhelmed with appointments. I was often on the road, travelling from city to city. I attended meetings and conferences alike to take all these new notions home to practice and be the best possible parent I could be. I became a multidisciplinary mother – part physiotherapist, speech therapist, occupational therapist, educator, psychologist, nutritionist, and massage therapist. I was working hard for my son and with my son. It was working! One step at a time, he was progressing!

At home, I was never resting. My tiredness was increasing with each passing day. My days off had become other workdays, another full-time job. I was running out of days for my own needs and for my own social circle of friends and family. When I made time for friends, I tried to maximize the experience. I wanted to enjoy their presence and fill up on positive energy. I needed to live those quality moments with them to attain a certain normalcy. I tried not to speak of my son's autism or of my daily difficulties. I simply wanted to enjoy good times with those closest to me. Nonetheless, my son's odd behavior and the non-standard interventions applied in our daily lives easily brought judgement, questions, comments and advice from others. I was losing the desire and pleasure I once had from sharing with my social circle. What used to recharge my inner batteries and filled me with joy, was now draining me.

Breaking Isolation Through Writing

This is how my circle started breaking away little by little. It had become brittle, and I was losing the support I once had and so needed.

Despite it all, I continued to work as a flight attendant. I loved my career, but it now had a different meaning to me. Working was now a necessity. The professional support for my son didn't come cheap. The bills had to be paid. I couldn't take a break or stop working as this would directly impact my son's health and development. I needed to both work and attend my son's sessions. As a maestro, I carefully directed a team of specialists towards one goal – the betterment of my son's life. I was the link between them all and the intermediary communicator. Having acquired a large expertise filled with knowledge about my son and his needs, I had become an essential piece in this orchestra. It was a never ending well – a destination to nowhere flight. I became caught in a complex gear system that I had created, and in which I had placed myself in the center – the maestro. I was stuck. My financial stress was growing, and my physical strain was taking its toll and growing by the minute. I had placed the oxygen mask on my son, but I had forgotten to put mine on first. I was running out of air!

Moreover, I was always troubled by the culpability. Guilty for going to work and being away 2, 3, and sometimes 4 days at a time. I was leaving my closest loved ones with the heavy load of the daily difficulties it entailed. Guilty for having the opportunity to recharge on layovers while my son needed me. Guilty of not being able to run back home for emergencies. I was always too far, even if only at an hour flight distance away.

Slowly and involuntarily, I was isolating myself. I felt I had no choice. I was exhausted. I spent my layovers sleeping. I wasn't going out to dinner with the crew or sharing wonderful unifying moments with my colleagues anymore. Without realizing it at first, I had closed the door on socializing. This of course, lead to me feeling excluded. I felt apart from the others. I didn't feel part of the group I once loved so much. I blamed the autism which seemed to have stained all aspects of my life. Alone and away from home, I was suffering of boredom, insomnia, and deafening silence.

Breaking Isolation Through Writing

I envied the normal life of other mothers. I envied their daily challenges which seemed so light in comparison to my own. I didn't participate in conversations. I listened without speaking. I pulled back. I couldn't talk about the same things because I was so far from living the same reality. My life was too different. Nothing in my life was seemingly normal. My morale was at an all-time low. On the rare occasion, I would confide in a friend or colleague about how I was feeling, and this brought me a sense of relief for only a short ethereal moment. It never lasted. Talking about my difficulties made my anxiety levels rise. It seemed to have a mirror effect on me. The more I revealed myself, the more I was scaring myself as I knew how difficult my situation was. My life was far from easy. I didn't want to face my strains, fatigue and distress. I had to be strong. I also avoided talking to those ultra-empathetic, too sympathetic, people as there's a fine line between too much empathy and pity. I just wanted to be heard with no judgement, no advice.

Solitude took over. Even as I worked on an airplane, surrounded by 200 some passengers and crew members, I was alone. Their proximity didn't change my state of aloneness. By not having pursued and kept alive my social circle of support lead to a deficiency in my social relations. I was going through very difficult times and I had no apparent support. My little moments of joy with friends and family were gone.

Life went on. I kept taking care of my son, the passengers, my colleagues... and always with a smile. A smile that hid so much. I forgot to take care of myself. I forgot to think of myself. I forgot to take some time for selfcare. I forgot to nourish my relationships with those closest to me.

To break the isolation cycle, I chose to join a group of mothers of autistic children. After a few meetings and discussions, I realized that this was not an avenue that would work for me. I wasn't feeling better. I wasn't breaking the cycle. I felt that this avenue was contributing to my self-marginalization. I was strangely isolating myself more, just differently. I was moving towards a further extreme of non-standard living instead of getting closer to normalcy. I felt vulnerable instead of feeling better with a group of peers! Certainly, I felt they understood me without having to explain everything in great detail.

Breaking Isolation Through Writing

Nevertheless, I felt that autism was too present at these meetings and sometimes the discussions were too painful. I wanted to feel better – uplifted. This just wasn't working for me. I was starting to understand that I had to take care of myself, not just of others.

One day, on layover, I started writing. Alone in my room, I let my emotions run free. I gave them time and space to be. On each layover that followed, I had a secret rendez-vous with myself and my thoughts. I was taking a liking to this new flow of writing. My healing had begun. I loved being in my pajamas, sitting comfortably, a cup of mint green tea on the nightstand, and my favorite Swarovski gem pen in hand. I was filling the pages one by one. Sure, sure, I'll admit it! It wasn't always just green tea. A little glass of red wine from time to time was there too!

I felt like I was retaking control of my life again. I was making a point to meet with myself on a regular basis. I was becoming Isabelle again – the woman I once was. I chose me. I was taking the time to take care of myself – for myself. I was speaking up (on paper). I was slowly reopening the door to dialogue which I had closed behind me for way too long.

This is how I created a private Facebook page called: "Ma bulle". The birth of the project started by me inviting my close friends and family to join. On this page, I shared publications based on my daily reality and daily experiences with my autistic son. I blogged. By writing these texts, I wanted to bridge the gap between my life in isolation and my social circle. I wanted them to know what I was living through and let them in. I wanted to reduce the distance and pull them back in and myself all together. I wanted my circle to understand my son and feel closer to him. I wanted to include my son in my circle in a way that he would be respected.

I was finding peace in this way of freely expressing myself and without judgement. I wasn't confronted with others' judgement either. One blog blurb and publication at a time, I was educating my circle on differences. I had carte blanche. I was free!

Breaking Isolation Through Writing

I was writing more and more when, one day, I found my number of followers to be growing. Friends of friends, work colleagues, and mothers of other autistic children who had heard of my growing group were being added to my private page. The page quickly reached 515 members. The more the group grew, the more I wrote. The positive comments and kind feedback of encouragement brought me great joy and a sense of renewed value. I felt surrounded by positive energy. I was proud of this group to which I really felt I belonged. It was beneficial and immensely fulfilling. I was motivated! I had finally found the right way, for me, to break my isolation!

That short time that I allowed myself to write a blurb brought me so much well-being each time. The more I wrote, the more I heeled. By sharing my innermost thoughts, I was giving new life to both my body and mind. Even if I wrote in the middle of the night! When I felt that I couldn't sleep, I would sit up in bed and start writing. My thoughts, which yearned to be shared, flowed, and were freed while my head simply searched for a cozy resting place on a pillow. The result was a better sleep and a progressively better recuperative sleep. My heart was slowly being freed of the weight of such intense locked-in emotions which were transferred to words that I shared. I was finding peace. This page, this tool, was my remedy. Whenever I felt the first signs of isolation, I took the medicine – I wrote.

More and more, I was reconnecting with my closest friends and family. I felt understood and well surrounded. Touching others by sharing my most intimate thoughts filled me with happiness. It was a real pleasure to write and share my daily life with my group. I was getting back such love and positive energy that I just wanted to share more. I was finding a deeply needed balance through this group of friends.

The more I wrote, the more my vision on autism changed. I started talking about the positive, beautiful differences that my son brought into my life instead of the autism. To look with your heart. To see difference as a strength – a lever. Through writing and taking the time to think and ponder, I understood that difference was refreshing and precious. Difference was normal and saine. By opening my heart and thoughts to others, I changed my own views. I reflected more and I reflected differently. I saw others and myself differently as well. I saw difference in all its splendor and color all around me.

Breaking Isolation Through Writing

I saw my own reality differently by putting pen to paper. I saw all the wonderful events I was living. I saw the positive. I was seeing the strengths, the challenges, the improvements, the baby-steps that my son was taking. I felt supported. I was developing a positive perception of my own parenting skills. I started believing in me again. I was rebuilding my self-confidence. My state of mind was brightening. My challenges were still there, that hadn't changed, but the circumstances had. The happy times with my son were growing at the same rate as my energy was being renewed.

Things also changed at work. My sensitivity improved to make room for empathy from no matter where or whom it came from. I was filled with happiness and I was spreading that happiness with no expectation of anything in return. I was getting close to my colleagues again and I was looked forward to hearing their stories and what mattered to them. I let myself be guided by them and by my heart. This is what gave meaning to my work. The more open I was, the more opportunities opened up and the more receptive I was. I was guided by what was important and essential such as a hug in support, a sincere listening ear, arms to rock a baby, a tissue to dry a hidden tear, a chocolate bar to lift the spirits, a scarf to stay warm, or a passing hello as eyes meet.

By speaking up, I found my place and my identity. I allowed myself to be me. I allowed my Québécois accent, which used to embarrass me, be heard when I spoke English. I was proud to be me. Just like that (well after much self-work), I had found balance. I was at peace with myself. Writing broke my isolation and freed me. By writing, I heard myself. I listened more deeply. I reflected on my own inner dialogue simply by letting it out – expressing myself and allowing myself simply to be. To find balance, one has to be able to listen to oneself. I realized that writing wasn't just a remedy. Writing was a look in on my past to give my future meaning and purpose. Writing made me whole.

So, what if I gave you a pen and a blank page...

BiOGRAPHY

Isabelle Rioux

March 23rd 2011 will remain a date forever engraved in Isabelle Rioux's heart. That day, her then 2-year-old son Samuel was diagnosed with an Autism Spectrum Disorder. A difficult time; shock, denial, distress, and anger. A flight attendant for 24 years and mother of two, she knew then that her life would never be the same. She knew that only her vision of how she saw differences in others could be what would bring beauty to her new reality. She decided to welcome this new challenge with an open heart, and she closed the door on all judgment for her son and for herself. Samuel, without knowing it, changed her way of seeing diversity in others. Samuel, with his own range of this spectrum, was always real and true to himself. His outward uncensored way of being and expressing himself was changing Isabelle's own view of herself. She learned to welcome her flaws alongside her qualities, making her feel whole, beautiful, and true to herself, like her son. Isabelle holds a bachelor's degree in business administration from the University of Québec in Montréal. She is also interested in teaching and has discovered a real passion for the profession of substitute teaching in Supporting All Individual Learners (SAIL), such as those diagnosed with Autism Spectrum Disorder. A woman committed to the cause of autism and special needs, Isabelle participates each year in making differences in others shine through the month of autism at conferences and with concrete actions in schools. Her growing need to rebuild her life and push further, led her to write continuously. She created a private group called Ma Bulle on Facebook with more than 565 following members where she shares her daily experiences with her son. Her purpose in creating this group was to shine a light on an otherwise unbeknown disorder. Isabelle wants to make a difference in people's lives. She aims to make those living with an autism spectrum disorder shine, to give them wings and to fly high!

 groups/417468075031563/ ma bulle

 isabelle.rioux.712

FREEPORT, BAHAMAS

CHAPTER 18

by Farnaz Mamizadeh

" Where there is a will, there is a way.. " Unknown

I was born in Iran in 1981. My mother was a flight attendant in the air force and my father was a pilot. They had their whole lives ahead of them, until they didn't. A war broke out in 1980 between Iran and Iraq that lasted eight long years and killed more than a million people. My parents were forced to leave Iran, leave their friends and family, and say goodbye to everything they knew. With that, they put behind all their dreams and the hopes they held for their future.

We moved to Canada in 1987, carrying nothing but a suitcase. That year, my brother was born. Like many immigrants, we had to go through a hard life. My parents started from scratch, living in a one-bedroom apartment. All we had was a bicycle, a rocking chair, and a blanket, which my father bought for $20. My father would park cars at a close by hospital and ride his bike to work in the freezing -30°C weather.

I am where I am today because my parents gave up their dreams and hopes to give us a happy and safe future.
Skipping forward to 2005. I had just quit my job at the bank (toxic boss), dumped my fiancée (even more toxic than the job), and I was trying to find my place in the world. You could say I was a naïve child who had never seen the world or experienced anything but bullying and defeat (or so I thought was defeat). I remember coming home after quitting my job and crying. "My life is over," I cried out, quite dramatically I might add, as I was always one for dramatics, especially once the waterworks started.

My father, my voice of reason, told me to pull myself together and just get up, go out there, and find something. As per usual, he reminded me that it wasn't the end of the world. That we were not starving on the side of the street, and that something would come up. My mother, my voice of kindness and gentleness, would trick me with her beautiful words. She convinced me that I would be alright, that I could do this. I was her kid, and I could do anything I put my mind to. Everything happens for a reason, as the saying goes.

I walked into the Hyatt hotel ready to hand in my resume, pick up some pamphlets, and ask tons of questions, as one typically does at a job fair. Boy was I off on that one. A crowd of over one thousand applicants gathered, all dreaming of the skies. I remember meeting a young man studying to become an optometrist, who spoke five languages and was very charming and bright. And I thought to myself, "well, there goes my spot." Women dressed in full flight attendant attire; their hair pulled back looking like they just walked off a runway. Men dressed to the T in white pressed shirts and suits. And there I was, my hair in a flimsy ponytail, wearing a white t-shirt, jeans, and a leather jacket. I didn't really cry out "professionalism". But I was there, so I figured I might as well go forward with the interviews.

The first step was a single interview. Then came an interview where someone asked questions, and another observed. You then had to go through a language test, a made-up scenario about a runaway frog on a train, and finally a medical test. The process was not easy, and by the end of the day, out of the thousand applicants only fifty were chosen.

And yes, yours truly was among them.

That night I came home, and my mother asked, "where were you today dear?"

"I got a job," I replied, as she peaked her head out of the kitchen to see what I was mumbling about. "I'm going to be a flight attendant."

My father overheard my big announcement in the other room and yelled out. "What? Why didn't you take the pilot job?"

I laughed "baba (dad)!" as always, my father managed to turn the situation into a funny one.

So, imagine this: we go to headquarters, tons of new faces and simulators that looked like planes. The excitement was REAL. I could feel butterflies in my stomach at this "super cool" thing that was about to start.

And then it started. Initial flight attendant training was hard. I would be driving to work at 6h30 every morning, rehearsing my commands out loud during my commute. To an onlooker, I looked like someone singing a really badly tuned song. That, or I was losing it on someone.

I got through to week five. The reality of the life I left behind started flooding in. My breakup, everything that came up after it, and all the emotions and meltdowns that followed. So as you can imagine, I was neither emotionally prepared nor psychologically able to take on the stress of my past alongside the pressure of this training. Five weeks and three failed exams into the training, I left. I was devastated.

There I was, back on my bed, crying, with my poor parents consoling me. Here we go again; Naz and her multiple crying tantrums. I have to admit, earlier when I explained that I was naïve, I should have also mentioned that I was an overly sensitive as a child. And because I couldn't express my feelings I would cry. Cry when I was angry, cry when I was upset. My waterworks seemed to have an unlimited capacity.

But I was young. A friend of mine offered me a job as a makeup artist. Not knowing much about it, I faked it until I made it.

On a summer day, during a sidewalk sale, I saw our flight attendant coordinator. "Naz, where have you been? Why haven't you come back to training?" he said.

"I didn't even know that was an option," I replied.

"Well interviews are happening in two weeks, and I want you there" he said.

I gathered all my courage and asked a friend to accompany me. I needed the moral support. And this time, I was set on getting in. Failure was not an option.

I showed up, dressed the part this time, and off I went to the step one interview. And to my surprise and excitement, my initial trainer from 2005 was my first interviewer. WOW, I thought, talk about the universe aligning itself for me. As we chatted, he told me I "had this" and with support sent me off to the next levels of the interview.

This time was different. I was two years wiser, I had worked through my heartbreak, I had matured, and I had a goal. I had two choices, I could run away, or I could face my fear head on, knowing that if I wanted something badly enough and that if I put in the effort, the entire universe would help. I chose the latter.

I had told my instructors if I needed to be first one in or last one out, I would do anything to get my wings. I volunteered for class representative, I stayed and helped others, and decided to put my life on pause for this training. I could not fail, I only envisioned a bright future, even though I had no real idea what the job was going to be like.

The big graduation day came. I bought all my classmates white roses to celebrate this success. My parents were getting dressed and we were running late. I started crying again: "I cannot believe after all this I will be late for my own graduation."

As always, my dad's voice came from the background: "relax!!!"

We arrived just in time. I was in a hysterical state. On one hand, I couldn't believe this day had come, and on the other, I was afraid of what was waiting for me.

My coordinator, as kind as ever, came up to me. "Hi Naz, calm down take a breath," he said.

And so, I did.

"Every year I do a speech. Would you like to do the speech today? But you can't cry," he laughed.

Half in tears, I said "sure I would love to".

"We started this training as strangers, each coming from a different walk of life, we became friends, and we will leave this training as family. For those of you who know me know this is my second chance at this, and I couldn't be more blessed or excited to start the journey."

The rest of the speech is a blur in my mind, but from that point on, my wings were pinned. As I gazed at the back of the room through my tears—yes, I obviously was crying—I could see my parents in the back, crying, reliving this journey in a different part of the world, in a different kind of setting. Their eldest child following in their footsteps was so nostalgic.

Failure was not an option, if you fail at something, pick yourself up, be courageous and try again. We are always growing and evolving, and we always have people to support us on our journeys. Don't be afraid to reach out and grab a hand.

As I mentioned, I was a sensitive child. I was also an introvert. I wasn't socially unintelligent. I was just quieter and liked being in my space. I loved to observe things from afar, always imagining people's stories and where they came from and learning from what I would see. I drowned myself in books, art, and music. This brought on years of bullying. It made me shy and scared, hence the crying.

My first flight was to LaGuardia or Ottawa, either way, a short haul. I chose the position that would keep me away from people's stares. But being a three-crew plane (A319), if I chose the back galley position, I had to read the announcements. And, as luck would have it, I had to do a live demo. I was so nervous, pacing back and forth in the back galley trying to find the page in my announcement manual to read. As I started with a trembling voice, partly through, do I not drop my book? OMG, and now everyone's eyes were on me. Heads turned towards the back of the plane, where I stood, my cheeks flushed like cherry tomatoes. I was so embarrassed. I finally found my book and the page and continued. Everyone realized I was new, and at the end of my announcement, I got myself a round of applause.

Standing in front of the cabin was just as bad, if not worse. All those eyes glaring at me, watching my every movement. I remember thinking "do I have a booger on my nose? Is my makeup ok? Is my hair ok? God my feet hurt with these stupid shoes! Should I smile a full smile (teeth showing) or a slight smile, ear to ear? Maybe regular smile in case I have food stuck to my teeth." I was so nervous. I would avoid eye contact and pray no one asked me a question that I didn't know how to answer.

It got better as I did more flights and I got more practice. I slowly came out of my shell, feeling more confident in front of people, engaging in conversations; "what a nice scarf." "What nice shoes." I realized I was finally able to talk to people, especially strangers, and feel at ease.

I started smiling. With my teeth showing. I still continued to observe, as this was my character, my real nature. And I realized that I was becoming more and more emotionally intelligent, knowing how people felt, reaching out to help before I was asked for it, handing someone Kleenex discreetly when they were crying, to show I was there and understood.

I held people's children when they needed to use the bathroom. I became more aware of my words and the value they held. I was firmer and stood my ground, but I was fair. I took time to listen, I was good at that too, and related to people's humanity.

Sometimes I would have Persian passengers. And, with them not knowing I was Persian, I would surprise them with a "chizi meil darin" which translates to "May I get you anything to eat/drink." And they would jump. I would help them with all their questions, and I took time to go to them to ask them their choice of meal and drink as they could not communicate with my crew.

And often I would stay behind and help them at immigration as a translator, as there are not many Farsi-speaking agents in Montreal. I would wait for them outside and accompany them until they reached their loved ones. My mother in the same role 25 years ago, was not welcomed in that matter. Times have changed...

I was once called to a flight to go to Spain, Madrid. Oh the excitement was intense!

I called mom: "Mom I'm going to Madrid."

"Oh lucky you that's so wonderful where are you staying?" she asked.

"At the Princessa" I said

"That is where I used to stay 25 years ago," she said. Go downstairs. There is a mall. There is a soap store. They have a black soap. Bring me one back please."

Black soap? My mom always had the weirdest shopping list. The next morning, I went down and there it was, her famous black soap. I picked up a couple and brought them back. Once I returned and had a chance, I flew to Montreal to see my family.

"Here mom I brought you the soap," I said handing her the soap.

She stood there so excited and opened up the packaging. She held the soap in both hands and slowly brought it close to her nose and closed her eyes. "I used to buy this when I was flying," she said. "It was my favorite soap. Thank you, you made me relive a moment in my past that I had long forgotten."

Sometimes a smell, a sound, or an image can bring back a whole lifetime worth of memories. It's the small moments, the ones that we forget to cherish, that count at the end of the day.

In these past thirteen years, I learned many lessons. I learned to be responsible and attentive towards others. I learned to smile a lot more, I learned that one gesture of kindness goes a long way. I learned that regardless of our ethnical background, status, race, gender, or experiences, at the end of the day we all come into this world the same way and leave it the same way. Only our memories remain.

I learned that life is always evolving, and in this generational gap, the cultural change and the struggles, my parents' stories and mine will live on through those who succeed us. My parents may have not had the chance to live their dreams out but were able to continue their lives in a safe environment where their children could have a future.

Every day I would call my mother, as I was based in another city, and tell her about all of my exciting stories and all the things I had seen and done. My mother would ouuuu and ahhh and say, "I'm so happy for you baby." And as usual, my father in the background saying things like "khaliband," which translates to "I call your bluff." And we would have a good laugh.

After 13 years, the excitement and thrill are just as they were that first day. I have had so many firsts. So many opportunities have risen from this job and so many experiences that I would need a whole book to share. I got to live out my bucket list (although still not finished). I would leave my suitcase half packed and ready for the next adventure. My dad called me the "gypsy" always on the go.

Two years ago, I surprised my mother when she was in London visiting family. I called her "Hi mom, how's the trip?" "Its fine it's quiet and I feel lonely". "alright then, hop in a cab I have called you a taxi to bring you to my hotel" (an awfully expensive taxi!!).

After 13 years, she got to live the experience with me. She stayed at my hotel and we went exploring the city. I took her to my favorite coffee shop, and we passed by the Palace. I wanted her to relive her layovers. The next morning, she came on the bus to the airport with me and I got to serve her as my passenger. I felt tremendous pride having her on board and I wanted to show her that all her sacrifices had not been in vain; that I was living my best life.

2020 was a strange experience for all of us being laid off and having this big void in our lives, feeling lost in our identities as most of us lived, breathed our flying. I had to reconnect with myself and find what could temporarily fill the void. I went back to one of the things that has helped me stay balanced all throughout my life, Yoga and meditation. I became certified and started teaching and sharing my practice. It was a wonderful way for me to still be of service to my community.

I learned that failure doesn't mean the end of something, that you can try again. And having courage and faith can help open a world of opportunities and experiences that you could never have imagined possible. When you learn something, you have the knowledge, but when you put that knowledge into practice, it becomes a skill.

And as my favorite quote from Eat, Pray, Love (the movie) says: "If you are brave enough to leave behind everything that is familiar and comforting and set out on a journey to seek the truth be it internally or externally, and if you are truly willing to regard everything that happens on that journey as a clue and accept everyone you meet along the way as a teacher, if you are prepared to face and forgive difficult realities about yourself, then the truth will not be withheld from you."

BIOGRAPHY

Farnaz Mamizadeh

Farnaz Mamizadeh (Naz) was born in Iran, Tehran. She immigrated to Montreal, Canada when she was a child. Being a flight attendant for over 13 years has brought her tremendous joy and has given her the chance to learn about herself and others along the way. Travelling is her true first love, and her curiosity to learn and experience is still present, just like that naïve child who always wants to discover new things. She has been fortunate enough to travel to Africa on two occasions, visiting Burkina Faso and Abidjan in the Ivory Coast, helping as a volunteer translator and photographer. Naz has been a very spiritual person from a young age. She loves finding a sense of connection with people she meets along her way. Consequently, she has travelled to Spain and walked the path of Fatima and paid respect to the Golden Temple in Punjab. She has a bucket list and never shies away from trying something new: eating bugs in Thailand, jumping off a cliff in Albania, going on adventures with her friends in Bali. Wherever she is, she narrates her adventures, finding what lessons and skills her travelling can teach her. She did her eat-pray-love travel when she went to Italy and fell in love with the country, so much so that she started learning Italian. She went to India and fell deeper in love with India, as she loves the music and the Bollywood movies (anyone who knows her knows that side of her). And Bali brought on a connection with nature and her spiritual side and resulted with her training as a yoga instructor in Thailand and at Modo in Montreal. She is now a certified 700-hour Hatha Yoga teacher sharing her knowledge with many of her friends, family, and colleagues. She teaches via Zoom and has a page on Instagram for her students and followers Yoga.with.naz. This is her first-ever written work, and hopefully not her last.

 Yoga.with.naz

E-mail: farnazmamizadeh@gmail.com

Me and my love on the edge of the Dajti mountains
TiRANA , ALBANiA

CHAPTER 19

Prisons, Planes and my pursuit of happiness

By Adrienne Wiley

*" Success is not final, failure is not fatal.
It is the courage to continue that counts. " Winston Churchill*

Prisons, Planes and my pursuit of happiness

Sometimes I find myself sitting in a metal tube, hurtling through the sky, wondering how it is that I've ended up in this exact moment of life. Then, in other simpler moments, like when my daughter is falling asleep with her head on my chest, I know that I'm exactly where I'm supposed to be in the universe. Though it may not have been what my younger self envisioned for my future, here I sit, as one of a few hundred flight attendants remaining active at my airline while continuing to navigate the ongoing global pandemic and all of life's other challenges.

Throughout my 19-year journey in the sky, I've navigated marriage, became a mother of two beautiful babies, made so many fabulous friends, seen amazing places in the world, and in my more recent years, I've seen the end of my marriage, and have had to pick up and rebuild my life. I'd like to say it was a smooth ride, but like many flights, there's definitely been some turbulence.

Growing up, I thought that I was destined to be a police officer. Perhaps this came from a place within me of wanting to do something important with my life and wanting to make a difference while helping others. What I didn't realize then, was that I have the power to fulfill these desires in whatever I chose to do in life. I have had so many opportunities in various roles that I've taken on to do exactly that.

With my original law enforcement goal in mind, I pursued a degree in Criminal Justice Studies. I spent countless hours volunteering with the police and going on ride-alongs. I volunteered for the local Distress Centre answering crisis lines, and eventually landed a job in corrections as a guard/youth worker. Each of these roles enabled me to build on my strengths and develop my character into the person I am today. Whether it was a standout moment or having to adapt myself to fill a certain role, I've taken these skills with me and have been able to use them in my job as a flight attendant.

Prisons, Planes and my pursuit of happiness

At the crisis line, I spoke to people in the throes of some of their worst moments in life. People who needed help walking through their panic attacks, addictions, and even people that simply didn't want to be alive anymore. One call that has stuck with me over the years involved a mother of a 6-year-old boy that was feeling suicidal. While there are procedures that we followed on such calls to assist in preserving life, which in my case were well under way, the moment that the small child got on the phone and asked me why his mommy was taking out a knife, chilled me to my core. Thankfully, the paramedics arrived shortly after this moment, and took over. For me, that was where the call ended, and I had to accept that. I had to resign myself to the knowledge that I did what I could to help this person in a tumultuous life moment.

When I got hired at the correctional facility, I must admit that I hadn't fully understood the details of the job that I had taken on. It wasn't until I was in training and was being taught about handcuffs, shackles, strip searches, pat downs, and restraints that I realized that I in fact was working in a jail. Much like the crisis line, the experiences I had at that job gave me a range of tools and knowledge to draw from going forward in life. I quickly learned how to challenge my limits and step out of my comfort zone. I had to figure out how to be assertive, to both the staff members (some of whom told me that I was "too young and too cute" to survive in that job) and the inmates, while learning to face conflict head on. This job gave me the confidence that I needed to believe that in a difficult or urgent situation, adrenaline and instinct really do kick in. While there is a vast difference in the ways I've learnt to manage aggressive and angry humans in a jail versus those on a plane, there will always be similarities.

At some point, while still very young and working in corrections, I tried to pursue my dream of becoming a police officer. Unfortunately, I was unsuccessful in that attempt, which upset me at the time, but I believe fate had other plans for me.

I had heard over and over again about this airline that had started up in my city and that was growing and expanding with great success. It had never occurred to me that I would (or even could) be a flight attendant, but I resisted the voices of uncertainty in my head and went through with my application.

Prisons, Planes and my pursuit of happiness

Unfortunately, for this formerly quiet and shy introvert, the interview/hiring process at the airline started with a dreaded (and mildly terrifying) group interview. I was forced to conquer my fear of public speaking when we were made to draw topics from a hat and stand in front of the group while speaking about said topic for a full two minutes. My topic was sports. Well, as luck would have it, and thanks to a former teacher, I had the perfect story for this!

I used to attempt to play volleyball in school, and honestly, it was not my strongest skill. I used to bump the ball so hard and high that it would shoot up into the rafters, quite consistently. My teacher (a giant of a man) would yell my name at the top of his lungs when this happened. "ADRIENNE!!!!!" I would stand there nervously quivering because I had no idea what was going on. It wasn't until many years later that I learned about the "Rocky" movie association with my name. Suddenly years of people randomly yelling my name when I introduced myself all made sense. It's funny how something that I didn't understand for so many years became an important memory to draw from, enabling me to ace the scary group interview process while even drawing a few laughs from the crowd.

Now, for the second time in my life, I found myself sitting in a training class, unsure of the job requirements that I had gotten myself into. I had never given much thought to the actual role or job description of flight attendants. I hate to admit this, but even I thought their primary job was to smile, greet the passengers, and dole out the food and drinks! I had no idea that we become first responders, eyes and ears to the pilots when situations occur, counsellors, guardians to young children as they travel across the country, and sometimes a human splash guard for whatever bodily fluids may occur! I soon realized that in the air, everyone looks to the flight attendants for pretty much everything. You can't call 911 from 38000 feet, nor can you call the police when there is a disturbance. Similarly, when something goes wrong with the airplane in a mechanical way, the pilots may be the ones to deliver the information, but as flight attendants we are constantly the face and source of reassurance in the cabin. We take people on exciting trips, reconnect them with loved ones, and are part of the everyday routine for business travelers.

Prisons, Planes and my pursuit of happiness

However, we are also there during the lowest, most traumatic moments of peoples' lives when they NEED to get to a loved one at the end of their life or in an emergency.

I would soon realize how fortunate I was to have been hired, not only as a flight attendant, but specifically at the company that I work for. I learned that this company was trying to be something different. There was a huge focus on developing a caring, people-focused culture within our company while encouraging individual empowerment to resolving situations for our guests as they arose. We, as employees were all a part of something bigger than each of our individual jobs. Even when we were just meeting our coworkers for the first time, there was an instant bond and cohesiveness amongst us because we were all part of this unique adventure that many people don't have the opportunity to experience.

For quite some time, my airline was known as the "fun airline". Yes, we were that airline that was known for playing the toilet paper game on longer flights in those early days (before TV's and Wi-Fi) to pass the time. Strange, but true! We were also known for our level of caring, compassion, and willingness to look outside the box to find immediate solutions to guests needs when we could. While we cared for the flying public, behind the scenes we were also caring for each other. I've had some amazing layovers, meals, and drinks with my coworkers and learnt so much from so many, as we all come from different walks of life. I've also experienced the kindness and compassion of my peers when I've fallen ill while at work and relied on their assistance to get me to a hospital and back.

As far as our superpowers go, there are many! From perfecting the ultimate calm, reassuring face, to providing first aid and coming up with a genius hack to rig an IV bag to hang from an overhead bin for the remainder of a flight, the skills that we are required to activate sometimes even surprise us. I got to test out my "flight attendant face" when I was a few months into the job and we were midflight. The lights in the cabin went dark and when the pilots were able to communicate with us, they said that they had lost oil pressure in one engine and had to shut it down.

Prisons, Planes and my pursuit of happiness

We were diverting to a closer city and could expect an "abnormal" landing. This type of information generally comes with a flurry or questions from the passengers, the top two of which are generally: "Does this mean we will be late?" and "Am I going to make my connection?" They are also sometimes met with frantic and panicked questions like "are we going to die?", hence the calming face.

We proceeded to land, and all was well. While we were in the airport, we assisted the agents in handing out meal vouchers to the guests as best as we could. We were then told that the company was going to fly out a new plane to pick us up and that we would be able to continue on to our destination. The issue that arose though was that we were in a relatively small airport (at the time) that had one small sub shop open as a food option with two employees working. Suddenly there was a barrage of about 130 people lined up at that sub shop. Myself and one of my co-workers were trying to find food for ourselves when we noticed the insane line up. This is where he and I were able to demonstrate that, deep down at our core, as flight attendants, we do want to be helpful people. And, well, quite frankly we were starving! So we did what we could to help in an odd scenario. We got behind the counter at the sub shop, slapped on some gloves and joined the other two employees to form a bigger sandwich assembly line. We plowed through the huge line up (after quite some time) and we reached our ultimate goal at the end...which was to feed ourselves. The passengers were struck by the fact that we would jump in to do a job that we really didn't have to do. So when we got on the new plane to continue our journey, spirits were high, and all were appreciative of our efforts.

On another flight, proving that our skill set as flight attendants is ever expanding, we were asked to craft a marriage proposal. A gentleman came up to us on the ground and told us that he wanted to propose to his girlfriend. It was a one-hour flight. But, using our resourcefulness and not wanting to disappoint, we came up with a trivia game in which we not-so-randomly selected his girlfriend as the contestant. We came up with 3 fairly easy questions for her and her prize at the end, was of course, the proposal.

Prisons, Planes and my pursuit of happiness

From the odd and entertaining, to the more serious, as flight attendants we are constantly tested on flights. Some people travel when they are terminally ill, so as to take that one last trip with their loved ones. People sometimes pass away on flights. Recently, I myself experienced this. While we were on the ground and at the end of the flight, a guest was having trouble getting off the plane. It was only then that his wife shared the seriousness of his ill health, telling us that she just needed to get him to their ride, and she was transporting him to palliative care. At one moment, out of basic human kindness and a deep desire to help in whatever way I could, I held this dying man's head on my chest so that his wife could make a phone call. When I discovered that he did pass away later that day after we left, it had a profound impact on my heart and soul. Our thoughts went out to this couple, and I only hope that we were able to offer some comfort and compassion to them both in this horrible moment of their life. In these situations, we do our best to evaluate, think in the moment, and do what we can to carry people through, even if it's to their final end.

I can't move on in my story without mentioning some of the simply odd behaviors that we see from the flying public. At times, the airplane has become free range for personal grooming. I've watched a man stand up, while on a stopover on the ground, and proceed to shave his face with an electric razor in the aisle. We frequently hear the dreaded sounds of finger and toenails being clipped. We find Q-tips and dental floss sticks crammed into the seat pockets and left behind on the floor. People have apparently taken off their undergarments at times and shoved them under the seat cushions, as I've found both men's and women's attire when searching the plane. A man once came out of the lavatory with blood splattered all over his white dress shirt. When asked if he was ok, he told us that he had just vigorously flossed his teeth. He then proceeded to wash his shirt out in the sink and tried to hang it over the emergency megaphone mounted on the aft galley wall. Just when you think you've seen it all, there's always more out there to shock you. Like the bodily fluids! Without getting into too much stomach-churning detail, I will say that going bare foot into the washroom (which we see all the time) is NEVER a good idea. The floors are often wet or covered in some liquid, and I know from having the thrill of cleaning it up that it's rarely just water. I've also been handed an air sickness bag full of urine because a passenger decided to relive himself at his seat.

Prisons, Planes and my pursuit of happiness

I share these stories to demonstrate the scope of the job that I do. Some people think it's all glamour, all the time. If only that was true! But like anything in life, we take the good with the bad. And sometimes, after a particularly trying day, I get to go to a quiet, kid-free hotel room and go out for dinner and enjoy the company of a fabulous crew. And if we're lucky, maybe it's in a tropical destination!

These past few years have been some of the most challenging ones in my life. After coming to the heartbreaking realization that I hadn't been happy for many years in my marriage, I finally worked up the courage to leave my husband. I had to confront my personal fears and self-doubts to come to this decision. Would I be able to afford to be a single mom? Was I capable enough to embark on this journey? Was I destroying my children's lives by making this decision?

Unfortunately, I had fallen victim in my marriage to emotional abuse and had gotten to the point where I no longer felt I was capable of meeting the expectations my husband had of me. Because of these feelings of failure, I realized that I had been withdrawing from my family and my kids. I was finally able to come to the conclusion that my kids deserved more from their mom, and that my relationship with them was suffering because of my own personal misery in my marriage. It's a difficult thing to choose happiness for yourself knowing that it will complicate the lives of your children beyond what you had hoped for them. But I knew that I needed to find my voice in this situation and regain my independence.

This decision that I chose for myself, to make my life better, was still a gut wrenching one to make. It came with far-reaching effects that I had not anticipated. I discovered that my husband, the partner that I had put all of my trust in, had racked up a massive amount of debt throughout our marriage, and due to this, I was driven into financial ruins. I had to start from nothing, while forging ahead on my path to independence. While I have come to accept responsibility for my own ignorance throughout my marriage, it doesn't make the hardship any easier to bear. To say I've struggled would be an understatement. I've cried, I've grieved, I've hurt, I've gotten so angry that I go back to crying, and some days I didn't even get out of bed.

Prisons, Planes and my pursuit of happiness

But through this time in my life, I've learned to break things down day by day, sometimes hour by hour. I've learned that I have amazing friendships in my life and that it's ok to ask for help. That my parents and family support me beyond a shadow of a doubt, while some family members who I thought of as my own, have chosen to sever ties with me. Most of all, I've learned that I am capable. I am strong and I have found my strength both as a mother to my kids and as a human, and I've realized that I can no longer be silenced.

I've found throughout my struggle that sharing really does lead to support and strength in numbers. When I tell my story to the people in my life, be it work friends or friends in my everyday life, there are so many others in similar situations. The generosity I've experienced from others willing to share their stories with me has been nothing short of inspirational, and I'm forever thankful to hear these words and stories of support.

Finally, in rolled 2020, bringing with it the COVID-19 pandemic. While I've seen a lot in my years of flying, it is fair to say that nothing has devastated the airline industry as much as this current pandemic has. I'm happy and relieved to still be in the air, but I do so with a heavy heart. On a personal level, I've watched my career and livelihood be slowly torn apart and depleted. I worry for my own financial future in the midst of my personal post-divorce struggles. I also find myself grieving for the thousands of coworkers, both pilots, flight attendants (and all others across the airline's network) that have lost their jobs. I consider so many of these people to be my friends, and I miss them. It's a magical thing to get to work with your friends and to share the infectious joy and laughter that so many of us have experienced on a daily basis.

For those of us left working, the pandemic has changed the scope of our job drastically as well. We have become "mask police," and have to deal with angry and frustrated people lashing out at us often because we have to enforce these new regulations. Seeing deserted airports and empty flights day after day is simply depressing. Many of our normal duties on the plane have been reduced to handing out wipes and water, and then sitting idle for most of the flight.

Prisons, Planes and my pursuit of happiness

There is a new type of fatigue that we feel after many of our current workdays, likely from boredom and the emotional toll of seeing a lack of people in what used to be a bustling industry. I only hope that I can do my part to keep my airline viable, while attempting to navigate this "new normal".

For me, what started out as a short-term job, being a flight attendant turned into a career that I love. It has given me flexibility that has allowed me to raise my kids and physically be there for them. I've made lifelong friendships that I cherish. I hope to have many more years of laughter, tears, and dance parties on the plane. I hope that our airline and aviation industries across the world can survive these trying times and flourish once again. Most of all, I can't wait to hug my coworkers and friends when they come back from being laid off.... even if being able to hug will lead to random strangers hugging us as they get off the plane!

BiOGRAPHY
Adrienne Wiley

Adrienne Wiley has been a flight attendant in a large Canadian airline for over 19 years. While she obtained a BA in applied justice studies and started her career as a correctional officer, she soon moved on to a more uplifting career in the sky where she could make people smile. She would often be found trying to make her coworkers laugh or dance on the plane, while aiming to genuinely help people through their travel journeys. She is a perceptive and intuitive person who tries to connect with others frequently while sharing honest truths about her own life experiences. She is known to rarely filter her words, to often incorporate humor into her interactions and to not take herself too seriously. Outside of work, Adrienne is a single mom to her two amazing and beautiful kids, a 14-year-old son and an 8-year-old daughter. She embraces the adventure of parenting with a whimsical attitude, open dialogue, and compassion. She often tries to make her kids laugh while guiding them on their paths through life. She thinks she is hilarious, though her teenager would call her "cringe-worthy"! Aside from spending time with family, friends, and her boyfriend, Adrienne enjoys cooking and eating delicious food (flat wings only, please), sipping Prosecco and wine, and is known as a baker and blossoming cake decorator for all those that won't critique her works too seriously! She has recently become a bird watcher and never tires of witnessing beautiful sunsets, from in the air or on the ground, in whatever part of the world she is in. Adrienne cannot wait to resume travelling and plan new adventures with those she loves once the world recovers from the current pandemic.

Adrienne Wiley

Wileycat79

LINDSAY PARK, CALGARY, ALBERTA

CHAPTER 20

Divinely Orchestrated

By Caroline Grenier

I can do everything through him who gives me strength.
Philippians 4:13

That moment when you know the universe has your back and you're being divinely guided is how it was for me skyrocketing into becoming a flight attendant. This blessing soared out of nowhere and felt like I was being guided from up above! I had just completed college and started working at my new office job. It was clear right away this was not for me...I literally felt like a robot. Having to wake up early every day, find something to wear, spend all day inside an office, go home, eat, and maybe get to do a workout if I was not too exhausted, and then repeat day after day. "This cannot be life," I said to myself.

Fast forward a few years, I was sitting in my office, and I got a call offering me an interview for a flight attendant position at an airline. I was so confused about how they contacted me, yet I immediately said "Yes"! As a rule, when opportunities present themselves, I jump onboard! How did this happen? I had never thought of being a flight attendant. I got home, informed my family, and my mother said with excitement, "Oh yeah, I forgot to tell you I mailed your resume to airlines and cruise lines as I thought you may like that better." My first reaction was... "is this for me or for you?" I was pleasantly surprised she thought of this way of life for me! It's amazing how our mothers know us best, and so she took the liberty to put it out in the universe and see what happens. I became a traveler at the early age of 3 and must have been mesmerized and captivated by the flight attendants, as I decided to imitate them doing their service. I had gone into the washroom to fill up cups with the lavatory water and offered them to passengers. I surely melted some hearts on board that day. My amazing parents never forgot how I was fascinated and displayed an interest to become a flight attendant, even as a young little girl.

Divinely Orchestrated

I attended my interview looking the part with my crisp white blouse, a blue scarf around my neck, and my head high. Heading for this dream job, I had to pull off the road as I was so touched that my prayers had been answered. I entered the room and the interviewers seemed excited to meet me. They had had my resume on file for a while, as my mother had sent it in when I was only 18 years old. I read an announcement in French, and it felt like I got the job right away. The interviewer said, "it's great that you will be turning 19 during training, as we are able to hire you now". WOW I was on their radar. This was more confirmation that this job was divinely meant for me! Buckle up, it's time for takeoff to new horizons! My Dad shared that he had always secretly envisioned me as a flight attendant. Thanks to my parents loving guidance, I evolved as a flight angel! I am forever grateful, and I thank them still to this day!

My first flight felt like a dream. I got a call with good news as I was now on my way to Paris! I literally was jumping up and down...this is my new life! The person that interviewed me was working on my flight and I was incredibly nervous as I wanted to make a good impression. He was pleased by my professionalism and he commented on how great I was doing for my first flight. I said, "don't you remember me...you hired me," ... he said "well, I sure do pick them right!" Another flight attendant who I trained with was also on this flight, and we instantly decided that we were going to explore the City of Love as soon as we landed! We picked up some delicious baguettes and French wine and we were on cloud nine, gallivanting through the streets of Paris. Our first stop was the Eiffel Tower. My mouth dropped open. I was overjoyed and had to pinch myself. I was so fortunate to have found this career and I was in disbelief of where I was standing at that moment. That truly was a memorable first flight, and it was a clear indication that my new life was going to continuously blow my mind.

I also thought that being a flight attendant was the closest jet-set lifestyle to living like a supermodel. My dream when I was growing up was to be known as a positive, healthy role model, and bring back smiles and curves to that industry. Now, during that time, it was all about the anorexic look. This was so not me, nor would I ever put myself through such torture to fit these unrealistic and unhealthy standards. I could see the negative impact it was having on our confidence and well-being as a society, and I was not going to add to this toxic image.

Divinely Orchestrated

I knew, even at 10 years old, that I had aspirations, goals, and wishes for all people to love themselves as they are; as that is truly beautiful! I attended a modeling scouting call at 18 and received interest from multiple agencies around the world, yet they all wanted me to lose over 20 pounds. My agent begged me to lose the weight and even tried to convince me that most models use cocaine to get this skinny; "well not this one," I said. "You will represent me the way I am". I was not going to be pressured or enrolled in damaging my health to be accepted. It was a struggle and I lost out on lots of experiences, yet I am clear standing for what you believe is right to you means you respect yourself and you have that knowing within that is to be trusted. Become your own biggest fan! I had promised myself that I was committed to leading the way to exemplifying a healthy feminine body image, and I have kept this promise to this day. I am a true believer in that if things don't happen the way you hoped, that's ok because your experiences and choices make you the person you are today. I believe that if you trust in yourself and in your divine guidance, then your desires will come true at the right time if they are for your highest good. I love the fact that we now see healthier models in our everyday lives, and that they have been well received and appreciated by the public. May we continue to lift each other up and celebrate our uniqueness and the beauty we all possess in our own way.

One day upon landing at my home base, I received a text message from my agent asking me if I could go meet this client right away. I was still in uniform, as I had worked the flight, and headed to this audition for a modeling shoot in India. They were pleasantly surprised when they saw that I was a flight attendant. I tried on some clothes which happened to fit perfectly. I also had my passport on hand, so we proceeded to start filling out the travel documents right away. It felt divinely orchestrated as all was coming together with ease. The weather was extremely hot during the month of May in India, and we had to shoot quickly as we were soaked in sweat within minutes. Taking pictures while visiting and absorbing the magical Taj Mahal. I had the pleasure to shoot on the exact same bench that Princess Diana had sat on and that image was later used in pamphlets. Another epic image captured during an Indian shoot was when I was riding an elephant in a sea of people and cows all maneuvering with no real direction or order. India is so colorful and an adventure I will always cherish.

Divinely Orchestrated

I have learnt along the way that while some opportunities are divinely guided for you, others must be actualized and navigated. I took a four-month leave of absence from the airline and set off to fulfill my dreams of working as an international model in South Africa. When I first arrived, I stayed at a model house where bed bug bites coved my face and body. Not happy with where I was living, I quickly moved into the house of a famous producer who kindly offered me a room. I was set up for success, booking international jobs and making some incredible new friends while having the best time of my life. It was in this sacred land where I found God again and started attending church regularly. This was also where I learnt about speaking in tongues and fasting. It was a very faith-filled and inspiring experience for me and has forever changed me to my core. Also, Africa's wildlife is extraordinary, and I ended up visiting a safari located right in Cape Town where the animals were super friendly and accustomed to visitors. I recall our guide asking if I would like to pet the lions (I thought "is he crazy?") we watched the guides play and feed them and you could feel the love they had for one another. I did get a picture with the two lions calmly behind me, with the fence between us of course.

Being a flight angel is being of service. In the end we are all here to serve and love one another. Another big reason why flight attendants love our jobs is the perks! One of my favorite perks has to be the ability to travel with my family. A special family trip was to Greece, Santorini "aka Smurf town" is what it felt like to me. There was an incredible view of the island as we arrived in Santorini by cruise ship. Santorini is on the top of a mountain and since everything is white and blue it made it look like the island was covered with snow. Since flight attendants and their families fly "standby" and there are no guarantees of us getting on a specific flight, we always have to have a plan B, and even C, in mind. I love the story of when my parents were planning a trip to Las Vegas. When they arrived at the airport, they discovered that the flight was full, so instead my mother asked the gate agent where the next plane was going to. She told them that the next flight was to Halifax …"OK great, Halifax it is, I don't want to go back home," said my mother, and they took off! You can imagine how adventurous you become while making the best of your time to explore the world.

Divinely Orchestrated

Following your intuition and trusting your soul is what it takes to catch that next blessing in life. I was asked to explore my acting skills and join my talented friends in creating two short films. We produced and acted in both films and we ended up achieving great success and receiving multiple awards. These "shorts" were selected at Sundance and Cannes Film Festival. We decided to enter a contest and only had one day to shoot, edit, and submit the project. We made it happen and submitted our project with only one minute left to spare before the deadline and ended up winning first runner up.

The first day I arrived in Utah I was face to face with my Idol. I was dazzled because as a young teenager I would stare at the Cover Girl picture in admiration as I loved the vitality this supermodel radiated. She was the reason why I wanted to become a model in the first place. We connected and became pen pals for years and she even attempted to get me into her agency which unfortunately later closed their doors, and I never was able to work in the USA. Yet I am still very blessed as my idol actually supported me and furthered my dreams!

9/11 a day we will never forget. I was visiting a friend on a layover and spent the night at their house. My friend's mother called that morning in a panic to tell us that the world trade center had been hit by an airplane, so we jumped out of bed to find out more. Our eyes were fixed on the news in disbelief as we literally watched the second plane hit the building "live". I was crying and could not believe my eyes. "Is this even possible?" I kept asking myself. As soon as the airways were back open, my airline was the first back up in the air. We even made the news as we took off from Vancouver. I will always remember that flight as I was in uniform with my crew, and we were traveling as passengers; all eyes were on us. My next flight on which I was working ended up having the Toronto Argonauts team on board. Big-muscled men everywhere! So I made a joke saying "if I need help or if anyone tries to enter the cockpit, I just need you all to stand up; no one will be able to pass". They all started laughing and loved my humor while also acknowledging they had my back. This definitely helped ease the stress of returning back to work after such a tragic incident.

Divinely Orchestrated

Fast forward a few months later, I was in my Edmonton hotel room when I got the bad news that our incredible airline was going bankrupt... I was no longer going to be a flight attendant! My head was spinning, and I was pacing in my room in disbelieve that our airline was going to vanish. On my next flight, my crew members and I were not able to be in the aisle to do our service as our hearts were broken and it was not possible for us to keep our emotions to ourselves. It became clear to us that we were going to be our company's last flight to land, and that when we touched down, it was official, over 5000 people were going to be out of work. Many coworkers tearfully greeted our last airplane returning home. We consoled each other and rallied through the airport wondering how this all happened so fast. We literally found out at the same time as the news. I was frozen in pain and numb for days. I felt as though my life was ruined, and that my destined job had been taken away from me.

Shortly after losing my job, another airline gave me hope as they offered us first priority to interview for flight attendant positions since we were all qualified and looking to get our wings back. Over 2000 of us showed up, but that day they decided they only needed French-qualified speakers. So, they asked those that were French to move to the side and asked the rest to go home. It was such a harsh way to say goodbye to so many hopeful flight attendants wanting to be back in the air. In the end they only hired a handful of us, and I was one of those lucky 13. Once again, my angels came through and made sure my journey as a flight attendant continued....

In addition to being a flight attendant, I had decided to take a makeup artist course. It seemed like a great fit and a perfect, manageable side hobby that could create extra income. I recall seeing my first M.A.C. counter in Australia. I had my picture taken in front of the store as I had a feeling that one day, I would work for them. After losing my job when the airline went bankrupt, I noticed a part-time, 12-hour position available and knew that was my ticket into this company. I showed up with impeccable yet bold makeup and dressed in black to adhere to their standard look and image. You usually need to go through numerous interviews and makeup trials before being considered for a position, yet she hired me on the spot, and I started working right away.

Divinely Orchestrated

I bet you love seeing your flight attendants with a big smile and bright red lipstick. A fond memory I will always have of flying is how we all faithfully put on our red lipstick for landing. "Lips for landing" always stuck with me.

You need a free spirit to make it in this business. It takes time to get the kind of flying your desire. After some time in my career, I decided to become qualified as a head flight attendant, or as we call it, the "In Charge." This leadership role not only came with more responsibility, but also an increase in pay which was appealing. However, after ten years, I was suffering severe insomnia, was craving a better schedule, and I had to admit that the true reason I was doing this career was to see the world. I made the choice to leave this In-Charge position because, like my grandma said, your health should be your top priority. My first flight back as a flight attendant, I was roaming the streets of Rome. The following week I was in Amsterdam eating my favorite cheese in tears, as I had not been back in over 10 years. Shortly after that I was in Warsaw, Poland and that layover was particularly memorable, as the city had been rebuilt exactly like it was after the war. Family orientated community and the homemade pierogis were out of this world!

Speaking about making the best choices for ourselves is even more critical now during these challenging times that we are all facing worldwide. I am choosing to stay positive and not let my wings get too ruffled up. This layoff has been a blessing in disguise as this career does take a toll on one's health. I also had some health issues come up as my body saw an opportunity to get my attention with intense body pains. I discovered I have a fatty liver, so I initiated my own research like I always do. I started a new healing menu right away, and within days was feeling better. I was guided to follow a well-known natural doctor and once you know him and his wisdom, you too will be consuming an abundance of fruits and vegetables daily. Choosing a plant-based approach to heal my liver is also restoring my overall health, and I am realizing the essential laws of nature and the importance of eating as close to the natural source as one can. I have more energy and drive than ever before; I have happily, and freely lost weight, and I am 40 pounds lighter than this time last year.

Divinely Orchestrated

What a great pleasure it has been to explore natural ways to heal while being granted this pause to rest and time to fall in love with myself again. This time off has been beneficial on the mind, body, and spirit and has been a time to recreate myself and try new adventures. Keeping the faith, tuning inwards and being open to grow is key while surrounding yourself with wise powerful people who lift you up and make you smile!

All airline crew members worldwide have been greatly impacted by this turbulent pandemic affecting our industry and employment for years to come. Many have been laid off for over a year in Canada and the airlines are still very fragile. Personally, I tuned inwards to meditations with essential oils, daily yoga, eating more fruits and vegetables, and adding fun exercise and dancing while doing more of what I love. I also believe it's influential and empowering to question everything and research on your own as you realize valuable knowledge that may shift or add more insight and awareness. I personally am connecting with likeminded people and find it incredible to see how many freedom lovers there are around the world! Stand in your truth and be the light the world needs right now more than ever. I know my strength is with God and that is my true power! As a child of God, I am also aware of my rights. I am armored with the word and truth which is all mighty powerful. May we aim for peace and harmony while exercising our inherent rights and honoring our intuition at the same time as expanding and shinning our greatness.

No matter what is going on out there and no matter what life looks like, remember you always have free will! What I sense is happening is that we are collectively evolving through all this chaos and that we are experiencing the greatest spiritual awakening that our planet has ever seen. I believe that truth will set us free in the end. Create a world you love and stay focused on keeping your vibes and spirits high and choose to come from love as often as you can. May we all globally stand for our natural rights to be free to uphold our fundamental life choices; peacefully express our opinions, thoughts, and beliefs without fear of persecution. Keep the faith, do what you feel is right, and be brave! Remember love is like oxygen...its essential!

Divinely Orchestrated

In 2021 I'm taking off to new heights as an author, and in 2020 I transformed into a writer for a new Canadian magazine called, Chaarmz. I believe that now is the time to elevate ourselves during these transformational ages and to actualize our passions. When my friend launched his beautiful magazine, I quickly congratulated him and proposed my makeup services. He already had a makeup team but was so gracious to extend an offer for me to collaborate with him and to write for the magazine. I had this "ah ha moment" as I've always had this longing thirst, profound curiosity, and love for nature's superpowers, and now I was blessed with a chance to write about this wise knowledge. Hope you're hungry for some healthy wisdom and read my articles and may they inspire you to be your healthiest! Empowered by nature's life force and connecting with the superpowers our bodies need and love. My dream is for children and all to fall in love with nature's supernatural superpowers by consuming the best that Mother Nature provides and reap the healing benefits of eating a rainbow of fruits and vegetables every day. May we be our healthiest while following and tuning into our hearts desires as we all have skills, gifts and treasures inside of us ready to blossom! Keep nourishing your soul with truth and wisdom and be grateful for all that you have while falling in love with what you're up to. Love yourself and believe in yourself always May you be on cloud 9 in all that you do in life and let your dreams take flight!

I want to be singing... (" leaving on a jet plane")...with you all onboard!

Love...& B U !

Thank you Mom, Dad & Jaidev (which means "Winning Angel") for your loving support and encouragement to let my dreams take flight.

BIOGRAPHY
Caroline Grenier

The name Caroline means "Strong Free Women" witch she definitely embodies, exemplifies and represents! Caroline has a strong spirit. Her joie de vivre, luminous smile and contagious laughter light up any room that she walks into. As a Franco-Ontarian, she is fluently bilingual; has as a degree in advertising and marketing and is also a Landmark graduate. Caroline has been flying the friendly skies for 20 years and enjoys traveling on her time off and admiring beautiful sunsets and chasing waterfalls. She has lived through 911, an airline bankruptcy, and now a pandemic. Her strength and resiliency are once again being tested while she keeps her faith strong, and stays focused on what matters most; her health.

Since the aviation world is often impacted and many layoffs can take place, she sees huge value in having other passions and businesses. She believes that having a side job and/or hobbies is a smart option for flight attendants and their lifestyles. She has a free spirit that loves going with the flow of life's blessings while also following her heart's desires and callings. Her love for beauty and health has made her an excellent Makeup Artist that loves accentuating people's natural features while making them look and feel like their best self! She has recently started writing empowering articles for a Canadian magazine called Chaarmz, enlightening and inspiring others to connect deeper with nature's superpowers is her mission!

Caroline's biggest dream is to build an education health app for kids worldwide! Caroline is hopeful and has faith that all will be divinely orchestrated in due time and that she will find the strength to make her biggest dreams a reality.

BiOGRAPHY continued..
Caroline Grenier

Personal Website: www.flightattendantsuperpowers.com

 @CarolineGrenier - SuperPower Tips – Food & Health Enthusiast

 SuperPowerTips - Caroline Grenier – Food & Health Enthusiast

Chaarmz Magazine : www.chaarmzmagazine.com/foodandbeverage

Talent Agency: www.filmcomm.ca

MA MA MIA CRUISE

SANTORINI - GREECE

CHAPTER 21

THE VIRTUOUS CYCLE OF SUPERPOWERS IN THE 'BIG SKY OF LIFE'

Christina-Narayani Degano

Superpower as Career and Life Trajectory

True to unseen, Superpower forces, the universe seemed to covertly pull me into this project just in the nick of time, to be given the honor of writing the Superpower Introduction.

I do feel a particular affinity to the theme of the book: In a very low-profile way, I have been trail-blazing and nurturing Superpowers all my adult life, blessed to have discovered them, even decades before they passed the modern 'hocus pocus' test, and in my case, not a moment too soon.

Both my life and career trajectories have not been conventional. In some ways, this has been very good, but only and because it has also been very hard.

At a very young point in my life, it was necessary to find a Superpower to survive, which then helped me to thrive, and ultimately peacefully transcend it all.

Becoming an airline employee in general, and a 'Sky Hostess' in particular, has served a special role in this.

Ultimately, it has allowed me experience both the intensely active, worldly side, while nurturing its silent and still counterpart, together forming life's complete experience. *The wisdom of existence lies in living both 'extremes'.*

THE VIRTUOUS CYCLE OF SUPERPOWERS IN THE 'BIG SKY OF LIFE'

Personal Superhero Anecdote

As a lighter and symbolic anecdote, whenever I come across a difficulty or some challenging situation, Felipe, my partner, tells me 'Eres Azafata' ('You're a Stewardess'). In other words: 'You've got this...and basically anything you need to do or be'. Go figure that I hold other titles now which have some Superpower elements of their own, yet he does not generally refer to those in such times. This speaks to the tangible magic of our job.

And to think that Felipe is a badass surfing legend, twice over now, because he is still mastering big waves into his uber mature age. A bit of a Superhero himself.

Sounds boastful to mention, however I could not have excluded this vignette as it represents a huge compliment to our trade, and a fun testament to the theme of this anthology of chronicles: *Flight Attendant Superpower.*

The Early Choice and Destiny of Delay
"Your desires reflect your destiny" ~CN Degano~

As a Gen-Xer female, I straddled between and enjoyed both the more traditional and emancipated versions of my female self. Commonly to past tradition, especially amongst girls, I had dreamt of becoming a 'Stewardess', with my first observance of a beautiful, graceful, even loving 'Sky Goddess' who reminded me of a butterfly, fluttering about the world so freely. Also, I was very much exposed to my Italian motherland culture growing up, even by residence, and was consequently moulded by perceptions of flight crew glamor and prestige, which persist strongly there even today. Yet I had other countless ambitions as well, which I somehow intuitively knew could be complimentary to and blissfully supported by a 'Fly job', honoring my full human, 'millennial' age potential.

Becoming a flight attendant happened almost exactly 10 years after starting at my airline, an initial chunk of career equally divided between Customer Service in Reservations and the Airport, both Toronto-based. I missed the flight attendant cattle call the year I joined the company and even turned down a Cabin crew job at another airline, so I could work for the national carrier, my priority. And despite having an exemplary record, multiple languages under my belt, and glowing letters of commendation, I seemed to hit every barrier imaginable as an existing employee.

THE VIRTUOUS CYCLE OF SUPERPOWERS IN THE 'BIG SKY OF LIFE'

Dismayed years later, I used my second passport, and succeeded in a very selective process at a still-today timeless airline. Luckily with some strategic postponement however, I was finally granted the opportunity with my current carrier.

It was implied by peeps, even those closest to me, that I should have 'aimed higher', that being a 'hostess in the skies' was somehow below me, and that 'they' preferred to be stimulated mentally, for example. *You know you have chosen well with anything in life when such disparaging comments make you smile.* Ironically, the typical Flight Attendant is polar opposite to 'simple-minded and unmotivated', for reasons expressed previously in the introduction. And I was lucky to have figured this out well before 'landing' the job.

Delays getting there were necessary and meaningful, as they usually are, and I can see it all so crystal clearly now. My most important years of growth were the austere pre-flight ones, which with all their takeaways, catapulted me more strongly than if I had started off in the fluffy clouds.

Everything is always exactly the way it should be.

Superpowers to Survive

"Opportunities to find deeper powers within ourselves come when life seems more challenging" ~Joseph John Campbell~

My karma coming into the world was quite challenged in certain areas. It is fair to say that my early conditions were probably exacerbated by a naturally and environmentally reinforced hyper-emotional, worrywart persona. True to nature, I do still carry a tiny bit of this with me to this day, but in a much more manageable and productive form.

However, importantly to this story is that as a prolonged climactic result to those dynamics, I cycled through anorexia and bulimia for the full gamut of my teenage years. Back then, eating disorders were barely named yet, let alone understood. My early adopter tendencies showed themselves here as well, but naturally not with the best practice, as I nearly offed myself in the process.

THE VIRTUOUS CYCLE OF SUPERPOWERS IN THE 'BIG SKY OF LIFE'

Details are unimportant here. Try as I did, it was too hard to conquer and overcome with the same mind which fell prey to it all, when there was no real support anywhere, let alone within my small 'tribe' at the time, especially because no one was even exactly aware. I dabbled in teenage modelling which did not help, but of course, eating disorders take root when one is attempting to carve out and establish a sense of control, and gain illusive perfection when self-esteem is possibly lacking, even if illogically so.

In fairness, I managed quite well, relatively speaking, and was not a complete write-off. In many ways I was admired for my aesthetically pleasing presence, appreciated for my authenticity, and respected with some successes thanks to otherwise good intelligence and wisdom.

However, despite all the necessary ingredients for a Super life, there was at best, little bliss. Importantly, there was extreme dis-ease, which would have eventually eliminated any type of future.

So, to survive, I truly needed Superpowers. And luckily, the universe presented the golden one, not a moment too soon, and I grabbed on for dear life.

'Fuelling up':

"Magic is science we don't understand yet" ~ Arthur C. Clarke~

My first foundational Superpower, Meditation, was the one which opened the doors to my airline industry in April 1989. I remember, when a few months earlier on February 25, immediately after being initiated to the Transcendental Meditation (TM) technique, I remained unfazed when a car had nearly hit me, symbolically marking some amazing and instant internal transformation. And it was on that same Toronto Bloor Street, almost next door, where I started as a Reservations Agent—down the street from where I lived at a U of T dormitory, which numerically, was the exact mirror image to that of the Reservations office. Big, wonderful signs.

Becoming a meditator started to quickly transform and renew me on all levels, inside and out: from my mood to my tastebuds; from attitude to hair volume and skin texture.

THE VIRTUOUS CYCLE OF SUPERPOWERS IN THE 'BIG SKY OF LIFE'

Now decades later, it is finally being embraced as a best tool and life practice. However back then, Meditation was an absolute outlier activity barely or improperly uncovered in a previous 'Free Love' era when it was apparently the focus of ill-placed stigma, despite the veritable saints that resurrected and musical paragons that popularised it. As a result, its life-changing benefits were left minimized and ignored for a long time.

The resistance surrounding me was not subtle: From my airline's Reservationsofficepassing'roundtherumorthatIwasweirdformeditating (when nowadays, one is weird if one does not) to a very noble company Director at the time, who politely compared it to cultish religion, after I had suggested it be introduced as a employee benefit (now, a basic company offering).

It is said that Magic is science not yet proven, and associated to this, a practice must reach a 'tipping point' of adoption for it to be accepted and normalised.

Luckily, I was a free-thinking spirit, did not belong to a herd and thus was unaffected by groupthink.

Meditation naturally represented the foundation. It was followed by an ever-growing toolkit of related Superpowers that would ever increasingly restore balance, heal holistically on all levels, and create miracles and mission for me. Importantly, it helped bring my Superpower job of future, which was an intrinsic part of it all.

'Ground Duty and Taxi': Building the Silence

"Usually when Countries become Superpowers, they rise after a major crisis, which makes them realise their weaknesses, work hard towards overcoming them and build better tomorrow...." ~Narasimha Rao~

In the quote above, the word 'countries' can be substituted with 'people' and this is exactly what I started doing.

During the 90s, while still awaiting my most coveted job, in the 'runway lineup', I was full-on exploring and practicing everything magical and mystical. It was as if I had just come out of the dessert and was drinking drunk on the stillness of life.

THE VIRTUOUS CYCLE OF SUPERPOWERS IN THE 'BIG SKY OF LIFE'

While most others were normally enjoying the full freedom and libido of their early youth, I unconsciously created my own modern-day monk life. Mortgage poor, I worked 12/7, and then locked myself away, studying all things Yogic and generally spiritual, relayed by authentic Saints and Gurus. I volunteered at an Ayurvedic centre which increased my overall awareness of natural health. To increase 'vibration' (a word basically used to only describe noise at the time) I took workshops on Ascended Masters and Angels, listened to the original Law of Attraction teachings on cassette tapes, became initiated into energy healing techniques, and poured my little extra money into advanced mantras at a time when it was still secret knowledge. I took necessarily short retreats to far away places to explore even more deeply, sages and holy places. At home, I would spend hours at a time, in my favorite, then labelled, 'Esoteric' bookstore, plunging into the Natural, Holistic, Energetic, and Healing on all levels. And then I did my best to practice it all.

The advantage of the pre-social media, especially pre-internet age, was that new stimuli did not bombard or chase after anyone. Finding the knowledge and information was countless times more difficult. Consequently, one had to actively seek it out which encouraged serious discipline and commitment.

Cruising In-Flight: Virtuous Cycle of Superpowers

"To be blissfully alive, the possession of a Superpower is mandatory"
~CN Degano~

The universe finally felt I was ready. And I donned the Flight Attendant cape in 1999.

I was able to start cruising high, above the clouds, into gradually clearer and bluer skies.

The allowances of long stretches of solitude on days off and layovers allowed me to flourish in all ways.

Some were very material pursuits.

I became an amateur real estate investor, including in Peru and the U.S. At a certain point I had five properties under my name, and with the toils and tribulations of being a landlord, I was lucky to not have lost my head.

THE VIRTUOUS CYCLE OF SUPERPOWERS IN THE 'BIG SKY OF LIFE'

I was hands-on in the renovation of my own home and building one for my family. Initially or partially, I did this all by my single girl self.

On another level, I also focused on Education, from the more formal to the 'simply love of' variety, all facilitated by both long stretches of time off, leave of absences and layovers. An inaugural Fly Girl-Yoga teacher in 2002, after my long, intensive studies 'pre-flight' I started feeling whole and truly fulfilled. And for more than 15 years I would use a large part of my extended, pampering layovers, undistracted and comfortable, gaining certificates and degrees such as Master's in Counselling mid-2000s and about a decade later, Doctorate in Natural Medicine. With my Hypnosis and Emotional Freedom Technique qualifications, I would practice on fellow flight attendants on long layovers, and passengers in need. Secretly I repeated my mantras on crew breaks and bus rides to and from layovers. And sometimes I would bring my Biofeedback device with me to my destination, to practice the protocols on myself.

To counteract and sustain all my intense activity and studies, at work and away, I made extreme self-care a priority mission on layovers, taking advantage of countless relaxing, regenerative therapies and activities 'on-location', so to oftentimes return home feeling better than when I had left.

However, ultimately, I focused on using my ample time to nurture the stillness and silence of the 'Transcendent'—our Source, and connection to All, which also had the obvious practical benefits of sustaining health and youth.

Herein lies important confluence with a major life project and resultant PhD thesis on Reverse Aging. In 2008 I had an original 'Quantum, Belief effect' based idea to transform my physiology, one which received the literal 'cool' stamp from a world renowned, pioneering Epigenetics scientist. My layovers were for many years strategically planned to experiment and execute it all. And this, in a big way is my signature 'Superpower', having allowed for the extension of youth and all it encompasses, in a world which still stigmatizes women 'of a certain age'—something I would like to help to completely eradicate and transform.

And all of this does not even begin to address the abundant special and personal activities and dynamics, on and off the aircraft, with significant others and very special friends and acquaintances, from colleagues to locals, anonymous to famous—not relevant here, to be shared possibly in other memoirs.

In short, the Superpowers of being a 'Sky girl' gave me the time, opportunity, and confidence to further my own particular variety of Superpowers, to then more fully develop them into practices and missions. This phenomenon could be called 'The Virtuous cycle of Flight Attendant Superpowers'.

Silence Inside & Jet-Sound Outside: The Big Sky of Life

"Life stream has two shores: one silent and one active... in between this activity and silence flows the river of life"
~ Maharishi Mahesh Yogi~

Possibly this quote represents the deepest reason and opportunity for becoming a Flight Attendant: Living to the fullest, intertwining the Silent, Transcendent with the Active, Maya; two 'shores', or 'horizons' in our case, which embrace the 'Big Sky' of Life.

Until not that long ago, some people, including students, would look at me as if I was a type of living contradiction as a 'Mantra-chanting Stewardess'. However, I felt this was my badge of honor: 'How do you reconcile the Spiritual with the Materialistic World?', they would ask.

We are spiritual beings, living a physical experience. These realities are not mutually exclusive and should exist in tandem. The extremes of 'inner' and 'outer' work better, united.

Maya *itself* often times manifests in extremes for a Flight Attendant. On the brighter side, we are all fortunate to have that which pleases, pampers, and fulfills our senses: Awesome venues, luxurious hotel stays, good benefits, and decent remuneration to enjoy the freedom of time and mobility. On the flipside, we are exposed to toxic and hazardous elements; we endure fatigue, jet lag and general physical challenge; we commonly encounter difficult problems and passenger discontent; And we are away from home in even dangerous times, just to name a few.

THE VIRTUOUS CYCLE OF SUPERPOWERS IN THE 'BIG SKY OF LIFE'

As examples of personal positive 'extremes', on my 'journeys': A supervisor who empathised with my critical need for last-minute, extended time off, and 'saved' my special decade-long project and thesis; and a 'scheduler God', who did the same at times of deep mourning and need. A huge and unexpected helping hand came from a 'not yet met' colleague, marketing my Flight Attendant crash pad, when he found out about my best intentions but many hardships. A whole junior crew who made a celebratory banner sign for my 25th company anniversary on a short, busy flight, was so moving. And it was deeply comforting when a great 'Sky Goddess' dropped me off a 'care kit' after I had become very ill and needed to stay back in London on my own.

And then there are those 'dark' experiences which could have decimated me. Some very uniquely disturbing scenarios include: Having a tray thrown at me by a passenger 'under the influence', after patiently tolerating his bad behavior. Innocently answering my hotel door to a 'trusted' male colleague who attempted to aggressively 'capture' me in my own room. Very surreal was when another co-worker sarcastically verbalised and mimed 'boohoo' to me, after her partner blew the huge monetary investment I had entrusted him with, and as if not enough, threatening me as well. Luckily, such incidents are not representative of the majority and were, extreme indeed.

And despite feeling deeply shocked by the fact that humans could be this way, by some grace, I did not even need big support, vindication, or time off to recuperate (although I do not discourage such legitimate responses). I was not permanently stained or jaded by this darkness. I was able to heal the experiences on my own, peacefully and positively.

This is because I had been dipped in that 'silence' so many times. I was well-armed with positive, Superpower energy, guiding me in countless ways: Solid karmic awareness allowed me to keep my hands 'clean', knowing that the law of cause and effect would take over without my intervention. Practical wisdom reassured me for example, that dark forces attack and target the light. Energy techniques, sacred and scientific helped me remove the emotional charge and helped me feel healed and protected. I was relatively unaffected, like the proverbial duck. *And importantly, I continued to love my fellow crew member, and passenger because we were all one on this 'journey' together.*

THE VIRTUOUS CYCLE OF SUPERPOWERS IN THE 'BIG SKY OF LIFE'

I was once described as too sensitive even for an ashram, yet fate had me vie for a job in one of the most worldly and emotionally testing of industries and jobs. Not per chance: *The very sensitivity and vulnerability that nearly wiped me out was the key to searching out the right Superpowers, making me stronger and more resilient than the naysayers themselves, and quite honestly, more than I had ever thought possible. Those superpowers then made me a bit of Superheroine, at least in comparison to what I once was...*

For those who believe in the science of the stars, experts in astrology let me know that my astrological natal chart points to this possibly being my last time on the blue planet. If true, it will certainly be because *I have been fully and equally affected by and immersed in both the 'Silent' as well as the 'Active' horizons of the 'Big Sky' of life.*

I still have some necessary road left in order to master this, but when these two 'extremes' are unified, there is *liberation or unattachment, an ultimate Superpower. In turn, this gives rise to pure and unconditional Love,* 'da best one of all', which I will offer back to my —our, Superpower job and all of my fellow Superheroes.

An eternal Thank You and Merci, fair Sky Hostess and Attendant of my soul's journey.

CONTACT

HOLISTIC COUNSELLING
(PREMAVIDA):

PREMAVIDA WEBSITE:
www.premavida.com

PREMAVIDA FACEBOOK:
premavida

REAL ESTATE FACEBOOK:
southontariorealestate

christina.degano@gmail.com
www.southontariorealestate.ca

BiOGRAPHY

Christina Degano (Narayani)

Multi-passionate, spiritually grounded, holistic citizen of the world could describe Christina (Narayani). Grateful to be Canadian, Christina has greatly evolved in foreign lands, as many in the aviation world do. She has resided within her deep ancestral roots of the Italian Friuli region, and enjoyed long-standing connections with other cultures, such as in Peru, Colombia, and Hawaii. Her exploratory spirit was principally nurtured by her airline career, starting in 1989, on the Toronto 'ground'—in Reservations, followed by YYZ Customer Service—before becoming a Flight Attendant in 1999. Christina has used the gift of travel, primarily for self-development and lifelong learning. Over the decades, she has taken early-adopter 'deep dives' into the fields of Yogic/Spiritual Science and Natural Medicine. Her passions and specialties focus on Energy & Quantum medicine, Yogic & Rejuvenation therapies, and various integrative modalities as a Doctor (PhD) in Natural Medicine. And as a Registered Professional Counsellor, she fervently subscribes to promoting mental health holistically, a pivotal factor in the optimization of total human wellness. . Recently she has become a Real Estate Agent in Ontario, Canada, advancing the love of real estate she has also practiced in different ways and several lands, all her adult life. Her fiancé Felipe, lives in Kauai Hawaii, and although they are still currently living a long-distance relationship (which is being tested to perfection in Pandemic times) they collaborate in their similar vocations of Holistic Health and Real Estate and together plan their related future mission. Christina's intentions are to always serve the highest good, educate and exemplify supreme well-being and dwell blissfully in both the Maya and Divine stillness of life.

FELiPE POMAR
HANALEi BAY - KAUAi

ARRIVALS..

SUPERPOWERS of FLYING
Our Loving 'SEE YOU SOON'

Jessica De Serre Boissonneault & Christina Degano (Narayani)

21 extraordinary flight attendants
21 incredible stories of life and resiliency
21 empowering chronicles of Superpowers
& Superheroes in the travel industry

Our SuperHero Mission in Critical Times

"Life takes off when fear is left on the ground" – unknown

In a hopefully charming, but certainly realistic fashion, this book is meant to humbly, but proudly, enlighten the world about the nature of our career and humanity as Flight Attendants. It is being presented at a key moment in history when a global pandemic has affected our aviation industry in bulls eye fashion. As such, it was created to be a message of hope. We are an extended family, in the good and bad, and 'fly in this together'. We are unconditionally united by our wings, a strong symbol of our Superpower.

Our industry seems to have been hardest hit in terms of central risk compounded with monumental loss of business, and consequently of customers and jobs due to restrictions and fear of travel during the pandemic.

Of course, our health care workers—who we feel akin to for one of the many hats we wear, as medical facilitators of sorts—have endured such an enormously disproportionate amount of the burden, and we would like to salute these true Superheroes of our pandemic times.

All the chronicles you have read honor the humans behind the uniform and demonstrate the extremes of our realties: the many literal and symbolic miles that have been explored; and the adventures, passions, challenges and even tragedies that are all somehow connected to our jobs. We applaud the persistence and positivity to create a better tomorrow and rejoice in the hope and belief to manifestgoals and dreams. Ultimately the success of each Cabin Crew member has been in grounding fear, so that they could take-off.

Unique stories, personalities, and relative expressions, reflecting our unity in diversity. We are a community of unique employees like few others, bringing together all cultures, creeds, ages, and personalities. Yet, each story has a strong message of resiliency, hope and love. Each of the authors is an emblem of pride for the industry and human community.

Safety as Service

Especially in times like these: Let us not forget! We are here to ensure your well-being and safety, as a professional and personal mission.

The most important practical mission of each Flight Attendant is the safety, and ultimately, emergency and daresay, survival role--to have you arrive at your destinations safely. As described many times in our stories, we go through extensive training to make sure we are always ready to perceive potential hazards and dangers and then act effectively to eliminate them. Society might have viewed and described the Flight Attendant job differently over the years, however the key role has never changed.

As relayed in these stories and witnessed in the media there have been many stories of varying degrees of 'resistance' against Flight Attendants around the world. Still today this phenomenon demonstrates the great threat and responsibility that such a role holds; yet how oftentimes undervalued it really is. Sometimes, what is not properly understood is that we Flight Attendants are acting on behalf of the public safety at large—in service.

Service as Passion

Service is a central superpower because it gives back so much. It touches the spirit, and the servant is transformed with gratitude, a powerful vibe. We have read about how a service that has proper energy behind it, can transform simple plane trips into beautiful souvenirs. We create a clan out of our fellow crew members by being of service to our colleagues and bring this energised Super 'care-giver cape' home to our families and friends, which emanates out to our communities, and the world at large.

Serving our human friend, lover or stranger in this pandemic is so crucial for society to feel the unity we may have been lacking before, and we crave so much now. A mere gesture of kindness and support can change the course of someone's otherwise socially distanced day. Whether we are pandemic fatigued or jet-lagged, let us try to serve and support every and any person or cause possible.

SuperFuelled Capacities

The word Superpower was chosen to highlight the magical element of any talent, quality or capacity that inspires or truly empowers.

Being in a pressurized tube at 40000 feet with 450 passengers aboard and doing a full meal service at 4 am makes one tough! The conditions of flight, strict demands of the duties and training, and serving and protecting a sea of people are just the main elements that mould our already existent talents into supersonic abilities, physical and mental.

It is seen in the different strengths needed to be a single mother of any child, and of course when an extra blessing such as autism is involved. It is proven in the willful talent to master 5 languages. It is demonstrated in the resourceful genius and awareness to perform CPR on a baby without delay and successfully bring back life.

The gifts of travel, along with the time to do it, are our greatest blessings. Here, travelling to 52+ countries becomes truly possible within one lifetime. The freedom of time and movement generally helps us grow intimately with our multi-passions whether it be as a therapist, real estate agent or poet.

Travelling opens up your heart and allows for tremendous personal growth. Whether it be new culture, food, climate, culture or its people, we are transformed at every new exposure. It offers new perspectives and inspiration. Evolution is made quicker than the speed of jet-engine sound.

A general and overriding quality is that of resiliency and temperance. This quote by Elizabeth Edwards totally describes the experience of flight and life, especially during the pandemic. *"Resilience is accepting your new reality, even if it's less good than the one you had before. You can fight it, you can do nothing but scream about what you've lost, or you can accept that and try to put together something that's good."*

Being a Flight Attendant, both requires and then preps one to have to positively deal with their 'own trips' of challenge. It takes this characteristic to survive and then thrive through a war or partner abuse for example.

And as mentioned, the pandemic truly saw us enter into a holding pattern. So much of this past year was difficult, yet it was such a beautiful opportunity to renew, re-invent, and rebuild. And our group has risen to the occasion of our signature type of resilience. It proves our individual and collective Superpowers, both professionally, and as unique human beings. All of us were faced with anxiety, stress, worry, grief and so on, regardless of seniority, age, or any existence of a 'Plan B'. We banded together like a real crew on social media to uplift, share, fly through, and flourish in our respective new skies.

Magical Passion In-Flight, In-Life

The propellants for Superpowers are magical passion, and un-abandoned love.

Life, like flying, can be very difficult to get through. Each different adventure creates uniquely distinctive challenging conditions.

In some ways, developing Superpowers is necessary. Otherwise, we are left only barely surviving. In possession of one, our experience is blissful.

And to accomplish it all requires magic and passion.

Being a Flight Attendant truly does feel magical for all the reasons described and all for which we need no affirmations.

We adore what we do. And being truly in love with our work, therefore, is the true magic that creates our Superpower job.

Find your Superpower, Be your own Superhero

Our Superpower Message for You is: Honor your own desires and inclinations of what your Superpower mission may be. Find your special strengths, qualities and ambitions and do not stop nurturing them. Then, find a home where they will be fully appreciated and amplified. With the secret ingredient of magical passion, you will cruise to maximal altitude in life. This is how you will surely become the Superhero of your own Story!

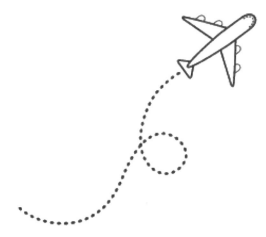

From a flight in which we have entertained you with several accounts of our common and individual passionate love affairs with our Superpower job, we now bid you a fond farewell, and send you off with a loving 'SEE YOU SOON'... It has been an honor to be with you, our Superhero passengers. May we leave you with a parting gift of a few hi-flying ingredients we recommend for incorporating into your Superpowered life:

COURAGE ♥ EMPOWERMENT ♥ COMMUNITY ♥ LOVE

SUPERHERO FLiGHT REViEWS

The airline industry is rich, diverse and colourful and is comprised of a myriad of professions. While the stories of this book are written primarily by Flight Attendants, the book itself would be incomplete without the accompanying testimonies of those other professionals of the aviation world. We have such an appreciation for all the airline concierges, airport managers, crew schedulers, ramp workers, baggage handlers, pilots, international flight attendants, and everyone else who enthusiastically help put planes and passengers in the air. Below you will find the stories of a few of these individuals, helping you to fully understand the extensive aviation world and how each person plays their role in this aerial circus we call air travel.

Valerie Blackwell

When I was 7 years old and in Grade 2, my first school field trip ever was to the Toronto Airport. I went armed with my Mom's Kodak camera, the kind you looked down from the top to take a photo. I came home with photos of planes taken from the observation deck that were blurry black-and-whites. I treasured them at the time, and still do to this day. I didn't realize at the time that this would be the beginning of a lifelong love of aircrafts, airlines and travelling. My 40+ year career has spanned 3 airlines - working in many positions on the ground and in the air. For the past 26 years I've been a Flight Director which has been one of the most amazing times of my life. The challenges and thrill of flying are always there. I still get excited about it every time I fly. The camaraderie amongst crew members is like no other, and I have made lifelong friends. The industry is, and always will be, volatile and unpredictable. The last year has been testimony to this. Over the last 30 years, more airlines in Canada have come and gone than I have fingers and toes. You have to be a bit of a gambler to get involved in the industry. But once you're in, it's addictive and you'll do anything to stay in it.

It's not for everyone, but you know when it's right.
I think I knew in grade 2.

May the flight continue non-stop!

Amanda Tosto

Aspire to Inspire

My love for aviation began in 2009 when I worked as a station attendant, loading and offloading bags. That was the first time I experienced being a woman working in a man's world. In 2010, I applied for the flight attendant position. My journey was full of unforgettable adventures, but I also faced several unexpected and emotionally draining situations along the way. Despite the hurdles, a fire of passion grew within me. A decade later, I made the toughest and most daunting decision to take when in a position of absolute mental and financial comfort. I wanted to become a pilot! However, the only way I could afford the $100,000.00 educational journey was to take a leap of faith and sell everything I owned and worked so hard to get: my condo, my car, and all my investments. I was terrified of giving everything up and moving forward. My journey was far from easy, filled with sacrifice and losses. I left behind everything I know and love. Being the only woman at my flight school, working in a male-dominated industry, fighting all odds, and constantly proving myself, I have not shied away from my long-term goals and I keep persisting. I continuously push my boundaries as a commercial pilot and step out of my comfort zone every day. This undertaking is not for the faint of heart, but I can guarantee that the results are rewarding. There is no limit when you have determination. My goal is to inspire women who think they are not good enough to fight for what they want and never to give up, no matter the obstacle or struggle. I aspire to inspire the women of the world to step up and shine. Remember, "life begins at the end of your comfort zone"- Neale Donald Walsch.

 amanda.kara    Amanda Karamanoukian Tosto

Nathalie Rebelo

My career went from airplane mode to fully connected by changing my lifestyle.

A flight attendant is often imagined as a jet-setter, effortlessly strolling the streets halfway across the globe. They enjoy the treats of this foreign country and – snap – they fly back home, waiting for another flight.

The reality is, this is physical work, and our body takes a serious beating. Until I realized how my unhealthy ways affected my dream job, I couldn't appreciate it.

Not caring for my well-being eventually caught up to me. The lack of sleep, empty nutrition, no intentional movements, little knowledge on how to nourish myself to create sustainable energy, drained me slowly. I'd spend my layovers in endless sleep sessions, in-room pizza, staying in, just waiting to come home.

I wanted more stamina, a clearer mind, more strength, and appreciation. Gandhi said "Be the change you want to see in the world"; So... I changed.

That's when I included online fitness, balanced nutrition, daily movement, whole foods, cleaned my menu, and my outlook to embarked on this voyage for the long run. Six years ago, I transformed my body, my soul and drastically improved my mindset.

I am now stronger and can avoid injuries. I boosted my immune system. I'm finally comfortable in my uniform. I have a positive attitude and I can savor the moment, mindfully. The shift was so profound, it brought out the entrepreneur in me.

Today, with my learnings, I mentor others through the same process. Now, leading by example to help flight attendants through our unique set of obstacles is my "mission possible".

My career is still the same, it's my state of mind that has changed. Even in the hardest year of flying in history, I am truly grateful for my office in the clouds.

Online Fitness|Nutrition|Support

 nathalierebelo   nathalie4u

Amine Yaakoubi

More than a year ago I unknowingly operated my last flight, the skies I called home. I traveled many countries and made so many friends and memories, from the briefing to the times we spent together on the layovers. My last flight was luckily my best destination, Zanzibar. At that special destination I contracted the virus that has affected many of us! I spent twelve days in the clinic, and I want to thank again everyone who was by my side. Thank you to all my colleagues who called and every-one who sent me messages checking on me even though we have never flown together. We are always united by wings.

Many of my colleagues working for other airlines were made redundant and many of us were put on a long, unpaid leave! It's not easy to move on and start a new chapter in your life because, for me, being a flight attendant is not just a job! I have personally learned a lot, learned how to be patient, learned how to love myself and being more open to people's uniqueness!

Life is lessons and this was the best lesson I learned. I learned in the past year that everything is temporary and not to be taken for granted. I enjoyed being a flight attendant so much and it became a part of me. I miss discovering other countries, going to my favorite restaurant in every destination.

These times have been hard on the aviation industry as a whole, but I'll always love flying. I hold on to the hope to return to the skies again. I am counting the days to return back to where I belong!

Hopefully happy old days will come back.

Charlotte Milot

I became a flight attendant at 21 years old. Five years later, I never thought my life would be as inspiring and unique. I travel the world on a daily basis; I eat in a different country every week, and mostly, I was able to make my family and friends travel and make them experience the wonder of our planet. My job is my lifestyle, and my coworkers are my second family. I haven't stepped a foot in an aircraft for over a year now and I miss it so much. I can't wait to put on my uniform and wear my wings; I can't wait to welcome unfamiliar faces on board that become familiar by the end of the flight. I can't wait to be back and call the sky my office.

Agnes Gauvin

I have been a Flight Attendant for 23 years. I was jet-setting across the globe, experiencing the 4 am wake-up calls, sporadic hours, flight delays, and the joys of working most weekends and holidays. My travel developed my communication skills, enhanced connecting skills, and expanded my knowledge of cultural differences. I was truly enjoying interacting with passengers on board and loved exchanging stories with them on their reason for travel. I developed lasting friendships with fellow crew members and gained an amazing "family" of support that I never thought possible. While I was grateful for all those experiences, the sense of lack of control in my life was ever present. During my layovers, I started reading business leadership books. At the same time, I was looking for ways to eat better while travelling. The food had to be portable, easy to prepare, and fit the acceptable requirements for customs. The products I found gave me better health and more energy to cope with the sporadic hours. The products came with "a business in the box" model. This was the perfect storm. While flying, I was able to work part time around a crazy hectic airline schedule, and started slowly to build my business. This gave me another source of income. Fast forward to today, I got laid off after 23 years of flying. I applied the triple A model from the airline: "Assess, Adapt, Act". The perfect storm has realigned itself. The difference this time is I have a sense of control in my life. My business is already established. The ability to work from home has never been more crucial. My connections with people now are all online. Zoom calls are now the norm. The best thing of all, my network 'family' and my flying 'family' are not exclusive. For that, I will be forever grateful!

Kepa

You would not believe what is left on the ground!

We often find items that our amazing passengers have left behind on the aircraft when they land and leave to spend 15 days on holidays in their exotic destinations. You all can imagine that books and glasses are on the top of that list!!! I have dreamed many times about owning my own "International Optical Second-hand Lunettes Shop" or my own "Flying Books Library" ... sounds great!!

Many times, we interact with our customers after finding a lost item, and many times we find them and hand them back their books, glasses, or tablets...!

This makes me happy, so you can imagine how happy I feel when I am able to help crew members... let me explain using a few stories.

I remember a time when one of our most "foodie" crew members left her "very special" food on board. She found a way to contact me, and I was able to offload her "menu" in Barcelona before the plane was flying back to Canada.

Many years ago, in 2013 or so, another lovely crew member left her laptop at security control. I think that was the first time a flight attendant had ever contacted me regarding this kind of rescue operation. I did my job and tried to find the laptop. We never found it, but since then, we have become good friends. We have only seen each other four times face to face, but it feels like we have known each other since 1970.

Those stories were about personal items, but sometimes there are challenging situations that require a better performance.

I remember that time when an official flight attendant was left behind at the hotel. Without that flight attendant, the flight could not depart! Somehow, we managed to coordinate with them, and they were on board before the flight left Barcelona ... we made it!!

And finally, let me tell you the most important "item" a crew member has ever left on the ground... their family members!!

Kepa continued...

Sometimes, when flights are full, there is no space for all the family members travelling on standby. When this happens, we will always take care of those who were left behind and who must stay for another day or so. When we help with a family member, the relationship we build is not comparable to any other. Back in 2013, the 15-year-old daughter of a flight attendant was left behind in Barcelona. The flight attendant did not want to leave her daughter behind but had no choice. She trusted me to take care of her, and that is what I did. She slept at my place, and I took her out to dinner with the crew. Nowadays, both she and her daughter are still coming to BCN, and I visit them sometimes in Montreal.

I couldn't be happier for what aviation has given me. FRIENDS.

Anthony Da Rosa

My name is Anthony - a laid off flight attendant and a proud Mental Health Nurse. I was a flight attendant for one year prior to being laid off, and still looking to go back, but for now I am focusing on nursing. One of the reasons I chose to be a flight attendant was to explore new cultures, sample new foods, and see the world. Flying is more than serving drinks, it's about embracing a culture, and teaching others about it. I used to love the get-up-and-go lifestyle where you never know where you may be going until the day of. Also, it taught me good time management skills, and you have to have very good communication skills because you will never work with the same people often. Since being laid off I chose to specialize in mental health, because it is so overlooked, and people believe in this stigma about it. I landed my first job doing addictions and rehab where I connected with people one on one and learned about so much history and trauma that led to the reason of them being there. After that, I realized I wanted to and needed to do more, so I began searching for more mental health related jobs in a hospital environment where I landed myself a job specializing in mood disorders and psychosis. For now, I realized just how well nursing and flying go hand in hand. Always remember to never give up. I remember my first interview for a flight attendant position, I never made it to the end, I went to nursing school and failed a semester. I gave up on both until I said "I can't give up". I pushed through school, applied to fly again. Now I am content doing both things I love.

Shirley Pierre

As a child, I was fascinated by the world globe in our living room. It was standing on four wooden feet. The globe was surrounded by a circular wood piece with perfectly spaced holes where cocktail glasses would sit nicely, ready to be used. I would turn the globe on that slanted golden axis. I slowly allowed my fingers to feel the grooves of the Rockies in North America, the Andes in South America, or the Himalayas in Asia. I loved the various city names delicately written on the countries, and I loved the coloured dots that represented the capitals alongside the blue hues to simulate the many bodies of waters that our planet embodies.

Little did I know that this daily ritual of playing with the world globe would spark not only my curiosity to discover the many cultures and the people of the world, but also, the insatiable appetite to walk in cities and countries to feel the different vibes from my own country.

Montréal, Canada. I still remember lining up at the Sheraton Hotel in February 1997. It was a very cold Saturday morning. I was in the queue to meet with an airline recruiter. I was excited, I was nervous, I was confident. The close to 5-hour wait did not deter my positive attitude.

London, England. My first overseas flight. Winnipeg, Canada. My first (and only) re-routing to get an ill passenger to a hospital for medical care. New York, US. The many, many, many layovers where I walked the equivalent of a full marathon, danced all night long, and attended a class at one of my favourite yoga studios. Buenos Aires, Argentina. A grandmother kept calling me "muneca" as I reminded her of a doll, and another passenger who loved the fact that I could only address his baby in French. My jetlagged brain had reverted to address young children in my mother tongue on that day.

Twenty-four years later, my flight attendant career is full of stories, amazing relationships with my colleagues, long flights, deep gut laughter, forever prayers to bidding scheduling gods, missed occasions with loved ones, and a view of the world that is skewed to some and my lifestyle to me.

Patrick Richard

It was after a layoff at a fairly reputable company in Greater Montreal, that I was going for the first time in my life; get out of Canada, fly and travel. Destination: San Juan and the Virgin Islands. I had just signed a 6 1/2 month contract with a very well known Cruise line company as a crowd leader aboard their liner. I hardly spoke English, but I had that passion and determination. Their ships were going to be my home away from home. A boundless love for the journey; which I call "My University of Life". A big part of that journey was also of service for me on my own quest for happiness. Sailing the oceans for almost ten years, I was privileged and very fortunate to have done almost 5 world tours.

From being a sailor and cruising the open seas, I grew some wings on my fish. It was in early 2014 that I was hired from a major airline company. I am still in the travel business and within the same big family that is our company. This is a very brief tour and synopsis of my personal journey in the travel industry. My quest as I like to call it, and for which I will be eternally grateful to life for having pampered me so much by offering me wonderful challenges in my search for joy, my quest for happiness. Everything you do in life is echoes of your own personal quest, your journey.

It's only quite recently that I've realized that not much is needed to keep me happy. Traveling will always be my best partner.

In order to keep my joy and happiness fulfilled, hopping on a plane and flying to New Brunswick to see and be with my entire family Is what's essential for me.

Prynce Michael

So much can happen in a year. I purchased my first home, started a new business, and most importantly became a better person in the process. Much like most of the world, I was also impacted by the vile Covid-19 virus. However, I wasn't impacted in the way you may think. Yes, I received a layoff letter from my current employer however, Covid impacted me by reaffirming that my mind is powerful and reminding me that I must continue to nourish it. With that being said, I challenged myself to not only generate more income, but to also not allow myself to see the negative impact that this pandemic has caused. Instead, I chose to embrace the many opportunities that presented themselves to me. During this pandemic my company launched our scholarship fund, and I became an international best selling author. Essentially, the covid pandemic has been a blessing in disguise. In order for us to grow we have to be uncomfortable. Nothing happens when we are comfortable. It is when we inconvenience ourselves that we truly grow to our fullest potential. If you don't take anything else away from this short exposé, take this; Potential is just potential until YOU DECIDE otherwise. Although, you may feel down and out just know that you aren't. A better tomorrow is waiting for you to create it.

Liz Dobrovich

My Treasured Airline Career!

Hello/Bonjour, my name is Liz, and I am a Concierge for this major airline. I have had the pleasure of 25 years of service, working with an extraordinary team of professionals who are customer-service centric in all that they do. From personalized check-in to fast tracking through security line-ups, BMW chauffeur service, Signature Suite Dining, and private priority boarding, we ensure that our most valued customers are made to feel pampered, appreciated, and valued!

I have three wonderful children, a beautiful granddaughter, and an adorable grandson. It is my love of family that motivates me to be my best! I am a first generation Canadian with proud Portuguese roots. My parents immigrated to Canada in the mid 50's with little resources and not a word of English but a strong work ethic and a sense of adventure, courage and humility.

I love the airport life. It is a fast-paced, exciting, and an ever-changing environment. You feel the pulse and the energy of people travelling for important business-related trips, relaxing beach holidays, or adventurous escapes. You get to meet interesting people from all walks of life and from every corner of the globe. Possessing an attitude of service and of making people feel valued and happy is part of the personalized service that makes my job so gratifying. A concierge heart is innate; this cannot be taught. Being proactive and creative to ensure a seamless travel experience makes a world of difference to a customer ...like when you succeed in rescuing a traveller's most prized Mont Blanc Pen that was left behind at check-in, well, that honest, heart-felt appreciation is priceless!

My most memorable moment in my career was when I was selected to be a torch bearer, representing our airline for the Vancouver 2010 Olympic Torch Relay - this was truly a monumental experience. The feeling of honour overwhelmed me. A sense of pride and privilege to be Canadian.

The opportunities that have been part of my career journey have brought me great fulfillment. I have had so much fun creating a life of service to others and working as a member of a winning team.

Michael Lindsay

I first joined the airline industry in 2007 and wasn't even sure that I wanted to be in the aviation industry. I was deathly afraid of heights at that time, and still am to this day, so I never envisioned myself travelling as much as I have.

I thought it would be a part-time, short-term employment because I was in school and when I was thinking of a career path for myself at the time, aviation was not one of them. Actually, I was applying for a position with a different airline when someone from this current airline spotted me and convinced me to work for them instead which was one of the best moves I have made in my life.

Working in this environment that feels like family has created many friendships and bonds which otherwise I never would have made or even dreamed of. The friends and bonds that I have made are very important to me and are a blessing. It has been quite the pleasure working in this industry and for this company. The experiences have been countless and a lot of fun as well. Travelling has created numerous memories and moments which will be cherished along with the friendships I have made. It is not for everyone. There are good days, bad days, and really really good days. The learning experiences, as well as the freedom it has brought, have been well worth all the ups and downs which comes with the industry, but these are ups and downs you would find in any career anyways.

Aviation life has been really good to me, and I am eternally thankful for that.

SUPERPOWER BUSINESS HUB

I believe that with a platform, comes the responsibility to give back. It is my pleasure to share with you the product of the resiliency of those who not only survived, but who have thrived during these trying times. A core objective of this book was to create a sense of support and kinship amongst those of us in the aviation community. I am so proud to introduce these lovingly created, flight-attendant-owned businesses. Each one of these business owners has managed to stand strong, reinvent themselves, and have turned the loss of their air travel lifestyles into businesses they are proud to call their own.

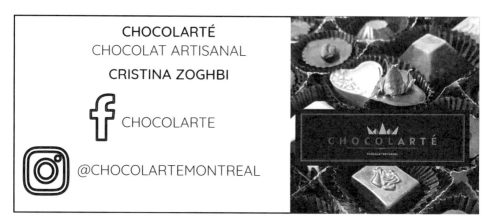

Bijoulie

Julie Miville Dechêne, Présidente
juliedbijoux@gmail.com
514 991-8542
f Bijoulie@bijouliejulie

Top Rated
Richmond Hill Real Estate Agent
Sze Lau

SZE KING LAU
Manager/Broker
劉思敬

416. 908. 9292
szelau.fhg@gmail.com

MELANIE KIS COACHING

Certifié Coach PNL - Membre ICF, SICPNL- Ritma receipt

soicoachingmk@gmail.com - SoiCoaching.com

SOI offers the luxury of well-being to women
in complete freedom & lightness
one step at a time with pleasure & love.

1 on 1 Coaching - Group courses - Workshops

NATUROPATH

Fun and simple lifestyle changes to reverse
your health symptoms and STILL have a life!

vanessariccio.com

LIGHT BEAMS OF LOVE

Natalie O'Connell

Reiki + Meditation + Intuitive Reader

light.beams.of.love@gmail.com
Instagram light_beams_of_love

Speak your truth.

Karine Boileau
@KarineBCommunatrice

Writer & Motivational Speaker
Energy healing - Access Bars
Ayurvedic cranial massage therapy
(514) 625-3364
www.versionb.life

MANI SAINI

Senior Designer

KYRA FINE GOLD

T: 416-821-5333
M: 647-896-1222
E: info@kyrafinegold.com W: www.kyrafinegold.com
Get Social With Us! Instagram & Facebook @Kyrafinegold

SUPERHERO SPONSORS

To those people who believed in me and this project, I want to say a big THANK YOU ! Your immense generosity has helped so many dreams (21 to be exact!) come true, and i could not be more grateful.

WHO AM I?
I have a PASSION in life:

It is to be at the service of HUMAN BEING, and for me, it is what matters the most!

I come from a family of six children, five girls and one boy. The value of helping and giving to others was taught to me at a young age. I am a father of three children.

I have been in business or more specifically, financial services for 8 years. Entrepreneur and the founder of KeA_Conseils (Investment & Insurance), I am a financial advisor and a group savings broker. I am a speaker of personal finance on topics such as 'How to control your expenses, SAVINGS and how to save on income tax or Registered Education Savings Plan (RESP)'.

My MISSION: To help my clients protect themselves against the disastrous financial consequences caused by the three worst enemies in the life of a HUMAN BEING: loss of salary, disease, and death; therefore, ensuring their financial security.

Kossi Awoutey
KeA_Conseils

 @kea_conseils

 kossiawoutey   kea-conseils assurances placements

Hailey Patry
Your True Happiness Coach
Marriage Mentor / The Happy Business Coach

Hailey is a world-renowned coach and happily-married mom-of-three. She helps you create your dream-life, dream-relationship, or dream-business!

She believes in happiness after depression, confidence despite anxiety, love after divorce and healing after infidelity. She believes you can be wildly successful, no matter what your past looks like. She helps you heal in 90 days or less. You will love your self, your results and your life!

Hailey offers private coaching for individuals, couples and entrepreneurs; speaking/keynotes; her 5 books, and her signature workshops. Hailey's spoken for 1-million+ audience members, is an award-winning best-selling author, awarded as "The-Woman-of-Resilience", "World's-Best-Marriage-Mentor" and "The-Woman-of-Leadership-Courage-Resilience".

Hailey offers unlimited urgent support between sessions, so you're not alone when you need help the most. When you hear someone's struggling and they don't know where to turn, especially if you hear of infidelity or low self-worth, she can definitely help.

Your get your first coaching session for FREE by texting 416-797-5856

If you're ready to shine... book some time. www.TheLiftedLid.com

Tara Filteau

We are Mother Daughter Empower, a Social Enterprise on a mission to empower the next generation of young girls! Did you know that by age 14 a girls confidence level will have decreased by 30% in comparison to boys of the same age? We are here to create a change in that stat, and we do so by providing moms with the tips, tools and resources that they need to raise the next generation of empowered girls!

Whether you're a mom, grandma, auntie, teacher, mentor or friend, you can make a difference by becoming a member of our community, join us at our next Mother-Daughter Retreat or grab a ticket to our Annual Mother Daughter Conference, our personal development and growth mindset programming is specially designed for girls ages 7-14 and inspires our community members to lead the way!

Together, we will empower the next generation!

Connect with us at; www.motherdaughterempower.ca
& follow us on socials @motherdaughterempower

Jonathan Taylor

I'm a flight attendant that got furloughed during covid-19.
While I wait to get back to the sky, I want to give you guys a sneak peek behind the loud conversations of the wonderful humans that hinder your sleep when you're sitting beside a closed curtain at 2 a.m.

The 76 is a Podcast by flight attendants for anyone interested in aviation. This podcast is for people who wonder about the lives of flight attendants. Which sane person would love to travel to three different countries in a week? If you're looking for a guide to becoming a flight attendant this is not the podcast for you. We talk about what it takes to wear the uniform, however, we focus on the people behind the uniform. I hope you guys enjoy this podcast as much as I miss my job.

After earning my first commission with my network marketing company, I dove in head first. What? I can get paid for sharing something I already love??? We all share things on a daily basis already !!
Ex: what is your favourite restaurant?

I really enjoy partnering with people who want more out of life.
Better physical health, better mental health, better financial health.
Now, I am focusing on turning something good into something great!

We can all create our own economy. I am most grateful for the company who has consistently supported me. The compensation plan has allowed me max out my savings for my child's complete education. That is huge! And I want the same for YOU

Agnes Gavin
Your success partner

"Be not afraid of growing slowly, be afraid only of standing still"
Chinese proverb

"Real people, Real solutions"

Marisa Morais

My name is Marisa Morais. I am an African Portuguese woman. I reside in Toronto, Ontario Canada. I emigrated to Canada 18 years ago looking for a better life for me and my daughter.
I am a mother of a 17-year-old girl. I have always worked in the restaurant and catering industry until the pandemic hit and the industry had to make drastic cuts.

I decided to get into the health and nutrition filed and joined Herbalife Nutrition as a wellness coach.

My purpose in life is to inspire, motivate and Empower people.

I can be reached at (647)572-5664

Email desamarisa417@gmail.com

Instagram THEBEAUTYBOUTIQUEBYMARISA

Facebook TheBeauty&NutritionBoutiqueByM&F

Oneisha Lewis

ONEISHA PERROTTE-LEWIS from Montréal, Quebec is an author, a mindset coach, a motivational speaker and a dedicated entrepreneur. She left her job in the nursing field to pursue her dreams of working for herself in order to help others attain ultimate control of their life and well-being while also, creating inspiring books that can possibly change or save a life.

Instagram: @iamoneishalewis

Facebook: Oneisha Lewis

Karina Oliver

My name is Karina Oliver. I own a business called Girls Empower, a female empowerment brand helping others feel empowered within themselves and their businesses.

I'm currently an Instagram Growth Coach and Social Media Manager. Mom of two boys.

My goals and aspirations are to create a life of success for my kids and I by helping ambitious female entrepreneurs through my coaching and management.

Contact me
Email: girlsempower@hotmail.com
Phone number: 438-483-3940
IG: @girlsempowermtl

Gordon So

Gordon So is a co-founder of Landed for Success with 20 plus years of direct sales in the network, marketing industry. With a strong background in the real estate and mortgage industry, he has built, trained, and motivated massive sales teams in several countries, and he has ultimately developed amazing client relationships and top-selling skills. In the past 6 years, Gordon has developed marketing strategies to help authors, trainers, and consultants grow their social media, digital marketing, and offline strategies to acquire more leads, sales, and speaking engagements. So, if you are serious about taking your personal development, skill development, and mindset to the next level, you will not want to miss any of his training and sales modules. With his favorite quote being "Motivation and Inspiration Without Direction Leads to Total Frustration", be prepared to follow Gordon in his wisdom to help you achieve your goals!

Co-founder, Landed for Success
Email: gordon.so@rogers.com

Jey Jeyakanthan

Jey goes by many titles, whether it's an entrepreneur, an IT professional, a Bestselling Author, or a Social Media Influencer. Today, he is the co-founder of Landed for Success and has built over 22 years of in-depth knowledge, involvement, experience, and expertise in trade sectors such as Business Development, Project Management, Social Networking, Volunteering, and Business Transformation for Fortune-200 companies.

Jey is also involved with many volunteer and advocacy organizations in Canada. Some examples include Jey acting as Director of Sophia Hilton Foundation of Canada, Executive Director of Never Give up Foundation, and Co-chair at Pierre Elliott Trudeau High School and Beckett Farm Public School. In addition, Jey's past positions include highly commendable roles as a Director of Canadian Tamils' Chamber of Commerce' and Member of Markham Board of Trade. With his intense commitment to the betterment of his community, Jey has been glad to help those around him!

Co-founder, Landed for Success
Email: landedforsuccess@gmail.com

Address: 10 Thornmount Dr,

Scarborough, ON M1B 3J4

YOUR NEW
Story

Welcome to Your New Story.

Our mission:

Give every human being the sparkle they need to shine so that they can write their new story, a story they will love and finally be proud of. Here, satisfaction is guaranteed.

Our team is made up of several specialists with in-depth knowledge in the field of personal development in order to allow you to live the life of your dreams, a life you love. We truly believe that every human being is important and that it is high time to come together in order to create a better world. A world in which each individual will find love for oneself and love for others. Join us in choosing to care of the most relationship in your life: THE ONE WITH YOURSELF. It's free to be a part of this family. Together we are stronger, and that humanity will heal when it understands that the verb TO BE is more important than the verb to have. The best gift you can give to yourself is taking care of you. Become the priority in your life. Here we will give you the tools so you can finally live the life of your dreams, a life that suits you. Become a part of this amazing family.

www.yournewstory.ca

IG: votrenouvellehistoire

Facebook: Votre-Nouvelle-Histoire

Courriel: info@yournewstory.ca